Hidden Boston and Cape Cod

The Adventurer's Guide

Hidden Boston and Cape Cod
The Adventurer's Guide

Ryan Vollmer
Patricia Mandell

Illustrator Norman Nicholson

Executive Editor Leslie Henriques

Ulysses Press
Berkeley, CA

Published by: Ulysses Press
Sather Gate Station
Box 4000-H
Berkeley, CA 94704

Library of Congress Catalog Card Number 91-065096
ISBN 0-915233-36-3

Printed in the U.S.A. by the George Banta Company

10 9 8 7 6 5 4 3 2 1

Publisher: Ray Riegert
Managing Editor: Claire Chun
Editor: Judith Kahn
Computer Consultant: Lindsay Mugglestone

Cartographers: Phil Gardner and Robert Lettieri
Cover Designers: Bonnie Smetts and Leslie Henriques
Indexer: Sayre Van Young
Research Associate: Phil Abrams

Cover Photography: Front cover by Dave Houser; back cover by Bob Holmes

Printed on recycled paper

CONTENTS

MAPS

———————

Throughout the text, hidden locales, remote regions,
and little-known spots are marked with a star (★).

———————

CHAPTER ONE

Adventuring Through Boston, Cape Cod and the Massachusetts Coast

Boston has been dubbed both the "hub of the universe" and the Athens of America, by its own residents—Bostonians certainly don't need lessons in self-esteem. Of course, travelers will forgive them that bit of pride, considering the riches the Boston area has to offer.

American history buffs will find themselves in heaven here. It would be almost impossible to discover another place so densely packed with historical treasures: from the spot where the *Mayflower* landed to the back rooms where the American Revolution was plotted to the fields where the fighting began. You can barely take a step without stumbling over a colonial battlefield, a historic site or monument, or an 18th-century house. There's a certain magic, too, in visiting spots where Paul Revere rode, Thoreau and Emerson philosophized, Hawthorne, Melville and Dickinson wrote, and John Kennedy grew up.

This is a territory of firsts: first college in the New World (Harvard), first public school, oldest lighthouse. Before your eyes will come to life all that you learned in school about the birth of the United States. And every few years, another nearby town celebrates its 350th anniversary.

But history is not all you'll find. Modern Boston, and Cambridge across the Charles River, beat to the pulse of the 20th century. Downtown, the classic 1795 Massachusetts State House looks out over a city that also has postmodern financial buildings, new and refurbished shopping arcades and sparkling highrise hotels. The high-tech boom of the '60s and '70s added a reputation for business acumen and technological know-how to an area already respected as the site of five major universities and dozens of smaller centers of learning.

Visitors will also discover, within a day's drive of the city, 168 miles of splendor along the Massachusetts coastline, which stretches above and below Boston and curves a great arm out into the Atlantic to form Cape Cod. Here are miles and miles of white sand beaches fringed with dunes and marsh grasses and seaside villages where elegant yachts as well as working fishing vessels bob in the harbor. Standing fast before time, old wooden saltbox houses have weathered into the colors of the very ground that made them. Directly to the south of the Cape, the wealthy island retreats of Martha's Vineyard and Nantucket float in pristine loveliness.

Whether you're in the northernmost villages of Rockport and Newburyport or in Provincetown on the tip of Cape Cod, the ocean is never far from anyone's mind. Fishing blessed all who settled here, from the Indians and the Pilgrims to the 19th-century whalers and today's fishermen of Gloucester, New Bedford and Plymouth. Residents of Cape Cod and the rest of the Massachusetts coast have always been premier shipbuilders and sailors, and today visitors can still take great pleasure aboard an excursion boat, a tiny sailboat or a vintage whaler.

The ocean also tempers the weather, making summers cooler and winters less fierce, although Boston itself can be notoriously humid in summer, and the winds along the Charles are sometimes bone-chilling.

Bostonians and Cape Cod natives revere their Revolutionary War-era, federal and Greek revival homes and landmark buildings, and their chowder made with milk, not tomato juice, thank you. To a real Massachusetts Yankee, there's nothing quite like the first clambake on the beach. To give them credit, many dour old Bostonians have expanded their tastes to include the flowers, glass arcades and gourmet restaurants of Quincy Market and whimsical things like balloon festivals. Still, in spite of the downtown highrises, there is little of glitz about this region. It's not an invented attraction but a real place, one that stands on the legitimacy and integrity of its origins.

This book was designed to help you explore Boston, Cape Cod and the Massachusetts coast. Besides leading you to countless popular spots, it will also take you to many off-the-beaten-path locales, places usually known only by locals. The book will tell the story of the region's history, its flora and fauna. Each chapter will suggest places to eat, to stay, to sightsee, to shop and to enjoy the outdoors and nightlife, covering a range of tastes and budgets.

Beginning in Boston proper, this book takes visitors from its Revolutionary War sites to Beacon Hill, Back Bay, the Fenway and all the other corners of this city of neighborhoods and ethnic charm. In Chapter Three, we cross the Charles River to visit Cambridge, site of Harvard University and dozens of bookstores and museums, then go on to Lexington and Con-

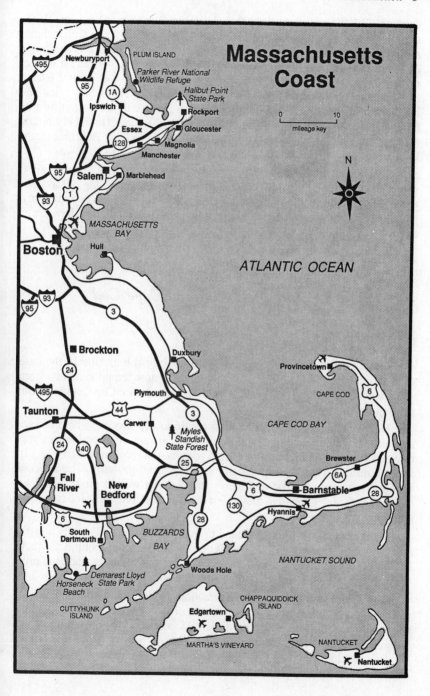

Massachusetts Coast

cord, now-idyllic spots where the Revolutionary War's first shots were fired. Chapter Four joins the hordes of visitors traveling to Cape Cod, where moors, salt marshes and breathtaking dunes lead out to the artsy enclave of Provincetown, and to the jewels of Martha's Vineyard—where a visitor might run into Jackie Onassis or Walter Cronkite—and the smaller island of Nantucket. In Chapter Five, we travel the Massachusetts coast: first we head north of Boston toward infamous Salem and the quietly beautiful old fishing and resort villages that hug the shoreline, then south to the Plymouth area, where Pilgrim memorials abound, and finally to New Bedford, made famous by Melville in *Moby Dick* and still a crusty old sea town.

Generations of travelers have come to the Boston area, searching for pieces of America's past that echo off brick pavements, seeking out its centers of learning, or just looking for a quiet spot in a cottage by the sea. Many have found there's too much here to contain in a single visit, and they return again and again.

The Story of Boston and Cape Cod

GEOLOGY

Geology is destiny, you might say. Certainly this is true in the case of Boston and Cape Cod. Some of the region's most famed symbols, from stone walls to Bunker Hill, Walden Pond, and the entire Cape, sprang from geologic events.

New England is one of the oldest continuously surviving land masses on earth. In Cambrian times, half a billion years ago, this entire area was covered by a vast inland sea. The Ice Age seized the region in a frozen grip about a million years ago, gradually spreading and growing. The mass of ice finally became so vast and heavy that its own weight pushed it down and outward, and it began to move. For thousands of years, the ice cap grew, engulfing all of New England.

As it moved, the ice cap picked up boulders, some as large as houses, and carried them along with it. Fields of boulders were left behind. Farmers had to clear their land of countless rocks before they planted, and they used them to make the stone walls that still line the landscape today.

The ice moved in a southerly direction, from Canada to Long Island, paring off hills and ledges as it went. Some of the glacial till was clay, which sticks to itself more readily than to ice. Deposited clay formed into low-lying, oval-shaped hills called drumlins, many a mile or more long and a hundred feet high. Some of the region's most famous drumlins are Bunker Hill and World's End in Hingham.

The glaciers came and went four times, retreating and advancing for over a million years, finally leaving this area about 10,000 to 12,000 years ago. The last glacial advance formed Cape Cod, Martha's Vineyard and Nantucket. At the front of the advancing ice sheet, released rock debris built up a terminal moraine—a ridge of rubble. These islands and coastal areas are what remains of the morainal ridges.

Large blocks of melting glacial ice formed kettle-hole lakes, deep bodies of water with a rounded shape, of which Walden Pond is a good example. It might also be said that kettle lakes make for fine ice-skating and ice-fishing.

HISTORY

Boston and its environs make up America's scrapbook, telling a tale of a nation conceived on hardship and perseverance, faith and dreams. It is a riveting story of high adventure and the push for freedom, of ingenuity and despotism, of victory over adverse conditions.

The opening pages find navigator John Cabot, on assignment from England's King Henry VII, seeking a Northwest Passage to the East. Cabot explored the coast of Massachusetts in 1497. He found no pass but claimed a considerable chunk of the New World—everything north of Florida and east of the Rockies—for the British crown.

Italian explorer Giovanni da Verrazano staked out the same coast some 27 years later, claiming the territory for his employer nation, France. Just prior to his visit, navigator Miguel Corte Real had been checking out the terrain for Portugal.

In 1614, English captain John Smith mapped the Massachusetts coast and was taken by its beauty. A soldier of fortune, Smith wrote a glowing report of the intriguing land, describing its "sandy cliffes and cliffes of rock" planted with cornfields and gardens.

Though captivated by the new region, none of these adventurers did what seemed the most logical thing: settle the place. Of course, this white man's frontier had been inhabited at least five centuries by Algonquin tribes. A peaceful people who dwelled in wigwams, they were expert growers of corn, tobacco, pumpkins and other crops. They hunted forests plentiful with moose, deer, turkey and goose, and fished the streams and ocean for bass, salmon, lobster and clams, throwing the area's earliest clambakes. They welcomed the first permanent European settlers in 1620.

Religious asylum, not adventure or fortune, is what those first settlers were seeking. The Puritans, cut off from Anglican England because of their strict Protestant beliefs, read with interest John Smith's glowing report on the New World. Could it be their Land of Oz? They were anxious to find out.

In the spring of 1620, the Puritans struck a deal with the Plymouth Company to finance a settlement in the New World. By summer's end, 102

Puritans boarded the Mayflower for a rigorous, two-month journey to America. They first sighted land at Cape Cod, then cruised the coast for a month and landed at Plymouth Rock. On December 21, the Plymouth Colony was born.

That first winter proved brutal for the colonists as they fought scurvy, pneumonia and other diseases that killed nearly half their group. But springtime brought relief and the opportunity to plant crops, thanks to help from the Indians who were hospitable to their new neighbors. To celebrate the first anniversary of their friendship, the Pilgrims and Indians feasted together for three days that fall.

As word of the successful colony trickled back to England, more Puritans set out for the New World. In 1630, about 1000 Puritans on 11 ships landed at Salem during the "Great Migration." Drawn by a vast harbor filled with sea life, settlers moved southward and declared Boston their main colony.

By 1636, another 12,000 immigrants had arrived. Puritan ministers, sensing the need to train future leaders, founded Harvard College and set up a general court to govern the colonies. Local matters were dealt with by town leaders at regular meetings, the forerunners of today's town council sessions.

Ironically, those same Puritans who sought the New World for religious freedom would not tolerate other beliefs. In 1651, a visitor from the Rhode Island colony was publicly whipped for being a Baptist. Victims of English persecution, Quakers fleeing the Old World were arrested on ships in Boston Harbor before they ever set foot on the new land. And in 1659, two men and a woman were hanged in Massachusetts for espousing Quaker beliefs. Religious dissidents fled to Rhode Island, which Puritans dubbed "the sewer of New England" and "Rogue's Island."

It was Puritan fanaticism that caused the untimely end of several other unfortunate New England souls. Witches, the Puritans said, were lurking about, possessed by demons and casting spells on innocent minds.

The accusations led to witch trials in Charlestown in 1648 and in Boston in 1655, but the most hideous ordeal occurred in Salem in 1692. After hundreds of people were imprisoned in a "Witch House," 19 were executed, including 80-year-old Giles Corey, who was pressed to death when he pled no-contest.

The Puritans were also a nightmare for the Indians. Determined to "save" them from their pagan ways, missionaries translated the Bible into Algonquin and set about converting new Christians. By the 1670s, nearly one-fourth of the Indian population had officially accepted the imposed faith. But it was not enough. The Puritans wanted not just mental converts but a race that would abandon its centuries-old customs, its very mode of existence.

As colonies expanded, the Indians got in the way. Several skirmishes ensued, but it was King Philip's War, from 1675 to 1676, that spelled the beginning of the end for the New England Indians. Pressured by colonists to abandon his land, chief Metacomet (King Philip) led a series of battles against his encroachers. He lost a decisive engagement when Massachusetts and Connecticut colonists burned wigwams, killing hundreds of women and children and disorganizing Indian forces.

Betrayed by a fellow Indian, King Philip was captured soon thereafter, his body beheaded and quartered. His head was displayed on a gibbet in Plymouth for 20 years as a reminder of white victory. Just four decades after the Indians had welcomed the first Puritans into their home, the Puritans had decimated them.

Although the Indians paid dearly for the colonists arrival in America, the settlers themselves thrived. The colonists found Boston waters teeming with cod and, by the 1640s, were shipping dried cod to the West Indies and the Mediterranean. In exchange, they received sugar, gold and molasses. By the 1670s, Boston dominated the West Indian shipping business, and by 1700 it was the third busiest port in the British realm, after London and Bristol.

But Britain resented this young upstart colony and began to impose trade and tax restrictions. In 1764, Britain imposed the Revenue Act, which levied duties on silk, sugar and some wines. Colonists rebelled and promptly boycotted the tariffs.

England didn't flinch. One year later, it slapped the colonies with the Stamp Act, taxing commercial and legal papers such as newspapers and licenses. Outraged, colonists denounced the tax and refused to buy European goods. "No taxation without representation," they cried. Every colonial stamp agent resigned, and before the law could take effect November 1, Parliament repealed the act.

But colonial anger was growing, and it soon erupted into riots. The British responded by sending troops to occupy Boston in 1768. Anti-crown tensions climaxed in the Boston Massacre in 1770, a clash between British soldiers and colonists. When the day was over, five colonials lay dead on King Street, present-day State Street.

England repealed most of the taxes, leaving duties on imported tea—then the most popular drink in America. New Englanders retaliated by buying smuggled tea. In 1773, when England's Tea Act flooded the market with cheap tea, agents would not accept deliveries—except for Governor Thomas Hutchinson in Boston.

When three tea-filled ships sailed into Boston Harbor, the Committees of Correspondence and Sons of Liberty—prerevolutionary activists—blocked the piers. Governor Hutchinson refused to let the ships return to England, so protestors invited him to a little tea party.

Disguised as Indians, 60 Sons of Liberty boarded the ships on the night of December 16, 1773 and dumped 342 chests of tea into the harbor. It was a defiant move and an ominous portent of what lie ahead: revolution was in the air.

On April 19, 1775, a single musket discharge set off America's first full-scale war. "The shot heard 'round the world" was fired at the Battle of Lexington and Concord, an effort by the Redcoats to crush revolutionary uprisings around Boston.

Forewarned by Paul Revere that "the British are coming," 77 Minutemen crouched in early morning darkness, waiting for the Redcoat attack. The British advanced, killing eight rebels and wounding ten on the present-day Lexington Green before continuing to Concord. There they destroyed a cache of arms and were finally driven out.

On June 17, 1775, the colonists fought the war's first major engagement—known as the Battle of Bunker Hill although it was really fought on nearby Breed's Hill—on the Charlestown peninsula near Boston. After enduring two British attacks, the Americans ran short of ammunition and retreated.

Though a technical victory for England, Bunker Hill cost the crown more than 1000 troops—over twice the colonial losses. More important, it proved that the Minutemen volunteers were a match for the better-trained British army. The British evacuated the city on March 17, 1776, and fighting never again touched Boston.

On July 4, 1776, the Declaration of Independence was adopted by the Continental Congress. Six years of war later, the colonies were free.

After the Americans won their independence, thoughts turned to commerce. But lost British markets pushed Boston into a depression, and the city began looking toward the Far East for trade, bringing in silks, spices and porcelain. Salem grew into a major port known for its China trade.

Fortunes were made by Boston's more prosperous merchants, a group of influential families who came to be known as the "codfish aristocracy." They dubbed themselves Boston Brahmins, smugly adopting the title of India's priestly caste. This small group counted among them the names of Cabot, Lowell and Hancock. They ruled the city with an unapproachable elitism, letting it be known that "the Lowells speak only to the Cabots, and the Cabots speak only to God."

The Brahmins built brick monuments to their prosperity on Beacon Hill, an elite residential district that defined the social character of Boston throughout the mid-19th century. Beacon Hill was home to such intellectuals as Francis Parkman, William James, Henry Wadsworth Longfellow, James Russell Lowell, Bronson Alcott, Julia Ward Howe and Horace Mann.

Great minds thrived across the region. Artists, thinkers and literary geniuses would set the dynamic tone in the Boston and Massachusetts coastal areas for centuries to come. Nathaniel Hawthorne lived in Salem, while Rudyard Kipling and Winslow Homer also made their homes on the North

Shore. Henry David Thoreau settled in Cape Cod, Emily Dickinson on Martha's Vineyard.

The sea was bountiful for Massachusetts during the 18th century. The coast thrived on its burgeoning whaling industry, with major ports at Nantucket and New Bedford, while the North Shore grew fat with fishing villages. In the 1850s Boston become the premier builder of clipper ships, sending these graceful craft around the world. To accommodate the growing trade, the city built many wharves along its waterfront. But the clipper era was cut short by the rise of steam-powered ships, which conservative Bostonians did not trust and would not build. Merchants shifted their capital to manufacturing, and the harbor went into a long decline.

The mid-19th century also saw the founding of some of Boston's most famed cultural institutions, among them the Boston Public Library, the Boston Symphony Orchestra, the Massachusetts Institute of Technology and Boston University, the first to admit women on an equal basis. The cultural richness produced a new nickname for the city: "The Athens of America." But political turmoil had not ended with the Revolution—abolitionism grew in the Boston area in the 19th century. William Lloyd Garrison published his *Liberator* newspaper for 34 years, despite being dragged through the streets by angry mobs and threatened constantly.

Into this tumultuous urban area swarmed thousands of immigrants, led in the 1840s by the Irish, who had been forced from their homeland by the potato famine. The influx of Irish changed the character of this Yankee city forever. First blatantly discriminated against by old-line Bostonians ("No Irish need apply"), they grew in numbers great enough to win political power. The first Irish mayor was elected in 1885, and the Irish gave us such leaders as former Speakers of the House John W. McCormack and Tip O'Neill, James Michael Curley and the Kennedy clan.

By 1860, 61 percent of Boston residents had been born abroad. Boston bloomed into an ethnic rainbow in the 1880s, when waves of Italians, Poles and Russians arrived, multiplying the population 30-fold.

At the same time, the city's area was itself multiplying. In the mid-19th century, Boston had begun filling in the bay between Beacon Hill and Brookline, a neighborhood now known as Back Bay. Other swampy land to the south was also filled and became the South End. By the turn of the century, Boston had tripled its size with landfill.

But soon after, Boston's economy suffered a tremendous decline that would last until the 1960s. The city lost its major port status to New York and Baltimore, and its textile, shoe and glass mills moved south in search of cheaper labor and operating costs. Population shrank in the 1940s and '50s, with Boston the only large city to decline in numbers during the post-war baby boom years. The city languished in the throes of this decline for decades.

Cape Cod meanwhile, was beginning to bloom as a tourist mecca, while Martha's Vineyard lured writers including Lillian Hellman and Dashiell Hammett to build summer homes along its exotic shoreline. In 1930, the respected Woods Hole Oceanographic Institute opened on the Cape's southeastern tip.

Good times eventually returned to Boston, too. In the 1960s, the Protestant elite and Irish Catholics finally cooperated in managing city affairs. Urban renewal projects created the new Government Center and the landmark Prudential and Hancock towers. The technological revolution of the 1970s and '80s enriched the area's economy.

With prosperity came urban problems. In the early 1970s, court-ordered busing among racially imbalanced schools sparked rioting and protests, particularly in South Boston and Charlestown. The crisis lasted several years. In the 1980s, blacks began to gain more power in local and state government and in private business, but racial tension continues in this city.

Today higher education remains a leading "industry" of Boston, the site of 47 colleges and universities at last count. And tourism is a major source of wealth in the city and along the coast and Cape Cod.

But beyond the high-tech centers and tourist attractions resounds the inescapable presence of Boston's colorful past: Revolutionary War monuments, 18th-century statehouses, steepled churches that held this country's first congregations. One need only explore Paul Revere's House or the Bunker Hill Monument to recognize the sites of this country's genesis. For Boston's past is America's past. And the region remains a vital part of the nation's present and future.

FLORA AND FAUNA

Massachusetts coastal waters hold a bounty of sea life, thanks in large measure to the magnificent salt marshes skirting its shoreline. Among the most productive acres on earth, these marshes are home to plants and minute animals that eventually wash into the ocean and feed fish and shellfish.

A delicately balanced ecosystem that takes about 5000 years to evolve, the marsh at high tide is full of fiddler crabs, fish and water fowl. At low tide, marsh mud flats are alive with shellfish and shorebirds.

Not surprisingly, conservationists and developers are at odds over the salt marshes. With the advent of dredging, developers were able to transform swampy marshes into profitable waterfront real estate, and from that point on there has been a battle to protect the salt marshes.

Massachusetts' bays and inlets also thrive with marsh-nourished crabs, oysters, quahogs, clams, mussels, scallops, periwinkles and whelks. Farther out to sea swim the species that have made this area one of the richest fishery resources in the world. Long famous for record-size striped bass and giant bluefin tuna, the coastal waters also have a variety of other highly prized fish, including flounder, cod, bluefish, swordfish, squid and shark.

The coast is also home to many endangered and rare species of birds such as the merlin, a small hawk, and sedge wrens. Blue herons, tree swallows, marsh hawks, catbirds, mourning doves, red-starts, orioles, osprey, Canadian geese, red-winged blackbirds and owls are a mere sampling of coastal birdlife.

An imposing sight, the great blue heron frequents both freshwater and saltwater areas and can be seen all over Cape Cod during spring, summer and fall. The largest of American herons, it's usually seen at a distance standing in shallow water waiting for prey to swim into view. It thrives on fish, reptiles, mice, insects and other small mammals.

Snowy egrets, once common chiefly along the shoreline south of Boston, now can be found throughout Massachusetts coastal marshes, especially in the summer. With its pure white body, yellow feet and black pointed bill, the snowy egret is fairly easy to spot. Around the turn of the century, hunters, coveting the bird's feathers for ladies hats, nearly wiped out the species. It's now illegal to hunt birds for the sake of fashion.

Belted kingfishers aren't the most cordial of the shore's feathered creatures. They stake out a territory in fresh- or saltwater marsh and try to drive other birds away. Fairly easy to recognize, the birds have a crested head, blue-gray upper coloration and a lighter belt under the throat. The more colorful female has a red band around the stomach.

Another common shorebird, the herring gull, nests on islands and in remote coastal areas. You can spot them by their white heads and bodies, light grey backs and black wing tips. The tiny semipalmated sandpipers are often seen in groups, scurrying along sand and mudflats. Sometimes called peeps, little peeps or ox eyes, they have grayish-brown backs, white speckled breasts and black legs. Other shore and ocean birds include shearwaters, petrels, fulmars, gannets, jaegers, skuas, phalaropes, arctic terns and more.

The noble whale is without question the most observed and admired sea mammal in Massachusetts. In the warmer months, hundreds of whale-watch excursions depart daily from ports everywhere along the coast, so visitors can watch 70-foot fin whales, acrobatic humpbacks, 20-foot minke whales and rare right whales as well as dolphins and porpoises at play in the waters. Hunted extensively in the 19th century, many species of whale are now endangered.

Although birds and fish populate the coast in great numbers, animal wildlife is somewhat limited. Along or near the shore you're apt to see deer, muskrats, painted turtles, ribbon snakes, raccoons, quail, pheasant and ruffed grouse.

Flora along the eastern edge of Massachusetts varies greatly from spot to spot. Common salt marsh flora includes fragrant sea lavender, a long,

(Text continued on page 14.)

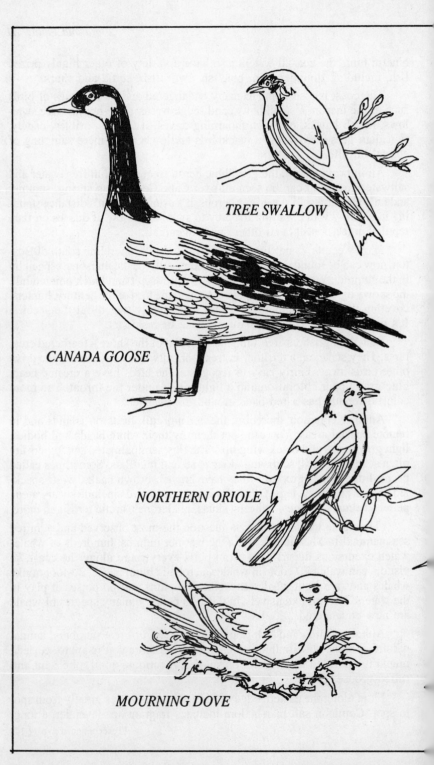

TREE SWALLOW

CANADA GOOSE

NORTHERN ORIOLE

MOURNING DOVE

HAWK

CORMORANT

BLUE HERON

slender, stalklike plant that produces tiny flowers in summer; glasswort, a low, edible plant that looks like a skinny pickle; orach, a sharply pointed, arrow-shaped, light-green plant found in the high marsh; stately seaside goldenrod, a tall, colorful high-marsh plant with small vibrant flowers that closely resemble upland goldenrods; and spike-grass, short, wavy grass with large flower heads.

Pitch pines and scrub oaks dominate Cape Cod's landscape, along with sassafras, and oak and pine forests cover Martha's Vineyard. Cranberry bogs lying in deep woods east of Plymouth lead to a crimson spectacle during fall harvesting, and patches of cranberries also grow on Cape Cod and Nantucket. Visitors will also discover swamps and forests of beech, cedar and holly. Growing close to the shore are wild roses, beach plums, heather and acres of wavy beach grass.

Nantucket is the only place in America with maritime heathland similar to that found in Scotland, a unique display of lush heather, bayberry and other flora. The island's rolling moors change colors with the seasons—from green and pink in the summer to the dazzling reds and golds that come in autumn.

When To Go

SEASONS

A constant battle rages here in the Boston and Cape Cod area between bristling battalions of cold, dry Canadian arctic air and laid-back, warm, humid air from the tropics. When these two mix it up, which is frequently, you have New England's legendary changeable weather. The morning may dawn fine and sunny, afternoon turn cold and foggy and nightfall bring a raging northeaster.

In Boston proper, the weather varies from warm, humid summers, when temperatures range from the 60s to the low 80s, to dry, crisp falls hovering in the high 40s (and the low 70s during Indian summer), to very cold winters, when temperatures dip to the 20s and 30s, occasionally falling below zero.

Along the coast and Cape Cod, the weather is milder than in the rest of New England, although winters are still long and cold. Summer temperatures range from the 60s to the 80s. Humidity can be a problem, especially along the North Shore, although ocean breezes keep things from getting too unbearable. In the fall temperatures range from around 45° to 65°.

Tourists flock to Boston for fall-foliage season (mid-September through October), when it can be very difficult to get reservations. During the low seasons of April, May and late October through late December, you'll have a much less crowded vacation and a much easier time getting reservations.

Traditionally the Cape, the Islands and coastal areas have been summer destinations, but more people are starting to visit in the fall, when prices decline along with the crowds. A bike ride through Nantucket in October when the moors are in bloom is an unforgettable experience. In the rural outskirts of Boston, and in farm country near Plymouth and New Bedford, autumn may be the most wonderful season of all to visit. Fall colors are at their peak, and all the harvests of apples, cranberries and pumpkins are in. Sunny days often warm up to "Indian summer" comfort, energized by cool, crisp nights.

Both autumn and winter are substantially drier than in other locales. Still rain is unpredictable and can happen at any time of year. In this area it manages to rain, snow or sleet about one day out of three, making for an annual precipitation of 42 inches. Although the 1938 hurricane looms large in natives' memories, when entire coastal communities were swallowed by the sea, hurricanes hardly ever happen. There are about five to ten per century, fortunately most much less devastating than the 1938 storm.

CALENDAR OF EVENTS

Each year, the Boston and Cape Cod area celebrates its colonial past by reenacting historic events. Other annual observances celebrate the area's riches and native skills: shipbuilding, arts and crafts, clam digging and agriculture.

JANUARY

Boston: The **Chinese New Year** is celebrated in January or February, with three weeks of festivities.

FEBRUARY

Boston: The **New England Boat Show,** one of the largest on the East Coast, brings out the latest and fanciest in power and sail. Four of the city's biggest hockey-playing colleges (Harvard, Northeastern, Boston University and Boston College) face off in the **Beanpot Hockey Tournament.**

MARCH

Boston: The **New England Spring Flower Show** has been running for more than 100 years, giving a lift to winter-weary Bostonians. The **St. Patrick's Day Parade** thrown by the Irish of South Boston is one of the largest and most festive in America.

APRIL

Boston: The nation's premier running event, the **Boston Marathon** is only one of several signal events on **Patriot's Day**. Other activities commem-

orating Revolutionary War events include a parade plus reenactments of
Paul Revere's famous ride and the Battle of Lexington and Concord.
Cape Cod and the Islands: During Nantucket's **Daffodil Festival,** hundreds
of these sprightly blooms decorate shop windows. It ends with an antique
car parade. **Go Fly a Kite Day** in Brewster features kite making, flying
and demonstrations at the Cape Cod Museum of Natural History. A pancake
eating contest, parade, kayak races, golf and tennis tournaments and local
art show are featured at the **Brewster in Bloom** festival.

MAY

Boston: **Lilac Sunday** at the Arnold Arboretum finds 400 varieties of lilacs
in bloom.
Cape Cod and the Islands: The **Heritage Plantation Rhododendron Festival** in Sandwich features blooms as far as the eye can see, plus lectures
and plant sales.
Massachusetts Coast: The **Salem Seaport Festival** includes food, arts, crafts,
antiques, live music and children's activities. **St. Peter's Fiesta** in Gloucester is a colorful event with religious activities, fireworks, music, food and
a parade. Anything that floats and *isn't* a boat can enter the madcap **Plymouth Bathtub Races.**

JUNE

Boston: The **Bunker Hill Day Reenactment and Parade** features contemporary patriots dressed in Revolutionary War uniforms fighting the famous
battle again. The **Boston Harborfest** offers nearly a hundred activities cel-
ebrating the harbor at 30 sites, highlighted by a chowderfest.
Outside Boston: The multicultural diversity of Cambridge comes alive in
the **Cambridge River Festival,** with live performances, crafts and food.
Cape Cod and the Islands: At the **Cape Cod Chowder Festival** in Hyannis,
you can vote for the best chowder and enjoy live entertainment.
Massachusetts Coast: Anything made with fresh strawberries can be served
at the **Annual Strawberry Festival** in Ipswich. **Railfan's Day & Railroad
Collector's Flea Market** in South Carver is the largest event of its kind
in New England.

JULY

Boston: The **U.S. Pro Tennis Championship** draws thousands of tennis fans
to the **Longwood Cricket Club.** Every weekend in July and August, **Italian
street festivals** honor patron saints with colorful parades and festivities.
Cape Cod and the Islands: The **Yarmouth Clam Festival** dishes up not
only clams, but many other seafoods, arts and crafts, music and entertainment. The **Falmouth Festival** includes over 200 professional artists and

craftsmen, live music and jugglers. In Sandwich, book lovers delight in the **Cape Cod Antiquarian Book Fair**, with over 40 dealers, rare and out-of-print books, manuscripts and collectibles. In Vineyard Haven, the **Tisbury Street Fair** includes quality clothing, jewelry, crafts, food and games. The **Edgartown Regatta** is one of New England's best and most serious yacht races. On Nantucket, the **Annual Billfish Tournament** is a big event where fishermen compete for the biggest catch of each species.

Massachusetts Coast: In Gloucester, the **Hammond Castle Annual Medieval Festival** has magic shows, music and merriment. Race Week in Marblehead includes sailboat races, parades and concerts.

AUGUST

Cape Cod and the Islands: Peter Rabbit's Animal Fair in Sandwich is great for kids, with pet rabbit shows, games, music and storytelling. In Orleans, the **Cape Cod Arts and Crafts Show** has 100 professional artists and craftspeople displaying their wares. On Nantucket, the **Annual Antique Show** offers quality antiques. Imaginations go wild at the **Sandcastle Contest** at Jetties Beach. In Oak Bluffs, **Illumination Night** is pure magic, with hundreds of paper lanterns strung throughout the Gothic homes. The **West Tisbury Agricultural Fair** includes fiddler's contests, the Massachusetts Woodsman Championship, horses and livestock shows, and even ox pulls.

Massachusetts Coast: New Bedford's **Annual Feast of the Blessed Sacrament**, the largest Portuguese feast in America, offers terrific ethnic food at budget prices. Tall ships regattas, races, concerts, parades and fireworks are offered at the **Fall River Celebrates America Festival**.

SEPTEMBER

Cape Cod and the Islands: Tasty crustaceans star at the **Annual Bourne Scallop Festival**. In Sandwich, the **Farmer's Market and Fall Festival** offers fresh produce, flowers, herbs, homebaked goods, entertainment, pony rides and appearances by Peter Rabbit. The **Cape Cod Antique Market**, a large gathering of antique and collectible dealers, takes place at Barnstable County Fairgrounds in Falmouth. Local restaurants compete for prizes at the **Hyannis Chile Cookoff**. The **Harwich Cranberry Festival** includes ten days of parades, contests, fireworks and exhibits. Wellfleet holds **Bygone Days**, a nostalgic weekend including a children's parade, a Cape Cod Shore dinner, fashion shows, church suppers, nature walks, quilt raffles and the Saturday Harvest Moon Dance. The **Nantucket Seafest** at Children's Beach is a great way to sample a wide range of seafood dishes.

Massachusetts Coast: The **Essex Institute Harvest Festival** in Salem features demonstrations of 17th- and 18th-century domestic arts, folk dancing, music and food. Arts, crafts, seafood, kayaking, canoeing and dory races are some of the activities at the **Newburyport Waterfront Festival**. Also in Newburyport, classical and jazz musicians perform on the street and the galleries have open house at the **Art Newbury Street**. The **Essex Clamfest** includes chowder, a clam-shucking contest and entertainment. At the **Gloucester Schooner Festival**, you can watch races, a boat parade and other maritime activities. **Plimoth Plantation Muster Day** includes antique militia weapons and defense displays, tactical moves, feasting and recreation. Cranberry harvesting, exhibits, puppet shows, Dixieland bands and crafts are part of the **Edaville Railroad Cranberry Harvest Days** festival.

OCTOBER

Boston: More than 3000 oarsmen compete in the **Head of the Charles Regatta,** the largest one-day rowing event in the world. Top women's tennis pros take part in the **Virginia Slims Tournament of New England.**

Cape Cod and the Islands: Island arts, crafts, workshops and exhibits take place during **Nantucket Heritage Days.**

Massachusetts Coast: If ever a place looked haunted, it would be Hammond Castle in Gloucester, where on **Freaky Fridays** ghosts and ghouls spook and delight you as you tour this romantic castle. If you can make reservations well in advance and have a great Halloween costume, don't miss **Hammond Castle Halloween Ball** in the Great Hall, a costumed event right out of a horror novel. **Haunted Happenings**, Salem's citywide Halloween festival, includes haunted-house tours, costume parades, parties, candlelight tours with witches, of course, magic shows and psychics. Mysterious legends of Essex County are told by costumed storytellers in historic houses at Salem's **Essex Institute Eerie Events.**

NOVEMBER

Cape Cod and the Islands: The **Green Briar Nature Center Thanksgiving Celebration** in Sandwich offers traditional holiday fare, special exhibits and craft demonstrations. **Felix Neck Sanctuary Fall Festival** on Martha's Vineyard includes nature walks and baked goods.

Massachusetts Coast: **A Sea Captain Celebrates Thanksgiving**, an 18th century banquet in Salem's House of the Seven Gables, also includes discussions on meal preparation, dining customs and music of the time (reservations required). Have a traditional turkey dinner with all the trimmings in America's hometown, Plymouth, during its annual **Thanksgiving Dinner.**

DECEMBER

Boston: The **Cambridge Christmas Revels** celebrate the winter solstice with period song and dance; audience participation is traditional. Hundreds of events mark **First Night**, a New Year's Eve celebration held indoors and out. There's a pageant, plus choral groups, ice sculptures, storytellers, acrobats, puppeteers and art and drama presentations. The **Boston Tea Party**

Reenactment finds patriots dressed as Indians throwing chests of tea into Boston Harbor one more time.

Cape Cod and the Islands: It looks like something out of Dickens along the town's Main Street when the **Nantucket Christmas Stroll** takes place, with a weekend of carolers and other Yuletide festivities.

Massachusetts Coast: **Christmas as Imagined** in Newburyport includes Santa arriving by boat, a parade and tree lighting. **Salem Holiday Happenings** includes crafts, fairs, house tours, auctions, concerts, ballet and more. A train ride through acres of colored lights and elaborate Christmas displays are part of Edaville's Christmas Festival of Lights in South Carver.

How to Deal With . . .

VISITOR INFORMATION

New England USA (76 Summer Street, Boston, MA 02110; 617-423-6967 or 800-847-4863 outside Massachusetts) has a free Travel Planner suggesting itineraries throughout New England.

As well as large cities, many small towns have chambers of commerce or visitor information centers; a number of them are listed in this book under the appropriate state or region.

For information on areas throughout the state, contact the **Massachusetts Office of Travel and Tourism** (Department of Commerce, 100 Cambridge Street, Boston, MA 02202; 617-727-3201). More detailed information on Boston can be had from the Greater Boston Convention and Visitors Bureau (Box 490, Prudential Center, 800 Boylston Street, Boston, MA 02216; 617-536-4100).

PACKING

Packing for a visit to this area is a little trickier than for other destinations. What you must take is dictated by the fickle Yankee weather, which might change at any minute. A warm, sunny day can turn cool and foggy without so much as a by your leave. The best bet is to bring layers of clothing that can be added or subtracted as needed. Even in the summer, bring some long-sleeved shirts, long pants and lightweight sweaters and jackets, along with your T-shirts, jeans and bathing suit.

Fall and spring call for a full round of warm clothing, from long pants and sweaters to jackets, hats and gloves. While fall days are often sunny and warm, fall nights can turn quite crisp and cool. Bring your heaviest, warmest clothes in winter: thick sweaters, knitted hats, down jackets and ski clothes.

Boston can be conservatively dressed at times. Some downtown Boston restaurants have dress codes, requiring men to wear jackets and ties and women to be "appropriately attired." But Boston Brahmins notwithstanding, most of this area is pretty casual, especially in summer by the sea, when everyone has sand in his shoes. No one will look askance if you wear your deck shoes and L.L. Bean pants to dinner at most restaurants, particularly in coastal resort areas. Massachusetts is less casual, however, than a warm-weather resort, and you can't get into most restaurants or bars without a shirt or shoes, or if you're wearing a bathing suit.

Residents here are used to rolling up their car windows every night in summer, knowing it may rain any time. Rain, though not usually heavy, is a big part of every season, so be sure to bring an umbrella and a raincoat, even in the summer.

Some of Boston's streets are almost as old as the city itself. On these rough, cobblestone ways you need sturdy, comfortable shoes that can take this kind of beating and be kind to your feet. Women should never attempt to navigate cobblestone streets in high heels. Likewise, some shores can be rocky. A pair of rubber shoes or old sneakers for swimming is sometimes advisable.

Though Cape Cod and the coast are not the Caribbean, you can get just as impressive a sunburn here. Bring a good sunscreen, especially to the beach, where sand and water reflect the sun's rays more intensely. Bring insect repellant in the summertime as insurance against the greenhead flies at the shore and blackflies in the mountains.

When you come here, you'll need nothing but the best street and road maps. Many roads in this area are winding, poorly marked or not marked at all. Finally, don't forget your camera for capturing scenes frozen from American history as well as quintessential New England vistas of light-houses and great sand dunes.

HOTELS

Visiting Massachusetts is your opportunity to stay in some of the most historic lodgings this country has to offer. A number of them date to the 18th century, such as Longfellow's Wayside Inn in Sudbury.

Boston hotels range from grande dames of the past century to glitzy contemporary skyscrapers. They are usually first-rate but tend to be priced for travelers on an expense account, especially in the downtown area.

The coastal regions are thick with historic farmhouses and sea captains' mansions turned into bed and breakfasts. These are often rambling, cozy affairs complete with fireplace, bookshelves and resident cat. But bed-and-breakfast booking agencies, especially in Boston, also list host homes with a spare room, which isn't quite the same thing. Be sure to ask whether a bed and breakfast is an inn or not.

Cape Cod has some of the most beautiful inns in the country, plus hundreds of other accommodations in every price range, location and style imaginable. If you plan to stay for at least a week, think about renting a house, apartment or condo; it's usually less expensive than a hotel. Call or write the Cape Cod Chamber of Commerce (Hyannis, MA 02601; 508-362-3225) for names of realtors handling rentals in a particular area.

In addition, accommodations include mom-and-pop motels, chain hotels and rustic seaside cottages where you'll awaken to the sounds of surf and crying gulls. Outside of Boston, lodgings are generally casual and low-rise.

Whatever your preference and budget, you can probably find something to suit your taste with the help of the individual chapters in this book. Remember, rooms are scarce and prices rise in the high season, which is summer, fall-foliage time and Christmas. Many hotels on Cape Cod and the Islands close in the winter, and reservations are mandatory in the summer.

There are lots of special weekend and holiday packages at the larger hotels, and off-season rates drop significantly, making a week- or month-long stay a real bargain.

Accommodations in this book are organized by region and classified according to price. These refer to high-season rates, so if you're looking for low-season bargains, be sure to inquire about them.

Budget lodgings generally cost less than $50 a night for two people and are satisfactory and clean but modest. *Moderate*-priced lodgings run from $50 to $90; what they offer in terms of luxury will depend on their location, but in general they provide larger rooms and more attractive surroundings. At a *deluxe* hotel or resort, you can expect to spend between $90 and $130 for a double; typically you'll find spacious rooms, a fashionable lobby, a restaurant or two and often some shops. *Ultra-deluxe* facilities, priced above $130, are a region's finest, offering all the amenities of a deluxe hotel plus plenty of luxurious extras, such as jacuzzis and exercise rooms, 24-hour room service and gourmet dining.

If you've got your heart set on a room with a water view, be sure to pin that down. Be forewarned that "oceanside" doesn't always mean right on the beach. If you want to save money, try lodgings a block or so away from the water. They almost always offer lower rates than rooms within sight of the surf, and the savings are often worth the short stroll to the beach.

(Text continued on page 24.)

The Land of Lighthouses

Massachusetts' prominence as a shipping and fishing center made lighthouses essential early in its history. The first lighthouse in America was built in Boston Harbor on Little Brewster Island in 1716. During the years to follow, 60 more were built all along the coast.

The majority of lighthouses have been well-preserved, and many are still in use, although the lighthouse keeper has gone the way of time. Today lighthouses are automated and unmanned. Lighted buoys, radio communications, radar and high-tech navigational equipment, electronic fog signals and the Coast Guard offer additional protection to seafaring vessels. Shipwrecks are practically unheard of these days.

A few beacons are privately owned, but most are maintained by the Coast Guard or local historic organizations. What follows is a guide to some of the most beautiful and historically significant lighthouses.

Built in 1797, **Highland Lighthouse Station** in Truro, Cape Cod, is better known as Cape Cod Light. It stands on clay bluffs overlooking an area once known as "the graveyard of ships" because hundreds of vessels went aground here before the lighthouse was built. Visible 20 miles out to sea, this classic white-and-black lighthouse is surrounded by scenic Cape Cod National Seashore and commands a magnificent view.

Located within the Cape Cod National Seashore, **Race Point Lighthouse** (★), built in 1816, guards the entrance to Provincetown Harbor. Surrounded by wild, windswept dunes, it is accessible only by four-wheel-drive vehicle or by foot. Even after the lighthouse was built, from 1816 to 1946 more than 100 shipwrecks occurred in this treacherous area.

Plymouth Lighthouse, established in 1768, is located on a beautiful bluff at the end of a peninsula that stretches from Duxbury to Plymouth Har-

bor. During the Revolutionary War, a British ship fired a cannonball at the lighthouse, but it barely made a dent. Destroyed by fire in 1801, it was rebuilt in 1843 and is one of Massachusetts' most scenic lighthouses.

Scituate Lighthouse, built in 1811 on Cedar Point at the entrance to Scituate Harbor, is maintained by the Scituate Historical Society. It's no longer in use, but an event that took place here during the War of 1812 gave this lighthouse historic distinction. In September 1814, Rebecca and Abigail Bates, the lighthouse keeper's young daughters, were alone in the lighthouse, when they spotted British war ships heading for the harbor. Frantic to do something, they started playing military songs on a drum and fife. The music made the British think the American Army was amassing, and they hightailed it back to the high seas. The girls became local heros.

Minot's Lighthouse, which dates to 1850, is built on a ledge one mile offshore from Cohasset. The ledge can only be seen at low tide. Most of the time the lighthouse looks as if it's floating in water. Since it was built in a highly dangerous area, men working on the lighthouse were washed out to sea by strong waves and currents. In 1851 a ferocious storm destroyed the lighthouses and two keepers died. Because of these tragedies the lighthouse was thought to be haunted by the ghosts of those who perished at sea. A museum in Cohasset contains many artifacts and historical information on the lighthouse.

Annisquam Harbor Lighthouse (★) is located on Wigwam Point at the mouth of Annisquam River on the North Shore. Built in 1801, this lighthouse doesn't have historic significance, but it is one of the most scenic in all of Massachusetts. It's located off the beaten path: to get there, take Route 127 to Annisquam and turn right at the village church, then right into Norwood Heights and follow the road to the water.

RESTAURANTS

Succulent native seafood stars at legions of Boston and Cape Cod restaurants, from lobster in the rough and tender bay scallops to codfish, mussels, steamers and milky clam chowder.

Besides seafood and traditional Yankee foods, Boston restaurants also serve up ethnic cuisines of every stripe. No matter what your taste or budget, there's a restaurant for you.

Within each chapter, restaurants are organized geographically. Each entry describes the cuisine and ambience and categorizes the restaurant in one of four price ranges. Dinner entrées at *budget* restaurants usually cost $8 or less. The ambience is informal, service speedy, the crowd often a local one. *Moderate*-priced eateries charge between $8 and $16 for dinner; surroundings are casual but pleasant, the menu offers more variety and the pace is usually slower. *Deluxe* restaurants tab their entrées above $16; cuisines may be simple or sophisticated, but the decor is plusher and the service more personalized. *Ultra-deluxe* establishments, where entrées begin at $24, are often the gourmet gathering places; here cooking is (hopefully) a fine art, and the service should be impeccable.

Some restaurants, particularly those that depend on the summer trade in coastal areas, close for the winter.

Breakfast and lunch menus vary less in price from one restaurant to another. Even deluxe establishments usually offer light breakfasts and lunches, priced within a few dollars of their budget-minded competitors. These smaller meals can be a good time to test expensive restaurants.

TRAVELING WITH CHILDREN

Massachusetts is a wonderful place to bring children. Besides many child-oriented museums, the region also has dozens of beaches and parks, and many nature sanctuaries sponsor childrens' activities year-round.

Quite a few bed and breakfasts in this area don't accept children, so be sure of the policy when you make reservations. If you need a crib or cot, arrange for it ahead of time.

Travel agents can help with arrangements; they can reserve airline bulkhead seats where there is plenty of room (but where you can't watch a movie) and determine which flights are least crowded. If you are traveling by car, be sure to take along such necessities as water and juices, snacks and toys. Always allow extra time for getting places, especially on rural roads.

A first-aid kit is a must for any trip. Along with adhesive bandages, antiseptic cream and something to stop itching, include any medicines your pediatrician might recommend to treat allergies, colds, diarrhea or any chronic problems your child may have.

At the beach, take extra care with your children's skin the first few days. Children's tender young skin can suffer severe sunburn before you know it. Hats for the kids are a good idea, along with liberal applications of a good sunscreen. Never take your eyes off your children at the shore. If you are traveling in winter, never leave a child alone near a frozen lake.

All-night stores are scarce in rural areas, and stores in small towns often close early, so be sure to be well stocked with diapers, baby food and other needs when you are on the go. But all-night stores such as 7-11 are plentiful in bigger towns.

To find specific activities for children, consult local newspapers. The *Boston Globe* Thursday Calendar has especially comprehensive listings that cover a good part of the state.

The **Travelers Aid Society of Boston, Inc.** (711 Atlantic Avenue, Boston, MA 02111; 617-542-7286) is a resource for any traveler in need and maintains booths at major transportation terminals. Volunteers can arrange to meet young children traveling alone.

OLDER TRAVELERS

The Boston area is a hospitable place for senior citizens to visit; countless museums, historic sights and even restaurants and hotels offer senior discounts that cut a substantial chunk off vacation costs. Many from hotter climes flock to Massachusetts for its cool summers.

The **American Association of Retired Persons** (3200 East Carson Street, Lakewood, CA 90712; 213-496-2277) offers membership to anyone over 50. AARP's benefits include travel discounts with a number of firms; escorted tours and cruises are available through AARP Travel Service (4801 West 110th Street, P.O. Box 7324, Overland Park, KS 66207; 800-334-3300).

Elderhostel (80 Boylston Street, Suite 400, Boston, MA 02116; 617-426-7788) offers many educational courses in a variety of Massachusetts locations that are all-inclusive packages at colleges and universities.

Be extra careful about health matters. In New England's changeable and sometimes cold weather, seniors are more at risk of suffering hypothermia, especially during prolonged exposure to wind. Older travelers should be very careful when walking to avoid falls. Sidewalks may be poorly paved or buckled in places, and cobblestone streets are easy to lodge an ankle in.

Be sure to bring along needed medications. Consider carrying a medical record with you, including your history and current medical status as well as your doctor's name, phone number and address. Make sure that your insurance covers you while you are away from home.

The **Travelers Aid Society of Boston, Inc.** (711 Atlantic Avenue, Boston, MA 02111; 617-542-7286) can provide emergency financial assistance and medical and social service referrals, help find low-cost accommodations, give directions and information and assist with banking and check cashing, and train, plane and bus connections. Volunteers can arrange to meet travelers with special needs.

DISABLED TRAVELERS

Massachusetts has made real strides toward making its many attractions and services handicapped-accessible. Parking spaces for the handicapped are provided at most services and attractions, although few buses are handicapped-accessible.

Special escorted group tours are offered by **New Horizons Travel for the Handicapped** (P.O. Box 652, Belmont, MA 02178; 617-231-8051, or 800-783-5567 outside Massachusetts), geared to the mentally handicapped and those with cerebral palsy. **The Guided Tour** (555 Ashbourne Road, Elkins Park, PA 19117; 215-782-1370) also leads tours for the disabled.

Access Tours (P.O. Box 356, Malverne, NY 11565; 800-876-2882 or 516-887-5798) specializes in travel arrangements for the handicapped with any disability.

For general advice on travel, consult the comprehensive guidebook *Access to the World—A Travel Guide for the Handicapped*, by Louise Weiss (Henry Holt and Company), available from **Facts on File** (460 Park Avenue South, New York, NY 10016; 800-322-8755).

Offering helpful information for disabled travelers are the **Society for the Advancement of Travel for the Handicapped** (26 Court Street, Brooklyn, NY 11242; 718-858-5483), **Travel Information Center** (Moss Rehabilitation Hospital, 12th Street and Tabor Road, Philadelphia, PA 19141; 215-329-5715), **Mobility International USA** (P.O. Box 3551, Eugene, OR 97403; 503-343-1284), **Flying Wheels Travel** (P.O. Box 382, Owatonna, MN 55060; 800-533-0363) and **Travelin' Talk** (P.O. Box 3534, Clarksville, TN 37043; 615-552-6670).

Amtrak offers discount train fares to the disabled. For a pamphlet describing their services, call a local office or write to Amtrak (National Railroad Passenger Corporation, 400 North Capitol Street Northwest, Washington, DC 20001).

The **Information Center for Individuals with Disabilities** (27-43 Wormwood Street, Boston, MA 02210; 617-727-5540) provides disabled travelers with information referral and problem-solving concerning the state of Massachusetts. A list of hotels, restaurants and historic sites that are handicapped-accessible is also available.

The **Travelers Aid Society of Boston, Inc.** (711 Atlantic Avenue, Boston, MA 02111; 617-542-7286) can arrange for volunteers to meet disabled travelers. Travelers Aid also publishes two free booklets, *Cambridge Access* and *Boston Access*, guides to handicapped-accessible sites and services in those areas.

FOREIGN TRAVELERS

PASSPORTS AND VISAS   Most foreign visitors are required to obtain a passport and tourist visa to enter the United States. Contact your nearest United States Embassy or Consulate well in advance to obtain a visa and to check on any other entry requirements.

CUSTOMS REQUIREMENTS   Foreign travelers are allowed to carry in the following: 200 cigarettes (or 100 cigars), $400 worth of duty-free gifts, including one liter of alcohol (you must be 21 years of age to bring in the alcohol). You may bring in any amount of currency, but must fill out a form if you bring in over $10,000 (U.S.). Carry any prescription drugs in clearly marked containers. (You may have to produce a written prescription or doctor's statement for the customs officer.) Meat or meat products, seeds, plants, fruits and narcotics are not allowed to be brought into the United States. Contact the **United States Customs Service** (1301 Constitution Avenue Northwest, Washington, DC 20229; 202-566-8195) for further information.

DRIVING   If you plan to rent a car, an international driver's license should be obtained before arriving in Massachusetts. Some rental companies require both a foreign license and an international driver's license. Many car rental agencies require a lessee to be 25 years of age; all require a major credit card.

CURRENCY   United States money is based on the dollar. Bills come in six denominations: $1, $5, $10, $20, $50 and $100. Every dollar is divided into 100 cents. Coins are the penny (1 cent), nickel (5 cents), dime (10 cents), quarter (25 cents). Half-dollars and dollar coins are rarely used. You may not use foreign currency to purchase goods and services in the United States. Consider buying traveler's checks in dollar amounts. You may also use credit cards affiliated with an American company such as Interbank, Barclay Card and American Express.

ELECTRICITY   Electric outlets use currents of 117 volts, 60 cycles. For appliances made for other electrical systems you need a transformer or other adapter.

WEIGHTS AND MEASUREMENTS   The United States uses the English system of weights and measures. American units and their metric equivalents are as follows: 1 inch = 2.5 centimeters; 1 foot = 0.3 meter; 1 yard = 0.9 meter; 1 mile = 1.6 kilometers; 1 ounce = 28 grams; 1 pound = 0.45 kilogram; 1 quart (liquid) = 0.9 liter.

The Sporting Life

CAMPING

Camping is somewhat limited in this area, but you'll find a few campgrounds at parks on Cape Cod and in the New Bedford area. For information on camping at Massachusetts state park sites, contact the **State Division of Forests and Parks** (100 Cambridge Street, Boston, MA 02202; 617-727-3180). A free guide, the *Massachusetts Campground Directory*, is published by the **Massachusetts Association of Campground Owners** (RR#1, Box 179-Z, Brookfield, MA 01506; 508-248-6373) and is also available from the **Massachusetts Office of Travel and Tourism** (Department of Commerce, 100 Cambridge Street, Boston, MA 02202; 617-727-3201). Camping is also permitted on several of the Boston Harbor Islands (see Chapter Two); for information about Peddocks and Lovells Islands, contact the **Metropolitan District Commission's Harbor Region Office** (98 Taylor Street, Dorchester; 617-727-5290); for the others, contact **Boston Harbor Islands State Park** (349 Lincoln Street, Hingham; 617-740-1605). Note: Massachusetts does not allow camping outside designated camping areas in state forests.

BOATING

Boating is one of the most popular activities in Massachusetts coastal areas. Sailboats, canoes, windjammers, power boats, cruise boats and ferries all ply the shoreline. You can bring your own boat or rent or charter a craft here. Each chapter in this book offers suggestions on how to go about finding the vessel of your choice. Charts for boaters and divers are widely sold at marine shops and bookstores throughout the area.

Massachusetts boating information can be obtained from the **Division of Law Enforcement** (Room 910, Ninth Floor, 100 Nashua Street, Boston MA 02214; 617-727-3905).

WATER SAFETY

Even in winter, you'll find diehard surfers and windsurfers riding the waves in their wetsuits. Swimming, waterskiing, jetboating and floating on inflatable rafts are popular activities in the summer.

People have drowned in Massachusetts waters, but drownings are easily avoided when you respect the power of the water, heed appropriate warnings and use good sense.

Wherever you swim, never do it alone. On the ocean, always face the incoming waves. They can bring unpleasant surprises even to the initiated. If you go surfing, learn the proper techniques and dangers from an expert before you start out. Respect signs warning of dangerous currents and undertows. If you get caught in a rip current or any tow that makes you feel out of control, don't try to swim against it. Head across it, paralleling the shore. Exercise caution in the use of floats, inner tubes or rafts; unexpected currents can quickly carry you out to sea.

There are some jellyfish that inflict a mild sting, but that is easily treated with an over-the-counter antiseptic. If you go scalloping or musseling, swim in or wade in murky waters where shellfish dwell, wear canvas or rubber shoes to protect your feet.

Remember, you are a guest in the sea. All rights belong to the creatures who dwell there, including sharks. Though they are rarely seen and seldom attack, they should be respected. A wise swimmer who spots a fin simply heads unobtrusively for shore.

If you're going canoeing, always scout the river from land before the first trip, and check the available literature. Rivers have danger areas such as falls, boulder fields, rapids and dams.

FISH AND FISHING

Ever since the Puritans discovered salt cod, New Englanders have been fishing these waters. In the 19th century, men went down to the sea in ships after bigger fish—whales.

Today many people fish just for fun, casting a line into the surf off a rock jetty for flounder, striped bass or bluefish, or perhaps going out to sea for such deep-water game fish as bluefin tuna or shark.

For tamer activities, try harvesting mussels, scallops, littleneck clams or quahogs. And anyone can throw out a lobster pot or two and bring home a deluxe dinner.

Freshwater fishing in streams, lakes and ponds nets rainbow, brook and brown trout, as well as largemouth bass, bullhead, perch, sunfish, catfish and pickerel.

The most common saltwater fish are winter flounder and bluefish. Other saltwater species include striped bass, cod, flounder, mackerel, haddock and pollock.

Massachusetts requires a license for freshwater fishing but not for most saltwater fishing, with a few restrictions.

For information on fishing in Massachusetts, contact the **State Division of Fisheries and Wildlife** (100 Cambridge Street, Boston, MA 02202; 617-727-3151) and ask for the Abstracts of the Fish and Wildlife Laws. A saltwater permit is required for tuna or lobster fishing; for this permit, contact the **State Division of Marine Fisheries** (100 Cambridge Street, Boston, MA 02202; 617-727-3193). The Marine Fisheries division also publishes the *Massachusetts Salt Water Fishing Guide*, which includes town-by-town lists of bait shops, boat rentals, jetties and piers, boat-launching sites and party boats.

CHAPTER TWO

Boston

A stately dominion of brick and brownstone, parks and trees, river and harbor, Boston has stood as the preeminent New England city for more than three and a half centuries. Holding fast to the tip of a tiny peninsula jutting into the Atlantic, the city grew and spread south and west through the centuries, but it's still compact and eminently walkable. Despite its tiny size, Boston has played a mighty role in history, a history etched in the minds of all Americans. For this is the birthplace of our nation, where the Revolution began.

A city of fanatical Puritan roots, Boston has been mocked and scorned by more worldly others as dull, pious and provincial, no match for New York or Los Angeles in sophistication. Rich in artistic and intellectual life, Boston has still been notched down on the big-city scoresheet for its lackluster shopping, dining and hotel accommodations.

But Boston is changing its face. While still revering its history and roots, the city is searching for a new identity as a modern, stylish metropolis. In the 1980s, world-renowned chefs set up shop here, winning over Bostonians and food critics alike. The palatial shopping emporium Copley Place opened, anchored by flashy Dallas retailer Neiman-Marcus, which would never have dared show its face here in the '50s. A building boom pushed up skyscraping, first-class hotels like the Westin, the Boston Harbor Hotel and the Four Seasons, as well as gleaming Financial District office towers. At the same time, old treasures like South Station and the Ritz-Carlton Hotel received much-needed face-lifts.

The push for class continues with a grand ten-year project called the "Big Dig" begun in the late 1980s, which involves carving a giant tunnel to place the ugly, elevated Central Artery expressway underground. The project's completion will bring light and spaciousness to the downtown area. And the city's main eyesore—the burlesque district known as the Combat Zone—is slated to be demolished and replaced with a new cultural district in the 1990s.

The city's Puritan roots were established in 1630, when a small band of English Puritans led by Governor John Winthrop arrived and settled on the peninsula. As the colony thrived along with others that would become the United States, economic tensions mounted that led to the Revolutionary War. Signal events on the road to independence took place in the Boston area: the 1770 clash called the Boston Massacre, in which five colonists were killed; the Boston Tea Party, where Bostonians disguised as Indians let the crown know what they thought of the tea tax—shiploads of tea were dumped into the harbor in a gesture that's still reenacted today.

The Revolution started in earnest in and around Boston. The first shots were fired at nearby Lexington and Concord in 1775 (see Chapter Three). In the Battle of Bunker Hill, the British drove off the heavily outnumbered Americans, but only after sustaining severe losses. When George Washington fortified Dorchester Heights in a single night, the British were ousted forever.

Two centuries after the Revolution, Boston still has a reputation for liberalism, spearheaded by the reigning scion of the Kennedy clan, Senator Ted Kennedy. The city's low-key mayor, Raymond Flynn, carries the standard for the Irish.

Boston the city is home to a scant 575,000 souls. Half are under 30; some 250,000 students flood the city each September, injecting it with vitality and youthfulness.

The nucleus of Boston proper is a pear-shaped peninsula. At its northernmost tip stands the North End, a small, Italian enclave clustered with shops, cafés and restaurants. The downtown area takes up most of the peninsula, winding between the waterfront and Boston Common from north to south and encompassing a Chinatown that is tiny yet rich in tradition.

High above Boston Common in regal splendor sits Beacon Hill, crowned by the State House and graced with Victorian bowfront brick homes, window boxes and hidden gardens. To the west of Beacon Hill lies its cousin, stately Back Bay, a place of wide boulevards and imposing brownstones. Farther west is the Fenway, sprawling around its marshy gardens and home to baseball's famous Fenway Park.

Just south of Back Bay is Midtown, which encompasses the architectural jewels of Copley Square: the Public Library, Trinity Church and the Hancock Tower. A bit farther south lies the city's largest neighborhood, the South End, another 19th-century brick residential area in the process of gentrification. Cut off from eastern downtown by the Fort Point Channel,

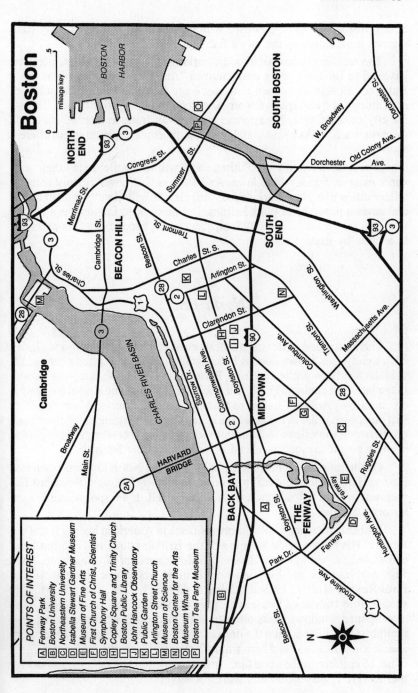

Boston

BOSTON HARBOR

mileage key

NORTH END

SOUTH BOSTON

Dorchester St.

W. Broadway

Dorchester Old Colony Ave. Ave.

Congress St.

Summer St.

Merrimac St.

Cambridge St.

BEACON HILL

Tremont St.

Beacon St.

Charles St. S.

SOUTH END

Washington St.

Charles St.

Arlington St.

Clarendon St.

Massachusetts Ave.

Columbus Ave.

Tremont St.

Cambridge

CHARLES RIVER BASIN

Storrow Dr.

Commonwealth Ave.

Boylston St.

MIDTOWN

Broadway

Main St.

HARVARD BRIDGE

BACK BAY

Boylston St.

THE FENWAY

Fenway

Ruggles St.

Park Dr.

Fenway

Huntington Ave.

Brookline Ave.

Beacon St.

Park Dr.

N

POINTS OF INTEREST

- A Fenway Park
- B Boston University
- C Northeastern University
- D Isabella Stewart Gardner Museum
- E Museum of Fine Arts
- F First Church of Christ, Scientist
- G Symphony Hall
- H Copley Square and Trinity Church
- I Boston Public Library
- J John Hancock Observatory
- K Public Garden
- L Arlington Street Church
- M Museum of Science
- N Boston Center for the Arts
- O Museum Wharf
- P Boston Tea Party Museum

South Boston (not to be confused with the South End) is a primarily commercial area, home to the city's fish piers.

The residential neighborhoods, harking back to English architecture, have led to Boston's being characterized "America's most European city." But since Boston has added new space-age layers to the urban quiltwork of centuries, the city wears a more American and international face. Though the city took its time, it has come a long way from its Puritan roots and the days when books by male and female authors were separated on different shelves.

Somehow we know the Puritan roots will never die; today their remnants exist in Sunday blue laws. And Boston will never be mistaken for wilder cities like New York or Los Angeles. It will always remain small, and never a province of punk hairdos. But nowadays, Boston has a lot less to apologize for on the big-city scoresheet and is becoming a first-class city in a class by itself.

North End

The North End is Boston's oldest, most colorful neighborhood. Today it's a tightly knit, homogeneous Italian community, established after a gradual takeover from pockets of Irish, Portuguese and Jewish residents starting in the late 19th century. The North End's mostly one-lane streets are crowded cheek-by-jowl with Italian restaurants and food stores. Many residents still greet each other in the language of the Old Country and hang their wash out between the alleys. All summer long, Italians celebrate their patron saints with picturesque weekend parades and street festivals.

On the roundish peninsula that is Boston, the North End juts north into Boston Harbor and is cut off from downtown by the elevated Southeast Expressway, which helps keep it a place unto itself. It's a spot where Boston history still lives.

Probably no name evokes more romance in American history than Paul Revere. His famous ride warning of the British attack in 1775 has been chronicled the world over. The quiet little expanse of North Square, lined with cobblestones and black anchor chain, is where you come upon **The Paul Revere House** (19 North Square; 617-523-2338; admission). This simple little two-story house with gray clapboards and leaded-glass, diamond-paned windows looks almost out of place in Boston today, and well it might. Built in 1680, it's the only example left in Boston of 17th-century architecture. Revere lived here from 1770 until 1800, although not with all of his 16 children at the same time. Inside are period furnishings, some original Revere family items and works of silver.

Next door to Paul Revere's house and entered through the same court-yard is the **Pierce-Hichborn House** (29 North Square; 617-523-2338; admission). Built about 1711 by glazier Moses Pierce, it's one of the earliest remaining Georgian structures in Boston. It later belonged to Paul Revere's cousin, boatbuilder Nathaniel Hichborn.

Also in North Square are the **Seamen's Bethel** (11 North Square) and the **Mariner's House** (12 North Square). An anchor over the door announces the Mariner's House, a place where, since 1838, a seaman has always been able to get a cheap meal and a bed for the night. Said the sailor-preacher of the Seamen's Bethel, "I set my bethel in North Square because I learned to set my net where the fish ran." Once a place where sailors worshipped, it's now a rectory office.

On a street noted for "gardens and governors" lived John J. "Honey Fitz" Fitzgerald, one of Boston's Irish "governors," a ward boss, congressman and mayor. His daughter **Rose Kennedy** was born in this plain brick building at 4 Garden Court Street.

The **Old North Church** (193 Salem Street; 617-523-6676; admission) is the one from which the sexton hung two lanterns the night of Paul Revere's midnight ride ("one if by land, two if by sea"). This beautiful church has Palladian windows and a white pulpit inspired by London designs. The four trumpeting cherubim atop the choir loft pilasters were taken from a French pirate ship. The church houses the historic lanterns in its steeple.

Directly behind Old North Church in the **Paul Revere Mall** stands a life-sized statue of Revere astride his horse—one of the city's most photographed scenes.

On the other side of the mall is **St. Stephen's Church** (Hanover and Clark streets), a brick federal-style church designed by the man who established that style, Charles Bulfinch, America's first native-born architect. The only Bulfinch-designed church still standing in Boston, St. Stephen's has a bell and copper dome cast by Paul Revere. Inside are wedding-cake-white fluted pillars, balconies and Palladian windows, a pewter chandelier and an 1830s pipe organ.

Copp's Hill Burying Ground (Hull and Snow Hill streets) served as the cemetery for Old North Church in the 17th century. Set high on a little green knoll, it overlooks Boston Harbor and Charlestown, which was bombarded by British guns placed here during the Battle of Bunker Hill. Its simple gray headstones bear pockmarks from British target practice. Buried here are Increase and Cotton Mather, Puritan ministers who wielded considerable political clout.

The widest street in all the North End is Hanover Street, a major center for shops and restaurants. Walking south on Hanover Street leads you straight to the **Haymarket–North End Underpass** (★), which leads under the Southeast Expressway to downtown. The underpass is lined with bright, primitive mosaics done by North End children, a kind of urban folk art.

The **Historic Neighborhoods Foundation** (2 Boylston Street; 617-426-1885) gives walking tours of the North End, as well as many other neighborhoods.

NORTH END RESTAURANTS

In the North End, you can feast on pasta and regional dishes from one end to the other, stopping at little neighborhood "red-sauce" cafés, plush formal dining rooms or late-night espresso bars. Some of the best deals in Boston dining are here, with many restaurants offering moderate prices.

Neighborhood regulars favor **Pat's Pushcart Restaurant** (★) (61 Endicott Street; 617-523-9616), which specializes in Northern Italian dishes and also serves up a lot of red sauce. In its casual, speakeasy ambience, the sole homage paid to decor is red tablecloths. But who cares when you can get such wonderful dishes as beef *braciolettini sorrento* and spaghetti marinara at moderate prices? Dinner only.

Mamma Maria's Ristorante (3 North Square; 617-523-0077) is the queen of North End gourmet. Highly regarded, it's set in a ritzy townhouse bedecked with brass chandeliers, mirrors and peach-and-gray walls. An upstairs atrium overlooks Paul Revere's little house. Mamma Maria's menu is refreshingly free of red sauce, featuring the lighter, reduced-sauce dishes of Tuscany and Piedmont, which might include grilled swordfish on a bed of pesto with steamed oysters, spinach and salmon caviar. Moderate to deluxe.

Café Vittoria (296 Hanover Street; 617-227-7606) is the most colorful of the espresso bistros. It might have been shipped here straight from Italy, so Old World is it. A massive and ancient espresso machine stands in the window, and latticework, marble floors and a mural of the Italian coast add to the feeling. Here's the place to indulge in a late-night espresso, cappuccino or Italian liqueur, accompanied by *gelato* or *cannoli*, all for budget prices.

If you can't visit the Sistine Chapel, you can still see its transcendent frescoes covering the ceiling at **Lucia's** (415 Hanover Street; 617-367-2353). Art critics come to rave and art students to stare in awe. More magnificent ceiling frescoes show Marco Polo's visit to China, the 12 Apostles and the Last Supper. Lucia's chef hails from Abruzzi and prepares specialties from all over Italy, robust to light dishes, something for everyone. Try the *pollo all'Arrabbiata* or *maccheroni all'Arrabbiata* (angry chicken or angry macaroni). Moderate to deluxe.

Nicole's Ristorante (54 Salem Street; 617-742-6999) is a glowingly pink place with an intimate and elegant café-style dining room. It serves light dishes from Northern Italy, and veal is a house specialty. Moderate to deluxe.

Café Paradiso (255 Hanover Street; 617-742-1768) is a favored haunt of local Italians. Downstairs is an espresso bar decorated with hanging plants, lots of mirrors and Italian cakeboxes with colorful designs. The spumoni is handmade, and the *gelato* and *granite* are freshly churned. Upstairs is a secluded, postage-stamp dining room set with pink tablecloths, where you can feel removed from the world at large. The menu offers a little bit of everything, covering Northern, Central and Southern Italian dishes. A house specialty is the Paradiso: veal, chicken or shrimp, baked with mushrooms, wine, butter, prosciutto and mozzarella. Moderate.

NORTH END SHOPPING

The North End is a food lover's shopping dream, chock full of wine and cheese shops and bakeries.

For a pungent whiff of Old World ambience, head for **Polcari's Coffee Shop** (105 Salem Street; 617-227-0786), a tiny shop brimming with open bags of cornmeal and flour, wooden bins of nuts and jars of coffee beans.

At **A & J Distributors** (236 Hanover Street; 617-523-8490), you can pick up almost any Italian cookware you want: pasta racks, painted pasta bowls, pizzaiole and waffle makers.

Overwhelming, tantalizing smells hit the nose in the **Modern Pastry Shop** (257 Hanover Street; 617-523-3783), which dates to 1931. It's hard to choose among the pizzaiole, zuppa inglese, amaretto biscotti and macaroons.

Downtown

The downtown area comprises several distinct neighborhoods, sprawling around the peninsula and looping around Beacon Hill and the Boston Common. Although Boston's compactness makes it very easy to sightsee on foot, there is no convenient way to see these neighborhoods, and you'll find yourself doubling back more than once.

For the hit-and-run tourist, there's the **Freedom Trail**, a walking extravaganza created in 1974 that links 16 major historic sights from downtown to Beacon Hill, the North End and Charlestown. A walking trail map is available at the Boston Common Visitor Information Kiosk (147 Tremont Street;

617-536-4100) or the Prudential Visitor Center (800 Boylston Street, Prudential Plaza; 617-536-4100).

But if you do nothing but walk the Freedom Trail, you will have missed many of Boston's riches. We have chosen to show you a route that covers many more sights than the Freedom Trail: It loops northward from the North End to the old West End, back down through Government Center and Quincy Market, and out to the Waterfront. Then it goes up State Street, down through the Financial District to Chinatown and the Theater District, and finally back up Washington Street to Boston Common. Since all these neighborhoods are so small, there's no need to treat them as separate geographic areas. But when a sight lies within the boundaries of a particular downtown neighborhood, we'll be sure to let you know.

When you come out the North End Underpass, you'll be crossing Blackstone Street. Look down at your feet to see a street sculpture called **Asarotan**—bronze castings of ears of corn, fruit, fish and vegetables, re-creating the clutter of market day, worn smooth by the passage of feet. The name means unswept floor, and the concept dates to Roman times, when food was similarly portrayed in mosaic floor tiles of banquet halls.

Asarotan was made in honor of **Haymarket** (covering several blocks of Blackstone Street), the country's oldest market, in operation more than 200 years. On weekends, open-air vendors hawk fruits and vegetables, meats, fresh fish and crabs, crowding over several blocks. Ancient hanging metal scales are used to weigh purchases. Prices are good here, but don't try to touch anything without a vendor's permission—he'll scream.

You'll find the **Boston Stone** (★) (Marshall and Hanover streets) easily enough by looking behind the Boston Stone Gift Shop. A round brown stone embedded in the rear corner of the house and dated 1737, it was brought from England and used as a millstone to grind pigment. A tavern keeper named it after the famous London Stone and used it as an advertisement.

Behind Marshall Street is the **Blackstone Block**, tiny alleyways that are the last remnants of Boston's 17th-century byways, the oldest commercial district. Their names, Marsh Lane, Creek Square and Salt Lane, represent the early topography of Boston's landscape.

The **Union Oyster House** (41 Union Street; 617-227-2750), built in the 18th century, became a restaurant in 1826, making it the oldest continuously working restaurant in America. Here Daniel Webster drank a tall tumbler of brandy and water with each half-dozen oysters, and he rarely had fewer than six plates. Before it was a restaurant, exiled French King Louis Phillipe taught French here to wealthy ladies. Upstairs in 1771, Isaiah Thomas published *The Massachusetts Spy*, one of the first newspapers in the United States.

At the western edge of Boston's peninsula, stretching from the Southeast Expressway to Storrow Drive, is an area that used to be known as the

West End. Once rich in many-quilted ethnic groups, it's now a mostly commercialized neighborhood.

A popular spot here is **Boston Garden** (150 Causeway Street; 617-227-3200), where the Celtics twinkle their toes and the Boston Bruins bash heads. In addition to basketball and hockey, it's used for circuses, ice shows and rock concerts.

Not on the peninsula at all, but out in the middle of the Charles River, is the **Museum of Science** (Science Park; 617-723-2500; admission), reached via the Charles River Dam. The star of the museum is the state-of-the-art Omni Theater, whose 76-foot domed screen and surrounding sound systems make you feel as though you're actually whizzing down Olympic slopes on skis or moving underwater through the Great Barrier Reef. The museum also houses live animal exhibits, the Hayden Planetarium and changing displays on foreign cultures.

The **Harrison Gray Otis House** (141 Cambridge Street; 617-227-3956; admission) was the first of three Boston houses Charles Bulfinch designed for his friend Otis, a prominent lawyer and member of Congress. Built in 1796, the three-story brick house is classically symmetrical, with rows of evenly spaced windows and Palladian windows in the center. Inside is one of the most gorgeous interiors in Boston, rich with imported wallpapers, opulent swag curtains and carpeting, gilt-framed mirrors, Adams mantels and neoclassical motifs framing every doorway and window. Surviving abuse as a bathhouse, Chinese laundry and rooming house, the building became the headquarters of the Society for the Preservation of New England Antiquities in 1916.

Right next door is the **Old West Church** (131 Cambridge Street; 617-227-5088), a handsome federal-style brick building with a cupola and pillars on three stories. The British tore down its original steeple to prevent signaling across the river during the siege of 1776. Rebuilt in 1806, it houses a Charles Fisk organ.

A short walk up Cambridge Street brings you to **Government Center**, a sprawling brick plaza with multilevel stairs and fountains designed by I. M. Pei, an architect who was to change the face of the city in the 1960s, leaving his imprint on many key buildings. The plaza contains two of Boston's most important government structures, the **John F. Kennedy Federal Building** and **City Hall**, a modernistic-looking inverted pyramid. An abstract sculpture entitled *Thermopylae*, inspired by Kennedy's book *Profiles in Courage*, stands facing the JFK Building. A mass of twisting forms, it takes its name from a Greek battle in which the Spartans fought the Persians to the last man.

Some say the **Steaming Teakettle**, a huge copper kettle hung outside the doorway at 65 Court Street at the edge of Government Center, is America's oldest advertising sign. It once announced the operations of the

Oriental Tea Company, Boston's largest tea company. Made by city copper-smiths, it holds 227 gallons, two quarts, one pint and three gills. It gives you a warm feeling to see the teakettle steaming away, especially on a cold day, and there's a coffee shop inside for more warmth.

For a figure so flamboyant as **James Michael Curley**, one statue is not enough. The corrupt Curley dominated Boston politics for years, from 1914 to the late 1940s, serving as mayor, congressman and governor and figuring prominently in Edwin O'Connor's novel *The Last Hurrah*. This four-term mayor was loved by the poor and fond of calling Boston bankers the "State Street Wrecking Crew." At Dock Square, two very lifelike bronze statues immortalize Curley, one sitting on a park bench, the other standing right on the brick pavement with no pedestal. Tourists have been seen patting the stomach of the standing Curley, so temptingly portly is it.

If you walk down the stairs at the rear of Government Center and across Congress Street, you'll be entering Quincy Market, one of Boston's most popular destinations.

Faneuil Hall (off Congress Street; 617-523-3886) was the city's central market in the mid-18th century. Its second floor became known as the "Cradle of Liberty," as it resounded with the patriotic rhetoric of James Otis and Samuel Adams in the years leading to the Revolution. On the third floor is a museum and armory of the **Ancient and Honorable Artillery Company,** the nation's oldest military group, founded in 1638. Look up to see the four-foot-long gilded copper grasshopper weathervane, a familiar Boston landmark and symbol.

Quincy Market is another historic marketplace, built in 1825 and 1826 by Mayor Josiah Quincy to expand Faneuil Hall. In a move that has been imitated by almost every major city, Quincy Market, along with its twin flanking arcades, the North and South Markets, was renovated in the 1970s into shops and restaurants that have become a major tourist draw for the city. The cobblestoned mall is a street festival by day, a lively nightspot in the later hours. It's wonderfully decorated during the holidays.

If you walk out the rear of Quincy Market and under the Southeast Expressway across busy Atlantic Avenue, you'll arrive at the waterfront.

When Atlantic Avenue was built in the 1860s, it sliced right through the center of many of the great old wharves, including **Long Wharf,** the oldest existing one in Boston. Built in 1710, Long Wharf was named for its length—formerly 1800 feet. The British marched up Long Wharf when they occupied the city in 1768, only to retreat back down it when they were routed out in 1776. Long Wharf also saw the departure of the first missionaries to Hawaii in 1819 and played a role in the 1850s California Gold Rush, when hundreds of New Englanders departed for San Francisco.

Buildings imitating Renaissance palazzos and Greek temples were built in the 19th century along Rowes, India, Central, Long, Commercial, Lewis,

Sargent's and Union wharves. **Lewis Wharf,** formerly Clarke's Wharf, was once owned by John Hancock. Nathaniel Hawthorne served as a customs inspector at **Long Wharf.** By the mid-19th century, the wharves were a center of clipper trade with China, Europe, Australia and Hawaii.

Many of the old wharf buildings, which once housed ships' chandlers and sail riggers, have been renovated into shops, offices and restaurants, including the **Pilot House, Mercantile Wharf** and **Chart House,** the only surviving late-18th-century building on the waterfront.

Central Wharf is home to the **New England Aquarium** (617-973-5200; admission), signaled by a bright red, 45-foot wind sculpture. Bostonians like to congregate to watch the harbor seals in the outdoor pool. Inside, the Giant Ocean Tank is home to 95 species of exotic reef fish, sea turtles, sharks and moray eels. Dolphins and sea lions perform next door on board the Discovery, a floating theater.

Waterfront Park (north of Long Wharf on Atlantic Avenue) is a neatly landscaped pocket park with brick walkways and benches that offers a lovely harbor view along with respite.

From the wharves, you can take cruises of Boston Harbor, a great way to while away an afternoon or evening and see the city skyline. Boat lines include **Boston Harbor Cruises** (1 Long Wharf; 617-227-4320) and **Massachusetts Bay Lines** (60 Rowes Wharf; 617-542-8000).

From Long Wharf, walk up State Street. In a couple of blocks, you'll come to the granite Greek Revival **Customs House** (McKinley Square at State and India streets), built between 1837 and 1847, where inspectors once examined all cargoes arriving at the wharves. Incongruously, this building also became Boston's first skyscraper in 1915, when the great clock tower was added. The clock, broken for many years, was restored in the late 1980s, and its bright blue and gold face now glows handsomely at night, visible from great distances.

The **Cunard Building** (126 State Street) was built in 1902 for the Cunard Steamship Line, owners of the ocean liner *Queen Elizabeth II.* Twin brass anchors flank its doors, festooned with dolphins and seashells.

The oldest surviving public building in Boston, the **Old State House** (206 Washington Street, corner of State Street; 617-720-1713; admission) is a pretty little brick building dwarfed by the surrounding skyscrapers. The bronze lion and stone unicorn atop its gables stand as symbols of the English crown. Until the American Revolution, this was the seat of British government. A ring of cobblestones outside marks the site of the Boston Massacre, the signal event launching the Revolution. A museum since 1882, the Old State House features winding galleries of exhibits on early Boston and maritime history, including memorabilia, ship's models, paintings and prints. (The State House is closed for renovations until Spring 1992.)

Right next door, **National Park Service Visitor Information** (15 State Street; 617-242-5642) has a good selection of maps, tour books and brochures and also sponsors ranger-guided tours to national park sites, including some Freedom Trail stops.

An outdoor flower market fronting the brick, federal-style **Old South Meeting House** (310 Washington Street, corner of Milk Street; 617-482-6439; admission) adds to its charms. Built in 1729, Old South has high-arching Palladian windows, white pulpit and candlelight chandeliers. Many crucial meetings leading to the American Revolution took place here, including the debate that launched the Boston Tea Party. Countless notables spoke here, including Samuel Adams, John Hancock and, later, Oliver Wendell Holmes. Though Old South was repeatedly ravaged—the British turned it into a riding school complete with jumping bar, and it was forced to serve as a temporary post office after a devastating fire in 1872—it has been restored to its 18th-century look. Taped presentations re-create the famous Tea Party debate and others.

Milk Street leads into the heart of the Financial District, a warren of streets stretching south from State Street to High Street and east to Washington Street. Dominated by towering banks and office buildings, the Financial District was considerably built up in the 1980s with bold new buildings, provoking controversy over their design in tradition-minded Boston. One of these—the **Bank of Boston** at 100 Federal Street—is laughingly called Pregnant Alice because of its billowing shape.

In its marching devastation, the **Great Fire of 1872** leveled 60 acres of downtown Boston. The spot where the fire was arrested on its northeastward path is noted on a bronze plaque on the front of the U.S. Post Office at Post Office Square, the corner of Milk and Devonshire streets.

Two bonanzas await in the lobby of the **New England Telephone building** (★) (185 Franklin Street). One, a massive mural called *Telephone Men and Women at Work*, circles the rotunda 360° and depicts decades of telephone workers, from 1880s switchboard operators to later engineers, cable layers and information operators. The other reward is Alexander Graham Bell's Garret, a dark little corner filled with memorabilia surrounding the birth of the telephone in Boston in 1875. The garret looks much as it did when Bell worked in it at its original location at 109 Court Street. (A **bronze plaque** at Government Center in front of the John F. Kennedy Federal Building marks that spot, where sound was first transmitted over wires in the fifth-floor garret.)

At 100 Summer Street stands a mobile that looks like a giant yellow lollipop tree, an ebullient surprise in a city where there is not much outdoor public art. Bostonians call it "the lollipops," but its real name is **Helion** (★), one of a group of pieces called "windflowers" by sculptor Robert Amory.

Walk south down Summer Street, until you come to **South Station** (Summer Street and Atlantic Avenue). South Station was a grand old station house in its day, the turn of the century. After a thorough restoration completed in 1989, this pink granite beauty stands tall and proud. Ionic columns, a balustrade and clock with eagle decorate the curved Beaux-Arts facade stretching for two blocks. South Station today serves as a transportation hub for subway, rail and bus connections. The interior, designed to resemble a European market square, sparkles with polished marble floors and brass railings and is filled with restaurants, shops and pushcart vendors.

Across the street, you can tour the **Federal Reserve Bank** (600 Atlantic Avenue, corner of Summer Street; 617-973-3463), which processes millions of dollars worth of currency every day. The Fed's unusual design—it looks like a giant white washboard, and there's a gap where the fifth floor should be—is intended to withstand down drafts and wind pressures. The Fed, which boasts a lobby full of sculpture and murals, also hosts jazz and classical concerts and changing art and crafts exhibits.

South Station is just a hop, skip and a jump from **Chinatown,** bounded by Essex and Washington streets and the Southeast Expressway. Compared to Chinatowns in other major cities, Boston's is quite small, just a few blocks long. But this Chinatown was much larger decades earlier, before the Southeast Expressway was built, cutting a wide swath through the district. The Tufts New England Medical Center, too, took a great chunk of Chinatown land when it was built. Now hemmed in by the Expressway and the Combat Zone, Chinatown has little room to grow.

The Chinese were first brought to Boston to break a shoe industry strike in the 1870s, coming by train from the West Coast. They settled close to South Station because of the convenience of the railroad. First living in tents, the Chinese eventually built houses or moved into places previously inhabited by Syrians, Irish and Italians.

Despite its small size, or perhaps because of it, Chinatown is intensely and authentically Chinese. Signs are in Chinese characters, and the area is densely packed with Chinese stores and restaurants. Even the phone booths are covered with Chinese pagodas.

The **Chinatown gates,** a bicentennial gift from Taiwan, stand at the intersection of Beach Street and Surface Road, marking the entrance to Chinatown. White stone with a massive green pagoda on top, they are guarded fore and aft by stone Chinese Foo dogs and sport gold Chinese characters on green marble. The classic characters are not readily translatable in modern Chinese, but they embody such moral principles as propriety, righteousness, modesty and honor.

The **Chinese-Culture Institute** (★) (276 Tremont Street; 617-542-4599) opened in 1980. It houses a gallery where rotating exhibits of Chinese paintings, sculpture, ceramics and folk art are shown. The institute also produces concerts, plays, dance recitals and lectures.

At the corner of Harrison Avenue and Oak Street is the large **Unity/ Community Chinatown Mural** (★), painted in 1986, which depicts the history of the Chinese in Boston. Among its pigtailed Chinese figures are construction workers, a launderer and women at sewing machines. Other scenes show the Chinese learning to read, protesting to save their housing and gaining access to professional careers.

Although you may not want to take one home, you can see live chickens squawking in stacks of wire crates at **Eastern Live Poultry** (★) (48 Beach Street), where locals line up to buy them "live or dressed."

Walk two blocks over to Tremont Street, and head south. In short order you'll be in the **Theater District**, centered on Tremont Street, Warrenton Place and Charles Street South. Boston has a lively and prestigious theater scene, with many tryouts moving on to Broadway. Among the half dozen or so nationally known theaters is the **Colonial** (106 Boylston Street; 617-426-9366), the oldest continuously operated theater in America, built in 1900. At that time the sumptuously decorated Colonial was considered one of the most elegant theaters in the country, with its 70-foot Italian-marble vestibule and foyer rich with ceiling paintings, cupids, plate mirrors, bronze staircases and carved wood. George M. Cohan, Noel Coward, Fred Astaire, Katharine Hepburn and the Marx Brothers have trod its boards.

Formerly the Metropolitan Theatre, the splendid **Wang Center for the Performing Arts** (270 Tremont Street; 617-482-9393) was built in 1925 as a palace for first-run movies in the Roaring Twenties. Opulently decorated with gold leaf, crystal, mirrors and Italian marble, it was designed to be reminiscent of the Paris Opera and Versailles. Renovated in the late 1970s and again in the early 1980s, this 4000-seat theater is one of the largest in the world.

Few people know that **Edgar Allan Poe** (★) had a long history in Boston, so in 1989 a memorial bronze plaque was erected to his memory at the corner of Boylston Street and Edgar Allan Poe Way. Born here, Poe was the son of actors at the Boston Theatre. He published his first book, lectured and enlisted in the army in Boston.

The **Grand Lodge of Masons** (★) (186 Tremont Street, corner of Boylston Street; 617-426-6040) is decorated with blue and gold mosaics of masonic symbols, and its grand lobby houses a small exhibit of masonic memorabilia.

Boston's famed **Combat Zone** on lower Washington Street should be added to the endangered species list. As the pace of development quickened in the late 1970s, its former horde of topless lounges, sleazy bars and adult bookstores and movies shrank to a pathetic few blocks that would be the scorn of any true big-city habitué. These are likely to disappear, too, in the wake of a new cultural district planned for the area for the late 1990s.

Downtown Crossing is the heart of downtown. Lunchtime shoppers crowd the brick pedestrian mall at the corner of Washington and Summer streets, fronting on **Jordan Marsh** and **Filene's**, two of Boston's oldest department stores. Downtown Crossing is street entertainment at its most diverse. Pushcart vendors and street musicians—one day a Peruvian folk band, the next a rock group—vie for space in the crowded mall. A one-man band is a permanent local fixture.

The **Old Corner Bookstore** (1 School Street, corner of Washington Street; 617-523-6658), now called the Globe Corner Bookstore, was a literary hub in the mid-19th century (see "Boston Bookstores" in this chapter). Covered with billboards in the 1950s, it was once threatened by urban renewal but saved by preservationists.

Old City Hall (45 School Street), a grand French Second Empire building, was renovated in the 1970s into offices and a French restaurant. As one of the first 19th-century Boston buildings to be recycled, it helped spark the preservationist movement. In front of Old City Hall stands the **Franklin Statue**, an eight-foot bronze tribute to Benjamin Franklin. Relief tablets at the base illustrate scenes from his career as printer, scientist and signer of the Declaration of Independence.

The **Omni Parker House** (60 School Street) is the oldest continuously operating hotel in America, first opening in 1855. Soon after, it became a hangout of the Saturday Club, a literary group whose members included Nathaniel Hawthorne, Ralph Waldo Emerson, Henry Wadsworth Longfellow, James Russell Lowell, Oliver Wendell Holmes and John Greenleaf Whittier. This little group founded the *Atlantic Monthly*.

King's Chapel (corner of Tremont and School streets; 617-523-1749) looks morosely like a mausoleum. Its steeple was never finished, so its Ionic columns flank a bare, squat granite building. The inside, however, is gorgeous, with carved Corinthian columns and pewter chandeliers. The first Anglican church in Boston, King's Chapel eventually became the first Unitarian church in the United States. King's Chapel became famous for its music, since it was the first church in Boston to have an organ—the Puritans didn't believe in music at Sunday services.

Beside the church is **King's Chapel Burying Ground**, the oldest cemetery in Boston. It contains the graves of John Winthrop, the colony's first governor, and Charles Bulfinch, the famed architect who later contributed to plans for the U.S. Capitol in Washington.

Park Street Church (corner of Park and Tremont streets; 617-523-3383) is one of Boston's most beautiful churches, with its white Christopher Wren spire and brick exterior. It was known as Brimstone Corner during the War of 1812 because gun powder was stored in its basement. Here William Lloyd Garrison made his first antislavery speech, and the song "America" was sung for the first time. These days, there are evening carillon concerts.

Next door is the **Old Granary Burying Ground**, which took its name from a large grain storehouse the Park Street Church replaced. Buried here are Paul Revere, Boston's Mother Goose (Elizabeth Goose, who became known for her nursery rhymes) and three signers of the Declaration of Independence, including John Hancock. You can't see exactly where each is buried, since the headstones were rearranged for the convenience of lawn mowing. Death's heads, skeletons and hourglasses were popular headstone motifs here.

Times have changed considerably at **Boston Common**, a large tract of forested green, America's oldest public park and the site of the first Boston settlement. In 1634, its acres served as pasture for cattle, training grounds for the militia and a public stage for hanging adulterers, Quakers, pirates and witches. A few steps from the visitor kiosk is **Brewer Fountain**, brought from Paris by Gardner Brewer in 1868 for his Beacon Hill home and later donated to the city. Notable among the statuary on the Common is the *Soldiers and Sailors Monument* high on a hill, whose figures represent history and peace.

Today, downtown office workers use the crisscrossing paths as shortcuts to work, and it's a popular spot for jogging, Frisbee-tossing and dog walking. You might wander into Park Street Station, the first station built on the nation's oldest subway, which opened in 1897.

Boston Common is the first jewel in Boston's **Emerald Necklace**, a seven-mile tracery of green that loops through and around the city, all the way to Jamaica Plain, Brookline and Dorchester. It was designed in 1881 by famed landscape architect Frederick Law Olmsted, who believed that parks could provide a psychological antidote to the noise, stress and artificiality of city life. The Emerald Necklace also includes the Public Garden, the Commonwealth Avenue Mall, the Back Bay Fens, Olmsted Park, Jamaica Pond, Franklin Park and the Arnold Arboretum. The Boston Parks and Recreation Department (617-522-2639 or 617-423-4659) conducts periodic walking and bicycling tours of the entire Emerald Necklace. Other parts of the Necklace will be dealt with under their appropriate neighborhoods.

Leaving the edge of Boston Common, you can walk up Park Street, which brings you to Beacon Hill.

DOWNTOWN HOTELS

Glitzy, contemporary skyscraper hotels have joined the city's old grande dames, moving into the downtown and waterfront areas in a 1980s building boom. Several are first-rate hotels, but, unfortunately, most of these new palaces are priced for the traveler on an expense account.

The city's older, vintage hotels, such as the Parker House, the Ritz-Carlton and the Lenox, have risen to the challenge by giving their properties much-needed face-lifts. The older hotels sometimes cost less than their towering competitors and edge them out when it comes to charm.

You will need to be as good as a detective to find truly budget accommodations in downtown Boston. And you must plan far ahead to book a room during fall foliage season, when leaf peepers from across the nation hit Boston in force.

One of New England's top-rated hotels, the 288-room **Four Seasons Hotel** (200 Boylston Street; 617-338-4400) overlooks the Public Garden. Interiors reflect the Victorian residential character of Beacon Hill, with a grand staircase leading up from the lobby and, in the rooms, leather-topped writing desks, fresh flowers in the bathroom and marble-topped vanities. Duvets are handed out in winter, and there's a spa, whirlpool, exercise room, masseur and lap pool with a view of Beacon Hill. Ultra-deluxe.

Owned by a Swiss company, the 500-room **Lafayette Hotel** (1 Avenue de Lafayette; 617-451-2600) is run with legendary Swiss efficiency and hospitality. Its location is convenient to everything, and the hotel has every luxury you could ask for: 24-hour room service, bathroom telephones, spa, Olympic-size pool with outdoor terrace, sauna, an exercise room, two restaurants and a lounge, where tea and pastries are served in the afternoon. The decor mixes colonial and European styles, with impressive antique furniture and paintings, Waterford crystal chandeliers and imported marble. Rooms are smartly finished in green, mocha or rose. Ultra-deluxe.

The **Hotel Méridien** (250 Franklin Street; 617-451-1900) is one of the country's most highly acclaimed hotels. It opened in 1981 in the former Federal Reserve Bank, built in 1922, a Renaissance Revival granite and limestone structure modeled after a Roman palazzo. Many original interior architectural details remain, including elaborate repoussé bronze doors, gilded, coffered ceilings and sculpted bronze torchières. The Julien Lounge is dominated by two massive N. C. Wyeth murals depicting Abraham Lincoln and George Washington. The hotel has 326 rooms, two restaurants, two bars, an indoor lap pool and health club facilities with whirlpool and sauna. The generous-sized guest rooms are elegantly cozy, with sophisticated color schemes of white, gray and black. A matching two-toned silver embroidered sofa and club chair contrast a black lacquer writing desk. Ultra-deluxe.

Omni Parker House (60 School Street; 617-227-8600) is a fabled Boston institution. Many celebrities have stayed here, from Charles Dickens and John Wilkes Booth to Hopalong Cassidy. Its lobby is decorated in the grand old style, with carved oak paneling and gilt moldings, a carved wooden ceiling, bronze repoussé elevator doors and candlelight chandeliers. In the heart of downtown, it's just steps away from Quincy Market. Rooms have writing desks and wing chairs, beige carpeting, pink floral spreads and marble baths. Ultra-deluxe.

The **Boston Harbor Hotel** (70 Rowes Wharf; 617-439-7000) is simply the most visually stunning hotel to be built in Boston in many years. Set right on the harbor and designed in grand classical style, the brick structure is pierced with an 80-foot archway. The waterfront side is lined with Venetian-style piers and crowned with a copper-domed rotunda observatory. A cobblestone courtyard reaches toward the ornate marble-floored and crystal lobby. Many of the 230 rooms have magnificent water views and feature dark wood furniture in a green decor, marble-topped nightstands and paintings of birds. The hotel has a health club and spa, sauna and lap pool, and an award-winning restaurant and bar. Ultra-deluxe.

A small luxury hotel with 152 rooms, the **Bostonian** (Faneuil Hall; 617-523-3600) stands right next to Faneuil Hall and Quincy Market. In its lobby are two exhibits on early Boston firefighting. Besides one of the city's top-rated restaurants, the Bostonian has a multiple-story terraced atrium. A typical room might have a rose carpet and contemporary furnishings like glass-topped tables and white love seats. The bathroom is spacious, with double sinks and a large oval tub. Some rooms have hot tubs and fireplaces. Complimentary use of a nearby health club is offered. Ultra-deluxe.

There are at least half a dozen bed-and-breakfast agencies in Boston, offering accommodations in host homes from downtown to Cambridge and the suburbs.

Bed & Breakfast Associates Bay Colony (617-449-5302) has rooms in 150 homes, often with full breakfast and private bath, many offering Waterfront, Midtown, Back Bay or Beacon Hill locations. Accommodations range from a bow-windowed room with pine floors, antique brass bed and fireplace in a South End Victorian townhouse, to Beacon Hill and Back Bay penthouses close to the Public Garden. One of the best deals for the money; budget to deluxe.

Breakfast is always included in rooms booked through **Greater Boston Hospitality** (617-277-5430), which offers dozens of listings, with many in Back Bay and Beacon Hill. Host homes include a brick federal house in Beacon Hill with fireplaces, four-poster beds, greenhouse and a lovely hidden garden, and a classic 1890 Back Bay brownstone appointed with 18th-century mahogany furniture and floors and Oriental rugs. Budget to deluxe.

DOWNTOWN RESTAURANTS

Downtown dining covers a wide spectrum, from traditional Yankee bastions to sprightly outdoor cafés and inexpensive ethnic eateries.

It's hard to say which is more stylish at **Cornucopia** (15 West Street; 617-338-4600), the food or the decor. Once a 19th-century literary salon, the historic building was renovated in 19th-century mission and sleek, postmodern style in a design hip enough to be featured in *Metropolitan Home*. Cornucopia's imaginative and innovative new American menu, which changes periodically, may include grilled trout in corn husk with roast peppers and corn relish, or roast pork with cranberry chutney and buttermilk biscuits. The menu recommends wines for each dish. Deluxe; moderate prices are available in the first-floor café.

Le Marquis de Lafayette (1 Avenue de Lafayette, at the Lafayette Hotel; 617-451-2600), opened in 1985 and swiftly won both national and local acclaim for the masterful French creations. You won't mind paying deluxe to ultra-deluxe prices for the fabulous French cuisine with Mediterranean and Asian influences. The menu changes periodically, and the wine list numbers several hundred selections. Artful desserts include apple charlotte and chocolate truffle cake. And you'll find the dining room's subdued elegance quite restful, with its widely spaced tables, original antique prints of hunting scenes and Italian rock crystal chandeliers. Dinner only.

Julien (250 Franklin Street, in the Hotel Méridien; 617-451-1900) manages to be both sprightly and elegant, with its impossibly high rose-colored ceilings and massive crystal chandeliers. Wing chairs and rose banquettes guard your privacy, and softly shaded table lamps cast a romantic glow. When the waiter removes the silver cover from your plate with a "*Voilà!*" you'll find a light but vibrant hand has seen to the sauces. Chef Olivier Roellinger's seasonally changing menu emphasizes regional foods, which might include Long Island duckling with yellow root vegetables or roasted Maine lobster with a lemon, herb, butter and mushroom soufflé. Ultra-deluxe.

Be sure to ask for a table by the window at **Aujourd'hui** (200 Boylston Street in the Four Seasons Hotel; 617-338-4400) so you will have a view of the Public Garden below. Tables are set with one-of-a-kind antique service plates, complemented by antique paintings and a display of porcelain. The regional American menu features game, poultry and seafood dishes, some with an Italian, French or Chinese twist. There's also a low-cholesterol menu. One block from the theater district, this is a great place for *après*-theater. Ultra-deluxe.

A bright red railing leads upstairs to Boston's greatest culinary adventure at **Biba** (272 Boylston Street; 617-426-7878), where chef Lydia Shire is unafraid to create from any palette: Chinese, French, Italian, Indian. Where else would you get lobster satay with green papaya and winter mint or beef short ribs with cumin seed and cilantro? Her dining room feasts the eyes, too, with rich colors and primitive Mediterranean motifs set off by yellow walls. Deluxe to ultra-deluxe.

So, you want it kosher? You can get it at the **Milk Street Café** (50 Milk Street; 617-542-2433), a cozy Financial District cafeteria that dishes up some of the best inexpensive homemade food in the city: soups, sandwiches, salads, muffins, bread and, always, desserts such as strawberry shortcake. Breakfast and lunch; budget.

If you like playing Picasso at the dinner table, **Fajitas & 'Ritas** (★) (25 West Street; 617-426-1222) is for you. Crayons stand ready for you to doodle on the paper tablecloth, and the work of many diners cum artists lines an entire wall. The chicken fajitas are a standout, as are the nachos. Budget in price.

You'll think you're dining al fresco in Italy at **Bnu** (123 Stuart Street; 617-367-8405), with its grape arbors and trompe l'oeil crumbling walls and starry blue ceiling. Close to the theater district, Bnu is famed for its Tuscan-style country cooking, featuring pastas, chicken and seafood. Moderate to deluxe.

Stepping into the **Essex Grill** (695 Atlantic Avenue; 617-439-3599) is like entering an Italian Renaissance palace. In a restored historic hotel, the restaurant has polished up the green marble lobby floors and kept the white Corinthian columns, gold-leaf ceiling designs and wedding-cake molding in the lounge. Seafood is the order of the day. Moderate to deluxe.

Among its American mesquite-grilled dishes, **Dakota's** (34 Summer Street, lobby level; 617-737-1777) numbers crab cakes and Atlantic salmon. Fresh seafood, game and meats round out the menu. Stylish Dakota mahogany granite graces the restaurant throughout. Deluxe to ultra-deluxe.

Haymarket Pizza (★) (106 Blackstone Street; 617-723-8585) fronts right on Haymarket, a weekend open-air food market, and the surrounding crowds make it hard to get in the door. But if you do, you'll find some of the best budget pizza in Boston.

Noisy and chaotic, **Durgin Park** (340 Faneuil Hall; 617-227-2038) is legendary for its rude waitresses and community tables set with red-and-white-checked cloths. A Boston institution founded in 1827, it dispenses such solid and hefty Yankee fare as prime rib, corned beef and cabbage, franks and beans, corn bread and Indian pudding. Moderate to deluxe.

You can't beat the **Union Oyster House** (41 Union Street; 617-227-2750) for historic atmosphere. In 1742 it was a dry goods store and in 1775 became a center for fomenting revolutionary activity. The restaurant opened in 1826, and Daniel Webster was fond of slurping down oysters at its U-shaped oyster bar, still standing today. Little alcoves with wooden booths and bare wood tables wend around the several wood-paneled dining rooms, and there are ship's models, a mahogany bar and antique wooden pushcarts in this casual and roisterous eatery. The menu of chowders, seafood and New England shore dinners spans moderate to deluxe prices.

The **Blue Diner** (178 Kneeland Street; 617-338-4639) is a real diner right in the middle of Boston, awash in blue neon and chrome, plus jukebox. Besides omelettes, flapjacks, New York egg creams and "wets"—homemade french fries swimming in gravy—you can get one of the last "bottom-less" cups of coffee in urban America. Moderate.

With its tall oak doors lettered in gold, **Tatsukichi** (189 State Street; 617-720-2468) looks like a foreign consulate. The food is just as impressive: almost 50 kinds of sushi and the famed house specialty, *kushiage*, skewers of battered and fried meats and seafood. Dine Japanese-style in a light wood and beige tatami room, or at a Western-style table. Budget to moderate.

A playful parody of rococo style, **Rocco's** (5 Charles Street South; 617-723-6800) has a stagy setting of 25-foot ceilings, mammoth swashes of drapery and frescoes of cherubs. Sculptures of pigs, fish and toucans serve as table decorations (they're for sale, too). An international menu mixes shrimp fra'diavlo with Oriental duck. Moderate to deluxe.

The **Commonwealth Brewing Co.** (138 Portland Street; 617-523-8383) makes its own beer in the basement, serving ten varieties on tap. A vast hall lined with huge copper vats, beer kegs, copper-covered tables and a brass-railed bar, the dining room is popular with sports fans from nearby Boston Garden. You can watch the beer being made behind glass walls. Chow down on hearty fare like three-alarm chili, steak and fish and chips. Budget to moderate.

Far above the crowded bustle of Quincy Market, you can dine in re-moved splendor at **Seasons** (9 Blackstone Street North, Faneuil Hall, in the Bostonian Hotel; 617-523-4119), one of Boston's top-rated restaurants. Widely spaced tables, gold-rimmed china, mocha banquettes, crisp white napery and mirrored ceilings add to the mood. A creative New American menu is served, changing seasonally, which might include seared quail with polenta and sausage or roasted monkfish with lobster roe. Deluxe to ultra-deluxe.

Las Brisas (70 East India Row; 617-720-1820), blazing with light, glass and brass, is certainly one of the glitziest Mexican restaurants around. The moderate-priced menu offers fajitas, nachos, bean soup and such spe-cialties as pollo à la Oscar, medallions of veal and mesquite grill.

The dining room at **Rowes Wharf Restaurant** (70 Rowes Wharf, in the Boston Harbor Hotel; 617-439-3995) says quite plainly old money. Dimly lit, it blends mahogany paneling and a midnight blue floral carpet with rose-shaded wall sconces and antique prints of English harbor scenes. Its wide windows overlook Boston Harbor. Artfully prepared meats and sea-food are its specialties. Deluxe to ultra-deluxe.

The **Boston Sail Loft** (80 Atlantic Avenue; 617-227-7280) stretches back and back, out onto the harbor for some wonderful views. Some of the best potato skins in town are to be had here, along with burgers, sandwiches, pastas and fish plates, in a nautical atmosphere. Budget to moderate.

The **Chart House** (60 Long Wharf; 617-227-1576) is one of Boston's most historic restaurants. Set on cobblestoned Long Wharf, it was built in

1760 and served as John Hancock's counting house. His black iron safe is embedded in the upstairs dining room wall. The Chart House carries a marine motif all the way, with gilt-framed black-and-white pictures of ships, as well as model ships. Famed for its dense mud pie, Chart House also dishes up hearty steaks and seafood. Dinner only; deluxe.

A thoroughly Chinese lobby greets diners at the **Imperial Teahouse** (70 Beach Street; 617-426-8543) in the heart of Chinatown, with Chinese lanterns and gold dragons. Known for its dim sum, the restaurant also serves Mandarin cuisine to lots of appreciative locals. Budget to moderate.

Five take-out restaurants with open kitchens surround a group of tables at the **Chinatown Eatery** (★) (44 Beach Street, second floor), where the same type of chaos reigns as at a Hong Kong food market. Wall-mounted menus are hand-printed in Chinese and English, and Asians predominate among the diners. Taken together, the restaurants offer some 400 items, covering Szechuan, Hunan, Mandarin and Cantonese cuisines. Lunch only; budget.

At **Ho Yuen Ting Seafood Restaurant** (13-A Hudson Street, 617-426-2316; and 58 Beach Street, 617-426-2341), no-frills service and decor don't diminish the excellent seafood specialties: dishes of shrimp, lobster, crab, clams, conch and snails. Budget to moderate.

DOWNTOWN SHOPPING

Downtown Crossing is the heart of downtown shopping. A brick pedestrian mall at the intersection of Washington and Summer streets, it fronts on **Jordan Marsh** (450 Washington Street; 617-357-3000) and **Filene's** (426 Washington Street; 617-357-2100), two of Boston's oldest department stores and rivals since the mid-19th century. No shopping tour would be complete without a visit to **Filene's Basement**, the country's oldest bargain store, founded in 1908, which has made a legend out of off-price shopping. In the 1940s, 15,000 women once stormed the doors to get the last dresses to leave Paris before the German occupation.

Detractors say merchandise slipped during the 1980s, when the Basement opened 22 stores in six states. But the Basement is always crowded with women, who used to try on clothes in the aisles until dressing rooms were installed in 1989, and who don't mind the flaking paint and exposed piping when they can pick up designer dresses for less than 10 percent of retail price after three markdowns. Or, on occasion, an $80,000 sable coat for $5000.

The biggest tourist shopping mecca in Boston continues to be **Quincy Market**, just a few steps from Faneuil Hall. A Boston marketplace since 1826, Quincy Market is the centerpiece of three shopping arcades filled with more than 160 shops and two dozen food stands and restaurants. Outside

(Text continued on page 56.)

Boston Bookstores

Boston is a book lover's delight, brimming with bookstores full of quirky personality, charm and the imprint of history. These shops display a colorful, individual stamp, with second-hand shelving, hand-lettered signs and perhaps a beat-up leather chair or two or a resident dog.

Boston's most famous literary emporium is the **Globe Corner Bookstore** (One School Street; 617-523-6658). In the mid-19th century, it was called the Old Corner Bookstore and was a literary haunt of Hawthorne, Longfellow, Lowell, Emerson and Holmes, as well as Dickens and Thackeray when they were in the United States. Today the store's two floors burst with books about world travel and New England.

The **Brattle Book Shop** (9 West Street; 617-542-0210) claims the title of being the successor to America's oldest continuous antiquarian bookshop, dating from the 18th century. Used books sit on battered gray steel shelving and range from fiction, humor and poetry to history, genealogy and heraldry. Old *Life* magazines dating to 1936 march up the stairway and through history, covered with the faces of Tallulah Bankhead, Betty Grable and Hedy Lamar.

Established in 1898, **Goodspeed's Book Shop** (2 Milk Street; 617-523-5970) has been selling used and rare books ever since. Despite the exposed pipes and peeling paint, this little basement shop holds many treasures, and a staff of 20 experts to help you unearth them. The collection is especially strong in marine, genealogical and American history books. A second location at 7 Beacon Street has a stunning selection of antique European and American engravings, first editions and rare autographs, Winston Churchill's and Ulysses S. Grant's among them.

Good food and good books go hand in hand, and never more so than at Boston's two bookstore cafés, **Trident Booksellers & Café** (338 Newbury Street; 617-267-8688) and the **Harvard Bookstore Café** (190 Newbury Street; 617-536-0097). Trident claims the prize for being the funkiest: the province of black-clothed young hippies, a plethora of Third World, gay and alternative publications, and a menu of homemade soups and sandwiches tailored to a struggling writer's budget. It also sells bonsai trees, incense and myrrh, self-improvement videos and campy black-and-white postcards. The Writers League of Boston stages Sunday readings of new poetry and fiction here. The Harvard Bookstore is comfortably middle-class, and its dining room is middle-class sophisticated.

Gleaming new mainstream books emphasize fiction, cooking, art, architecture, travel and home design. PEN/New England parties annually here, and the store sponsors an author series.

An astonishing 25 bookshops surround Harvard Square (see Chapter Three). Established in 1856, **Schoenhof's Foreign Books, Inc.** (76-A Mt. Auburn Street, Cambridge; 617-547-8855) is America's oldest comprehensive foreign-language bookstore. It carries reference books in 130 languages, among them Swahili, Urdu, Tibetan, Navajo and classical Greek and Latin, whatever you need to complete a master's or Ph.D. Still, the shop is not too pedantic to sell children's favorites like *Le Petit Prince* and *Babar.*

Where else but Cambridge could a poetry-only bookshop exist? The **Grolier Book Shop** (6 Plympton Street; 617-547-4648), founded in 1927, is America's oldest continuously operating poetry bookshop, carrying 9000 titles from all periods and cultures. Supported by friends of Conrad Aiken, who lived next door in 1929, the shop grew into a meeting place for such poets as Ezra Pound, Marianne Moore and A. E. Housman. The shop sponsors an annual poetry prize and reading.

Many Harvard Square bookshops specialize in rare and out-of-print books, among them the **Pangloss Bookshop** (65 Mt. Auburn Street, Cambridge; 617-354-4003) and **Starr Bookshop, Inc.** (29 Plympton Street, Cambridge; 617-547-6864).

Seven Stars (58 John F. Kennedy Street, Cambridge; 617-547-1317) breathes New Age culture. Besides such titles as *Everyday Zen, Spiritual Emergency* and *The Dynamics of the Unconscious*, the shop sells Tarot cards, incense and gorgeous chunks of amethyst and other crystals, which some believe have healing powers. The shop sponsors lectures and workshops in Kundalini yoga.

A couple of miles out from Harvard Square, **Kate's Mystery Books** (2211 Massachusetts Avenue, Cambridge; 617-491-2660) is a mecca for mystery lovers and writers. Opening on Friday the 13th in 1983, the store has a black cat logo and walls lined with several hundred black cat figurines. About 10,000 new and used titles range from Dashiell Hammett and Agatha Christie to Tony Hillerman and Robert Parker. A special section focuses on mysteries set in New England. Mystery Writers of America meets here, as does the Spenser Fan Club.

This is just a sampling of Boston's bookstores, large and small. In this area of scholars and writers, there's a bookstore for everyone, with almost 300 listed in the Yellow Pages. That's one for every 2500 inhabitants.

the market are a profusion of cheery flower and balloon stands, and under its glass-canopied sides are pushcart vendors selling novelty products. Flanking Quincy Market are two more arcades, the North Market and the South Market. Among the more intriguing shops are **Purple Panache** (617-742-6500), where everything is purple—T-shirts, stuffed animals and novelties—and **Hog Wild** (617-523-7447), where you can buy such piggy products as stuffed pigs, pig jewelry and pig T-shirts and mugs. Also browse **Banana Republic** (617-439-0016), purveyors of travel and safari clothing, and **Folklorica** (617-367-1201), which has a fine selection of antique and contemporary gold and silver jewelry. **The Nature Company** (617-227-5005) sells animal videos, telescopes, sundials and a wide selection of nature books.

If there is such a thing as a vintage joke shop, **Jack's Joke Shop** (197 Tremont Street; 617-426-9640) is it. Open since 1922, the narrow shop is festooned with dozens of elaborate Halloween masks and wigs, inflatable skeletons and glasses with noses and mustaches.

You'll think you're in Paris at **French Kisses** (140 Tremont Street; 617-423-0422), with its French movie posters, art prints and thousands of camp, vintage, black-and-white and contemporary postcards.

Many years ago, the waterfront had legions of marine supply companies. One shop that holds true to the past is **Boxell's Chandlery** (★) (68 Long Wharf; 617-523-5678), in operation for more than 50 years. Boxell's sells worldwide navigational charts, foul weather gear and a staggering array of books on navigation, knot tying and racing.

For such a small area, Chinatown has more shops than you might imagine. If you've never experienced Chinese pastries, your mouth will water for them at **Hing Shing Pastry** (★) (67 Beach Street; 617-451-1162), where you can see the bakers at work.

Professional-quality Chinese cooking equipment is sold at **Chin Enterprises, Inc.** (33 Harrison Avenue; 617-423-1725), including two-foot-diameter woks and brass strainers.

DOWNTOWN NIGHTLIFE

Boston's arts scene has rich centuries of history behind it and is expanding all the time. The **Bostix Booth** at Faneuil Hall (617-723-5181) offers half-price tickets for many performance events on the day of the show, cash only, first-come, first-served. The **Boston Jazzline** (617-262-1300) offers 24-hour recorded information on local jazz events.

THE BEST BARS

There's a Boston bar for everyone: young singles, bricklayers and stevedores, the State House crowd, Financial District workers, Cambridge academics, sports fans, the Irish.

The **Bell in Hand Tavern** (45 Union Street; 617-227-2098) is Boston's oldest tavern, opened in 1795, and retains a cozy, colonial feeling.

Irish brogues roll so thickly at the **Black Rose** (160 State Street; 617-742-2286) that it sounds like Dublin. Irish beers, Irish folk music and a rollicking good time are house specialties.

The **Last Hurrah** (60 School Street, in the Omni Parker House; 617-227-8600), imbued with turn-of-the-century tradition, swings to the big-band sound on weekends.

NIGHTCLUBS AND CABARETS

The **Roxy** (279 Tremont Street, in the Quality Inn Hotel; 617-227-7699) is a beautiful and elegant art deco-style club where people like to really dress up. It has its own 14-piece orchestra, dance troupe and deejay. Cover.

A view of the city from the 33rd floor is offered the prosperous at the **Bay Tower Room** (60 State Street; 617-723-1666), where a four-piece orchestra plays.

Surfboard tables and Hawaiian-shirt-clad deejays add up to California fun with live rock-and-roll five nights a week at the **Boston Beach Club** (Landmark Inn, Faneuil Hall, 300 North Market Building; 617-227-9660). Cover.

A tropical paradise complete with 20-foot royal palms awaits guests of **Zanzibar** (1 Boylston Place; 617-451-1955), which offers rock and Top-40 music. Cover.

Beneath the Wilbur Theater is the elegant, upscale **Comedy Connection at Duck Soup** (246 Tremont Street; 617-391-0022). Drawing a mixed clientele, nationally known comedians headline seven nights a week. Cover.

The **Orpheum Theater** (Hamilton Place off Tremont Street; 617-482-0650) hosts nationally known rock performers.

THEATER

Boston's theater district is tightly clustered on lower Tremont Street and several blocks west. The **Colonial Theatre** (106 Boylston Street; 617-426-9366) and **The Shubert** (265 Tremont Street; 617-426-4520) host pre-Broadway tryouts and national touring companies. Popular contemporary plays are offered at **The Wilbur** (246 Tremont Street; 617-423-4008).

The opulent **Wang Center for the Performing Arts** (270 Tremont Street; 617-482-9393), formerly a Roaring Twenties movie palace, sponsors extravaganzas in dance, theater, opera and music.

Musical comedies are the specialty at **The Charles Playhouse** (76 Warrenton Street; 617-426-6912), while its **Stage II** (617-426-5225) downstairs has been home to the country's longest-running nonmusical play, *Shear Madness*, a comedy whodunit.

OPERA AND DANCE

Artistic director Sarah Caldwell has established the **Opera Company of Boston** (539 Washington Street; 617-426-5300) as one of the world's premier companies. Occasional rock and pop performances are also held here.

The **Boston Ballet** (42 Vernon Street, Newton; 617-964-4070) performs classics like *The Nutcracker* and contemporary works at the Wang Center. Its sister company, **Boston Ballet II**, gives free summer concerts at the Hatch Shell on the Esplanade.

Beacon Hill

Beacon Hill got its name from a beacon that stood atop it in 1634 to warn colonial settlers of danger. "The Hill" used to be much taller; it was leveled by 60 feet to make way for residential building in the 18th century.

After a building boom, Beacon Hill fast became the most elite section of the city, home to doctors, lawyers, writers and intellectuals. Oliver Wendell Holmes called it "the sunny street that holds the sifted few." The first formal residents of the neighborhood were John Singleton Copley and John Hancock. Later residents included Daniel Webster, Louisa May Alcott, William Dean Howells, Henry James and Jenny Lind.

No single section of town is more elegant than Beacon Hill. This charming area still looks like a 19th-century neighborhood with its gaslamps, brick sidewalks and narrow, one-lane streets that wind up and down the hill. Its later brick rowhouses were designed in fine federal style, with symmetrical windows, fanlight door windows, black shutters and lacy black iron grillwork. Beacon Hill residents love windowboxes and gardens, and many of the houses have beautiful hidden walled gardens. These are opened to the public during the **Hidden Gardens of Beacon Hill** walking tours in the spring, sponsored by the Beacon Hill Garden Club (617-227-4392).

The crown of Beacon Hill, at its summit, is the **Massachusetts State House** (617-727-3676), a grand replacement for the old State House downtown. After the American Revolution, state leaders wanted a more elegant home for the prosperous new government. Charles Bulfinch designed it for them in 1795 in federal style, with a gold dome, brick facade, Palladian windows and white Corinthian columns and trim. A tour of the interior is well worthwhile. An impressive rotunda, floors made of 24 kinds of marble, unique "black lace" iron grillwork stair railings, stained-glass windows and decorated vaulted ceilings are all part of the appointments. Don't miss the Sacred Cod in the House of Representatives, a wooden fish hung there in 1784 to symbolize the importance of the fishing industry to Massachusetts.

The **Old Court House** (Pemberton Square), now the Suffolk County Courthouse, has a grand rotunda with vaulted ceilings decorated with gilt rosettes and figures of cherubs, urns, scrolls and trumpet-blowing figures. Stone caryatids line the rotunda, representing Justice, Fortitude, Punishment, Guilt, Reward, Wisdom, Religion and Virtue.

Many come to admire **Louisburg Square**—between Mt. Vernon and Pinckney streets—for its sheer beauty. The centerpiece of the square is a serene oval park with a tall black iron fence, ringed with brick bowfront houses. Louisburg Square looks so much like London that a British film company produced *Vanity Fair* here in the 1920s. Louisa May Alcott lived at number 20.

Tiny one-lane **Acorn Street**—just south of Louisburg Square between Cedar and Willow streets—is one of the few old cobblestone streets left on Beacon Hill, and a very picturesque one it is. Coachmen and servants for nearby mansions used to live here.

Although the **Rose Standish-Nichols House Museum** (55 Mount Vernon Street; 617-227-6993; admission) was not fashionable for its time, it is a fine example of the late 19th-century row house. Standish-Nichols was quite a personage in her day. A noted landscape architect and pacifist, she traveled around the world and was a friend of Woodrow Wilson. Designed by Bulfinch, her home is filled with rare antiques such as Renaissance Flemish tapestries, statuary by noted American sculptor Augustus Saint-Gaudens and unusual imitation leather wallpaper gilded with gold.

Number **85 Mt. Vernon Street** was Harrison Gray Otis's second Bulfinch-designed home, while **45 Beacon Street** was his third, an unheard-of extravagance.

A grander library than the **Boston Athenaeum** (10½ Beacon Street; 617-227-0270) would be hard to find. The interior features high, vaulted ceilings, pillared archways, scores of marble busts, solid wood reading tables and red-leather, brass-studded armchairs. Founded in 1807 by a group including the Reverend William Emerson, father of Ralph Waldo Emerson, it's one of the country's oldest independent libraries. Its picture gallery and sculpture hall served as Boston's first art museum, and the library still maintains an impressive collection of art today, including works by Gilbert Stuart, John Singer Sargent and Chester Harding. The library is also noted for its collections of 19th-century American prints, Confederate state imprints and books from the libraries of George Washington, General Henry Knox and Jean Louis Cardinal Cheverus. Public tours are given by appointment.

The **Appleton-Parker Houses** (39–40 Beacon Street), twin Greek Revival houses alike in every detail, were built for two wealthy merchants.

At number 39, Fanny Appleton married Henry Wadsworth Longfellow in 1843. Number 40 is now the home of the Women's City Club.

At 63–64 Beacon Street you can see a few panes of the famous **Beacon Hill purple glass**, with hues caused by a reaction of sunlight. It acquired cachet, along with everything else traditional on "the Hill."

It is intriguing that while most people think of Beacon Hill as a Brahmin bastion, in the 19th century its north slope was the heart of Boston's emerging free black community. Blacks arrived in Boston as slaves in 1638. By 1705, there were more than 400 slaves, and a few free blacks, who settled in the North End. In the 19th century, most blacks lived in the West End, and on Beacon Hill, between Joy and Charles streets. The free blacks worked hard to provide decent housing and education for their own, and to help end slavery.

A number of their houses and public buildings still stand, and you can see them on the 14-stop **Black Heritage Trail** (★). Walking tour maps are available at the Boston Common Visitor Information kiosk and at the **Museum of Afro-American History** (46 Joy Street; 617-742-1854), a stop on the trail.

Among the public buildings are the **African Meeting House** (8 Smith Court), the oldest standing black church in America. Built in 1806, it was known in the abolitionist era as the Black Faneuil Hall. Here, in 1832, the New England Anti-Slavery Society was founded, with black leader Frederick Douglass and abolitionists William Lloyd Garrison and Charles Sumner speaking from the platform.

A stirring tribute to the first black regiment recruited for the Civil War stands at the corner of Beacon and Park streets. A bas-relief sculpture by Augustus Saint-Gaudens, the **Robert Gould Shaw and 54th Regiment Memorial** shows the regiment on the march with their young white leader, Bostonian Robert Gould Shaw, and an angel flying overhead. The black military role in the Civil War won new recognition with the release of the film *Glory*, which chronicles the story of the 54th Regiment.

The trail also takes you to one of the first schools for black children and to homes built by free blacks, among them the **Lewis and Harriet Hayden House** (66 Phillips Street), which served as an Underground Railway station and was visited by Harriet Beecher Stowe.

On an entirely different note, television history is also alive and well in Beacon Hill. Like homing pigeons, all tourists head for "Cheers," so we may as well get it out of the way. The setting for the television show is the **Bull and Finch Pub** (downstairs at 84 Beacon Street; 617-227-9605), not to be confused with the impostor, Three Cheers, at 390 Congress Street. Even though the Bull and Finch has made such a big business out of all this—selling "Cheers" T-shirts, mugs and hats in the Hampshire House Hotel lobby upstairs—it's a bar with real atmosphere. Originally an English

Charlestown and Bunker Hill

Charlestown is even older than Boston. It was founded by a small band of Puritans in 1629, who later abandoned it for Boston. Charlestown was almost destroyed by the British in the Battle of Bunker Hill, so few 18th-century houses survive.

A walk over the river on the Charlestown Bridge brings you to the Charlestown Navy Yard, the berth of the **U.S.S. Constitution** (617-242-5670), the oldest commissioned vessel in the Navy. It won its nickname of Old Ironsides when British cannon fire bounced off its sturdy oak hull in the War of 1812. A handsome black-and-white frigate, the *Constitution* once required 400 sailors to hoist its sails. While you can tour the top deck and down below, lines are always long; try at lunchtime.

Across the yard from Old Ironsides is the **Constitution Museum** (617-426-1812; admission), which houses exhibits on Old Ironsides' many voyages and victories, memorabilia and paintings. Nearby is the **Commandant's House**, a handsome brick federal-style mansion where Navy officers lived.

The **Bunker Hill Monument** (43 Monument Square; 617-242-5641) actually stands atop Breed's Hill, where the Battle of Bunker Hill was in fact fought. This encounter became legend with the words of Colonel William Prescott to his ammunition-short troops: "Don't fire until you see the whites of their eyes." The cornerstone of the 220-foot Egyptian Revival granite obelisk was laid in 1825 by General Lafayette, with Daniel Webster orating. There are 294 steps to the observatory, which affords a magnificent view of the city and the harbor.

Companion exhibits at the **Bunker Hill Pavilion** (55 Constitution Road; 617-241-7575; admission) include a multimedia slide show with 14 screens reenacting the battle.

If you feel hungry during your Charlestown outing, you can combine dining with history at the **Warren Tavern** (2 Pleasant Street; 617-241-8142), dating to 1780. The small, clapboarded house with gaslights was patronized by Paul Revere and George Washington. The inside appears dark and colonial, with heavy beamed ceiling, wood planked floors, candelabra wall sconces and punched-tin lights, thick lace tablecloths and a roaring fire. The solid fare, priced moderate to deluxe, includes steaks, seafood and a tavern burger with peddler fries. The Warren Tavern also makes its own brand of Indian pudding for dessert.

pub, it was dismantled and shipped here, complete with old leather and walnut paneling.

Yet another point of television trivia can be found in Beacon Hill. Private eye Spenser of "Spenser for Hire" lived above a Boston firehouse, which he entered through a bright red door. The firehouse is right next to the Charles Street Meeting House on Mount Vernon Street, at the corner of River Street.

BEACON HILL HOTEL

The only hotel in Beacon Hill is a real find, far less pricey than downtown hotels. The **John Jeffries House** (14 Embankment Road; 617-367-1866) offers 46 spacious studio apartments and suites, all with kitchenettes, in a renovated turn-of-the-century house overlooking Charles Street. Guest quarters are furnished in tasteful pastels, with dark reproduction furniture, large windows and contemporary bathrooms. There is also a large and comfortable lobby. Moderate to deluxe.

BEACON HILL RESTAURANTS

Two steps from the State House, **The Black Goose** (21 Beacon Street; 617-720-4500) specializes in Northern Italian cuisine. Take care not to load up on the home-baked *focaccia* bread, chewy yet light. Likewise the *caprese* salad, a mound of plum tomatoes, mozzarella and basil. Save room for the tasty entrées—among the menu of pastas and grilled meats and fish are linguine *basilico*, cannelloni, chicken *franco* and veal with fresh lemon and sage. Contemporary dash has been added to the dining room, originally part of a historic hotel. Moderate to deluxe.

Murals of top-hatted gentlemen and begowned ladies bring Paris of the Gay Nineties to life at **Another Season** (97 Mount Vernon Street; 617-367-0880), a romantic basement restaurant. Limited entrées are lovingly chosen: beef bourbon, salmon Dana and chicken *chèvre*. Desserts include apricot cheesecake and flourless swiss chocolate gâteau. Deluxe.

Along with its chic boutiques, Charles Street is lined with restaurants representing many ethnic cuisines.

Il Dolce Momento (30 Charles Street; 617-720-0477) is a great coffeehouse where you can linger over an espresso or cappuccino and feel welcome in a European way. Its café chairs are always crowded with young students munching on hearty Italian sandwiches and homemade soups. Specialties are fresh *gelato* made in-house, croissants and flaky pastries like *biscotti di prato*. Budget.

Good and spicy Thai food stars over the decor at **The King and I** (145 Charles Street; 617-227-3320). Start off with *satay* and Thai rolls, then move on to dancing squids, seafood *panang* or any number of chicken, duck, beef, tofu and noodle dishes. Budget to moderate.

Step into a Tuscan village at **Ristorante Toscano** (41 Charles Street; 617-723-4090), whose dining room has exposed brick walls hung with paintings of the Italian countryside. Feast on Florentine cuisine including homemade pastas and game dishes. The Tiramesu is a dessert standout. Moderate to deluxe.

Surrounded by whizzing cars in a rotary, **Buzzy's Fabulous Roast Beef** (★) (327 Cambridge Street; 617-523-4896) looks unsavory, to say the least. Still, this take-out stand, open until 5 a.m., has the best steakhouse fries in Boston, as well as cheesesteak sandwiches, chili dogs and short ribs. And it's got art: cartoons of John Wayne, Ben Franklin and Rocky Balboa adorn the hand-printed wall menus. Budget all the way.

BEACON HILL SHOPPING

At the foot of Beacon Hill, little Charles Street is thickly lined with antique shops, art galleries and specialty stores.

Quirky bargains lie in store at the **Beacon Hill Thrift Shop** (15 Charles Street; 617-742-2323), where Beacon Hill matrons bring their best silver along with bric-a-brac.

Grand Trousseau (88 Charles Street; 617-367-3163) sells nothing but the best vintage clothing: gorgeous beaded silk, lace and velvet gowns of yesteryear.

Fanciful handcrafted wood items abound at the **Charles Street Woodshop** (102 Charles Street; 617-523-0797), from yo-yos and birdhouses to breadboards and garden benches.

An amazing selection of beautifully colored and embroidered western-style leather boots awaits at **Helen's Leather** (110 Charles Street; 617-742-2077), along with leather coats and jackets, briefcases and belts.

One of Charles Street's oldest and most respected antique shops is **George Gravert Antiques** (122 Charles Street; 617-227-1593), which carries fine European pieces such as crystal chandeliers, armoires and furniture.

You ought to be able to find the perfect brass drawer pull at **Period Furniture Hardware** (123 Charles Street; 617-227-0758), which carries a full line of reproduction hardware.

BEACON HILL NIGHTLIFE

The **Lyric Stage Company of Boston** (54 Charles Street; 617-742-1790), Boston's oldest resident professional theater, performs revivals and premieres, and Dylan Thomas' *A Child's Christmas in Wales* every Christmas.

Back Bay

Although it started life as a mud flat, Back Bay fast became a fashionable neighborhood. As the city grew, it started running out of room in its original peninsula surrounding Boston Common, so it began filling in the tidal flats of the Back Bay in 1858, the largest land reclamation project of its time. Some 450 acres of marshland were turned into usable land over 20 years.

Given all this room to plan, Back Bay is the only place in town laid out with any perceivable logic. Streets follow an orderly grid, with cross streets named alphabetically for palatial ducal mansions: Arlington, Berkeley, Clarendon, Dartmouth, Exeter, Fairfield, Gloucester and Hereford.

The centerpiece of this grand reclamation project is **Commonwealth Avenue**. Patterned after the Champs Élysées, it's a wide boulevard with a grass strip mall that runs right through the heart of the Back Bay. "Comm Ave," as it's called by natives, is lined with stately brownstones and many historic buildings. Newbury, Beacon and Marlborough streets parallel Comm Ave. Fashionable Newbury Street is lined with chic boutiques, expensive jewelry, fur and clothing stores, art galleries, antique stores and loads of restaurants. Back Bay ends at Massachusetts Avenue, which natives shorten to "Mass Ave."

To the north, the Back Bay ends at the Charles River, where the wide, grassy **Esplanade** is a popular sunning spot in warm weather. Also on the Esplanade is the **Hatch Memorial Shell**, where the Boston Pops Symphony Orchestra and Boston Ballet II perform summer concerts.

If Boston Common is Boston's Central Park, then the **Public Garden** (bordered by Beacon, Charles, Arlington and Boylston streets) is its Tuileries, the first botanical garden in the country. Lavishly landscaped with flowers and trees, it's home to the **Swan Boats**, which circle the weeping willow-draped lagoon in season. The famous Swan Boats were launched in 1877 by Robert Paget, who was inspired by the swan-boat scene in Wagner's opera *Lohengrin*. The same family continues to operate them. Also in the Public Garden is some notable statuary: **George Washington** on horseback and a Daniel Chester French bronze statue of a maiden.

If you walk straight through the Public Garden gates at the corner of Beacon and Charles streets, you'll come upon **Mrs. Mallard and her brood of eight ducklings (★)** stretched out in a row behind her, all heading for the pond. Placed here in 1987, the bronze, larger-than-life statues represent the ducks made famous in Robert McCloskey's children's story "Make Way for Ducklings." Each April, the ducklings are feted on Duckling Day with a parade and festival sponsored by the Historic Neighborhoods Foundation (2 Boylston Street; 617-426-1885).

Ever since opening in 1927, the **Ritz-Carlton** (15 Arlington Street; 617-536-5700) has catered to a select clientele. The 17-story brick building overlooking the Public Garden, while not particularly striking on the outside, is the epitome of old elegance inside, where the lobby is graced with a large curving staircase and antique touches such as an exquisite brass railing. The original owner would never permit a reservation without researching the client's reputation in the Social Register or business directories. Many notable people have lived at the Ritz, including Charles Lindbergh, Winston Churchill and John F. Kennedy. Many more have stayed here, among them Rodgers and Hammerstein, Albert Einstein, the Duke and Duchess of Windsor, Tennessee Williams and Gregory Peck. Even Lassie and Rin Tin Tin have stayed at the Ritz, as has Louis the Swan, of E. B. White's children's classic *The Trumpet of the Swan*, sleeping in the bathtub.

Down the street, the Georgian-style **Arlington Street Church** (Arlington and Boylston streets) features a tall and graceful steeple designed by Christopher Wren. The Massachusetts Convention that ratified the U.S. Constitution in 1788 met here.

The **New Old South Church** (corner of Boylston and Dartmouth streets) is where the congregation of the Old South Meeting House moved in 1875, after they decided their Washington Street neighborhood had become too noisy to hear the sermon. The Gothic facade is dominated by a tower and carved stone rosettes. Inside are Venetian mosaics and 15th-century stained-glass windows depicting the Prophets, the Evangelists, the miracles and the parables.

The **Boston Evening Clinic** (314 Commonwealth Avenue) was created in the 1920s in an 1899 mansion modeled after a Loire Valley château. Its medieval-looking exterior has sculptured stone cherubs and gargoyles looking down from its battlements. Inside the building are spectacular bas-relief mahogany walls, gold-leaf carved ceilings, stained-glass windows and an ornately carved marble staircase.

Nowhere is the opulence of the Back Bay Victorians more amply evidenced than at the **Gibson House** (137 Beacon Street; 617-267-6338; admission), now a museum. Built for the prominent Gibson family in 1859, the Italian Renaissance Revival home is richly furnished with gold-embossed wallpaper and black walnut paneling, imported carpets and most of the Gibson family china and porcelain.

The **Institute of Contemporary Art** (955 Boylston Street; 617-266-5152; admission) has won an international reputation for its wide-ranging artistic events, held here for more than half a century. Housed in an old Boston firehouse, the ICA often shows experimental or controversial works, among them art exhibits, films, videos, music events, lectures and literary readings.

BACK BAY HOTELS

The vintage 1927 **Ritz-Carlton** (15 Arlington Street; 617-536-5700) sparkles after an extensive restoration. A standard room is spacious and airy, with a high ceiling, brown floral drapes and spread and French provincial furnishings. On the walls are prints of antique engravings of Boston and Bunker Hill. The bathroom has polished white marble floors and antique fixtures. Besides an in-house health and fitness facility with sauna and massage, the 278-room Ritz offers complimentary use of a full-service health club nearby. The hotel has two restaurants, an afternoon tea lounge and a bar. Ultra-deluxe.

One of the city's smallest, most charming hotels, the **Eliot Hotel** (★) (370 Commonwealth Avenue; 617-267-1607) was built in 1925 by the family of Charles Eliot, a Harvard president. The hotel has a warm, welcoming feeling, and underwent major renovations in early 1990. Its rose-colored lobby is set with wing chairs, sofas and crystal wall sconces. Rooms are furnished with dark, antique-style furniture. Some have kitchenettes. Deluxe.

Beacon Inn Guest Houses (248 Newbury Street; 617-262-1771) has eight less-than-lovely rooms (30 in the summer) with twin beds and tacky wood paneling and furniture. Still, these are moderately priced rooms in the heart of Back Bay, with kitchenettes and private baths.

One way around the high cost of Boston hotels is to rent a furnished room. **Comma Realty, Inc.** (371 Commonwealth Avenue; 617-437-9200) has 45 studio rooms and apartments with kitchens that can be rented nightly from November to March, weekly from April to October. The rooms are plain but clean, with serviceable brown carpeting, twin beds and funky blue bathroom fixtures. Budget to moderate.

BACK BAY RESTAURANTS

Though it emulates a Parisian bistro about as successfully as a McDonald's, the **Café de Paris** (19 Arlington Street; 617-247-7121) offers better fare than McD's: croissants, omelettes, crêpes and sandwiches, with cafeteria-style service. Budget.

High-end Chinese in a unique setting is the specialty at **Mr. Leung's** (545 Boylston Street; 617-236-4040). Cantonese and Szechuan dishes debut in a tiny formal dining room that looks like a dancefloor with its light-bedecked black ceiling. Deluxe.

Suffused in pink and graced with a cathedral ceiling, the **Back Bay Bistro** (565 Boylston Street; 617-536-4477) exudes a stylish informality. Roast chicken with garlic glaze and eggplant torta are among the menu offerings. Conveniently, the café chairs and tables move outdoors in summer. Moderate to deluxe.

Chef Chandler's Commonwealth Grill (★) (111 Dartmouth Street; 617-353-0160) dishes up hearty portions of Cajun and Creole fare in an easy, funky ambience where the carpeting is leopard skin and the lighting is dim. The chef, who did duty as a railroad dining car chef in years past, is famed for his seafood filet gumbo, alligator Creole, barbecue ribs with red beans, and broiled redfish with hushpuppies. Moderate.

The **Ritz-Carlton Dining Room** (15 Arlington Street; 617-536-5700) offers one of the most serene and traditional dining spots in Boston. Over-looking the Public Garden, this sparkling, elegant place features cobalt blue Dutch crystal chandeliers, French provincial-style furniture, blue-and-gold fringed drapes and swan-shaped table vases in honor of the Swan Boats. The continental menu changes daily but might include such wonderful en-trées as lobster in bourbon sauce, venison, pheasant or whole dover sole sautéed with pine nuts and lemon butter. There are almost 20 desserts, rang-ing from *bavorois à l'orange* to *crêpes Suzettes flambées*. Ultra-deluxe.

A cozy little basement restaurant, the **Kebab n' Kurry** (30 Massachu-setts Avenue; 617-536-9835) smells of the spices of India. The tables are set with pink cloths and silk scarves embroidered with lion hunts and ele-phants, set under glass. Authentic curries from North India, Bombay and South India include chicken, lamb, fish and shrimp dishes. Moderate.

BACK BAY SHOPPING

Back Bay is another of the city's densest shopping districts, concen-trated on fashionable Newbury Street, lined from end to end with chic bou-tiques.

Shreve, Crump & Lowe (330 Boylston Street; 617-267-9100), a Bos-ton jeweler since 1800, has always been the place to go for fine gold and silver jewelry.

A gold swan sculpture over the door signals the **Women's Educational and Industrial Union** (356 Boylston Street; 617-536-5651), founded in 1877 by a group of socially concerned women, the same year the Swan Boats set sail. Its shop sells Italian pottery, jewelry, women's accessories, stationery, cards, children's clothing, even antiques.

Conran's (26 Exeter Street; 617-266-2836) is in the former Exeter Theater, once Boston's oldest continuously operating theater. It has colorful, contemporary household goods galore, from glassware and china to office accessories.

If you like the Italian flair for fashion, consider **Settebello** (8 Newbury Street; 617-262-5280), selling imported women's clothing and fine leather boots and shoes in a salon-style setting of loveseats and Oriental rugs.

Shoes with a cluster of plastic bananas à la Carmen Miranda? You'll find them at **Alan Bilzerian** (34 Newbury Street; 617-536-1001), a chic shop filled with avant-garde clothing for men and women.

London Lace (167 Newbury Street; 617-267-3506) specializes in reproduction Victorian lace patterns made on the only Victorian machinery left in the British Isles. Items include lace curtain panels, table runners, tablecloths and antique napkins.

Who would mind buying used men's and women's clothing when it's as fashionable and "gently worn" as that at **The Closet** (175 Newbury Street, downstairs; 617-536-1919)? Only the latest clothes in the finest condition are accepted.

The **Society of Arts and Crafts** (175 Newbury Street; 617-266-1810) is the oldest nonprofit craft organization in the United States, founded in 1897. In its salesroom you can buy whimsical animal sculptures, papier-mâché masks and furniture with real personality, as well as pottery and jewelry. There's a second gallery at 101 Arch Street (617-345-0033).

Prem-la (221 Newbury Street; 617-266-8961) sells Himalayan imports, from brightly patterned sweaters and fiber wallhangings to brass figures, beaded necklaces and carved masks.

A surprising amount of fine—and expensive—19th-century French and English antiques is crowded into **Belgravia Antiques, Ltd.** (222 Newbury Street; 617-267-1915). Stylish armoires and highboys surround crystal wall sconces and original oil paintings.

For a smell of the Southwest, step into **Selletto** (★) (244 Newbury Street; 617-424-0656), always enhanced by piñon and juniper incense, where wares come from a worldwide network of artists. There are hand-carved marble peaches from Tuscany, birchbark baskets made by Ojibwa Indians and "found objects" like an 18th-century mesquite wagon wheel.

The **Tower Record Building** (360 Newbury Street; 617-247-9500) is a bold, winged stone creation by revolutionary architect Frank O. Gehry. It holds three floors of all the music anyone could want: classical, country, folk, rock, soul, reggae and gospel.

BACK BAY NIGHTLIFE

If you're rich or want to be, head for the dark-paneled **Ritz Bar** (15 Arlington Street; 617-536-5700), where tradition and Brahmin propriety rule.

Housed in a renovated police station, **Division 16** (955 Boylston Street; 617-353-0870) features recorded Big Band and swing music amidst pink neon, pink walls and art deco wall sconces.

During the Boston Marathon, you can't get in the doors of the **Eliot Lounge** (370 Commonwealth Avenue, in the Eliot Hotel; 617-262-1078), which is decorated with sports memorabilia and photos and the flags of marathon winners' countries.

Fynn's (359 Newbury Street; 617-536-1100) packs in the glamorati for its esoteric ambience based on movie legend.

Middle-class disco pleases the crowds at **Club Nicole** (40 Dalton Street; 617-236-1100) in the basement of the Back Bay Hilton. Dress code. An elegant vintage ballroom provides a romantic setting for ballroom dancing at the **Ritz-Carlton** (15 Arlington Street; 617-536-5700).

The **Boston Camerata** (729 Boylston Street; 617-262-2092), formed in 1954, offers medieval, Renaissance and early baroque concerts, both vocal and instrumental.

The **Paradise** (967 Commonwealth Avenue; 617-254-2052) draws SRO crowds for its national headliners in live rock music and dance. Cover.

The Fenway

The western side of Massachusetts Avenue edges over to the Fenway, the area surrounding the **Back Bay Fens**, another piece of the Emerald Necklace. Fens, from an Old English word meaning low wetlands or marshes, describes the area aptly. Along its sprawling length are several creeks and ponds, a rose garden and private garden plots, remnants of Boston's wartime "Victory Gardens."

No one thinks of the Fenway without **Fenway Park** (24 Yawkey Way; 617-267-8661), the home of the Boston Red Sox and the Green Monster, the famous left-field wall. Fenway Park remains one of the homiest and most old-fashioned ballparks in the country.

The campuses of two well-known Boston colleges are also in the Fenway—**Boston University**, along Commonwealth Avenue, and **Northeastern University**, south of Huntington Avenue.

Visible from Kenmore Square is the brightly lit, red-white-and-blue **Citgo Sign**, a gasoline advertisement and relic of the 1950s. The last of six similar signs in the United States, it has been declared a national landmark.

Housed in a 15th-century-style Venetian palazzo, the **Isabella Stewart Gardner Museum** (280 The Fenway; 617-566-1401; admission) is a little jewel of a museum. It contains the personal collection of Mrs. Isabella Stewart Gardner, amassed over a lifetime of travel to Europe. "Mrs. Jack," as she came to be called, was considered somewhat eccentric and outrageous by proper Bostonians, and she collected what she liked. Her booty includes Italian Renaissance, 17th-century Dutch and 19th-century American paintings, as well as sculpture, textiles, furniture, ceramics, prints and drawings. Built around a beautiful flowered courtyard, the museum also offers weekly chamber music concerts.

Not far from the Gardner Museum is the **Museum of Fine Arts** (465 Huntington Avenue; 617-267-9300; admission), world famous for its exceptional collections of Asian, Greek, Roman, European, Egyptian and American art. The MFA also holds impressionist paintings and works by such American masters as John Singer Sargent, John Singleton Copley and Winslow Homer. The MFA regularly attracts mega-exhibitions, such as traveling shows of Renoir and Monet works. Don't miss the Japanese gardens, and the little first-floor café.

FENWAY HOTELS

The **Newbury Inn** (★) (533 Newbury Street; 617-266-2583) is a real steal, a lovely Victorian bowfront brownstone with eight moderately priced rooms. The rooms are tastefully done with oak floors and period antiques, and many have fireplaces. All include a continental breakfast. There are shared baths, laundry facilities and a formal dining room.

The best deal for budget-minded travelers in Boston just has to be **Florence Frances'** (★) (458 Park Drive; 617-267-2458) 125-year-old brownstone with four guest rooms that share baths and priced on the low side of moderate. Mrs. Frances has traveled around the world and decorated each room individually with an international flair. The Spanish Room, done in red, black and white, has a display of Spanish fans on the wall. The living and sitting rooms are beautifully furnished with antiques and a collection of Royal Doulton figurines. There is also a community kitchen.

The **Boston International American Youth Hostel** (12 Hemenway Street; 617-262-8861) represents the rock bottom of Boston accommodations, both in terms of price and amenities. Dormitory-style rooms hold six beds, with males and females kept separate. You must provide your own sheets, and no alcoholic beverages are allowed. Non-AYH members can stay here by paying a small extra charge for an introductory membership. The hostel can accommodate 220 people in summer and 125 during the academic year. There are laundry and kitchen facilities, a dining room and lounge with piano and juice machine.

Unlike the YWCA, the **YMCA** (316 Huntington Avenue; 617-536-7800) allows both male and female guests. More generously appointed than the YWCA, it has a spacious and comfortable wood-paneled lobby, an indoor pool, laundry facilities and cafeteria. But rooms are cell-like and furnished with Salvation Army-type furniture. Budget.

FENWAY RESTAURANTS

You'll halfway expect the girl from Ipanema to stroll into **Buteco** (130 Jersey Street; 617-247-9508), so Brazilian and laid-back is it. Framed photos of Brazil line its white walls, Brazilian guitar music plays softly and tables are simply set with oilcloth covers and fresh yellow primroses. A standout is the *feijoada*—the Brazilian national dish, a stew of black beans with pork, sausage and dried beef, served with rice. Also try the homemade soups and desserts, among them caramel custard and guava paste. Budget to moderate.

The walls of **Bangkok Cuisine** (177-A Massachusetts Avenue; 617-262-5377) look like a museum, lavishly covered with elaborate framed pictures of Thai motifs in gold leaf: a peacock, villagers with elephants, Buddhist figures. Warm orange lights and crystal-and-brass chandeliers add to the exotic flair. Entrées include deep-fried whole fish, hot and sour dishes, curry dishes and rice and noodles. Budget to moderate.

FENWAY SHOPPING

The music of psychedelic '60s groups, '50s jazzmen and other performers of yesteryear rules at **Looney Tunes** (★) (1106 Boylston Street; 617-247-2238), where you can buy used records on the cheap.

FENWAY NIGHTLIFE

Citi (15 Lansdowne Street; 617-262-2424), one of the city's largest dance clubs, plays progressive and Top-40 sounds for avid dancers, and hosts top names like Eric Clapton and Prince. Next door, one of the trendiest dance clubs is **Axis** (13 Lansdowne Street; 617-262-2437), which features progressive music. Cover at both clubs.

The **Rathskellar** (528 Commonwealth Avenue; 617-536-9438), fondly called the Rat, first showcased the Police and Talking Heads and is still a loud hole-in-the-wall offering alternative rock bands. Cover.

CLASSICAL MUSIC AND THEATER

Under the direction of Seiji Ozawa, the prestigious **Boston Symphony Orchestra** (301 Massachusetts Avenue; 617-266-1492) presents more than 250 concerts annually. Its **Boston Pops**, directed by John Williams, performs lighter favorites in spring and free outdoor summer concerts at the Hatch Shell on the Esplanade.

The **Handel and Haydn Society** (295 Huntington Avenue; 617-266-3605) is the country's oldest musical group, started in 1815. They perform instrumental and choral music, and Handel's *Messiah* at Christmas.

The **Huntington Theatre Company** (264 Huntington Avenue; 617-266-3913), Boston University's resident company, specializes in classics, comedies and musicals.

Midtown

Midtown is an area lacking in identity, a bridge between Back Bay and the South End. While some consider it part of the Back Bay, particularly those who would like a better address, it has a distinctly different character, the result of controversial urban renewal in the 1960s that created modernistic buildings alongside 19th-century ones.

The **First Church of Christ, Scientist** (175 Huntington Avenue; 617-450-2000) is the world headquarters of Christian Science, founded in 1879 by Mary Baker Eddy. The mother church is topped by an imposing dome and set in a brick pedestrian plaza with a reflecting pool designed by I. M. Pei. Take a walk through the echoing **Mapparium** in the *Christian Science Monitor* building, a unique 30-foot stained-glass globe with a footbridge through it, for a peek at how the world looked in 1935.

Right across the street from each other at the corner of Huntington and Massachusetts avenues are two handsome and famous brick buildings: **Symphony Hall** (301 Massachusetts Avenue; 617-266-1492) and **Horticultural Hall** (300 Massachusetts Avenue; 617-536-9280). Designed in 1900, Symphony Hall is so acoustically perfect it's known worldwide as a "Stradivarius among halls." The Boston Symphony Orchestra celebrated its 100th anniversary here in 1981. Horticultural Hall is the third home of the Massachusetts Horticultural Society, the oldest active society of its kind in America, founded in 1829. The society maintains the largest and finest horticultural library in the world. This 1901 Beaux-Arts building features limestone and terra cotta cornices and moldings ornately carved with fruits and garlands.

The heart of Midtown is gorgeous **Copley Square** (Boylston Street, between Clarendon and Dartmouth streets), named for artist John Singleton Copley. Boston's religious and intellectual center at the end of the 19th century, the square is dominated by two architecturally imposing structures, Henry Hobson Richardson's Trinity Church and Charles McKim's Boston Public Library.

The French-Romanesque, medieval-style **Trinity Church** (206 Clarendon Street; 617-536-0944), built in 1877, is visually stunning inside and out. One of Richardson's most brilliant creations, Trinity Church has an enormous tower reminiscent of the domes of Venice and Constantinople. Inside, rich colors and exquisite Moorish details cover the vaulted ceiling, rotunda and walls, and there are John LaFarge frescoes and stained-glass windows.

Much more than a library, the **Boston Public Library** (666 Boylston Street; 617-536-5400) houses art and architectural treasures. A wide marble staircase, Corinthian columns and frescoes grace its grand entrance hall (at the side door). Inside are murals by John Singer Sargent, paintings by John Singleton Copley and sculptures by Augustus and Louis Saint-Gaudens and Daniel Chester French. Inspired by Italian Renaissance palaces, it was built in 1895. Take time to sit in the lovely central courtyard, where you'll find a fountain and benches.

The grande dame of Boston's vintage hotels is the **Copley Plaza Hotel** (138 St. James Avenue; 617-267-5300), built in 1912 in high Victorian style. It boasts a wide stone facade, whose curving center echoes the bowfront homes of Back Bay and Beacon Hill. Inside, marble and crystal appointments set off an elegant lobby topped with a trompe l'oeil painting of the sky. The internationally known Copley Plaza has served as a resting place for a dozen presidents and European royalty.

The Beaux-Arts **Berkeley Building** (420 Boylston Street) looks like a wedding cake, so curlicued and beribboned is its frothy white bas-relief terra cotta molding. Tiers of windows are trimmed in sea green, and a black marble entrance sign is flanked with dolphins and sea serpents. Built in 1905, it formerly housed Boston's design center and was beautifully restored in 1989.

There's no better way to view Boston than from the 60-story **John Hancock Observatory** (200 Clarendon Street, Copley Square; 617-572-6429; admission), the tallest building in New England. From 740 feet up, you can see the State House, the White Mountains of New Hampshire and the South Shore. Besides the great view, there are exhibits, a film, photographs and a sound and light show on Boston history. Down on the ground, the Hancock's shimmering glass sides serve as a fantastic mirror, reflecting the surrounding buildings as clearly as a photograph. When the Hancock was built in the late 1960s, architects argued bitterly that the rhomboidal building designed by I. M. Pei would ruin the character of Copley Square. The blue glass windows of this landmark have become collectors' items, ever since they fell out onto the sidewalk in the early 1970s. They were replaced at a cost of more than $8 million.

Like the Hancock, the **Skywalk Observatory** at the Prudential Tower (800 Boylston Street, Prudential Center; 617-236-3318; admission) gives you a bird's-eye view of downtown, this time a 360° one. Commonly called "the Pru," the Prudential Center was built in the early '60s as another piece

(Text continued on page 76.)

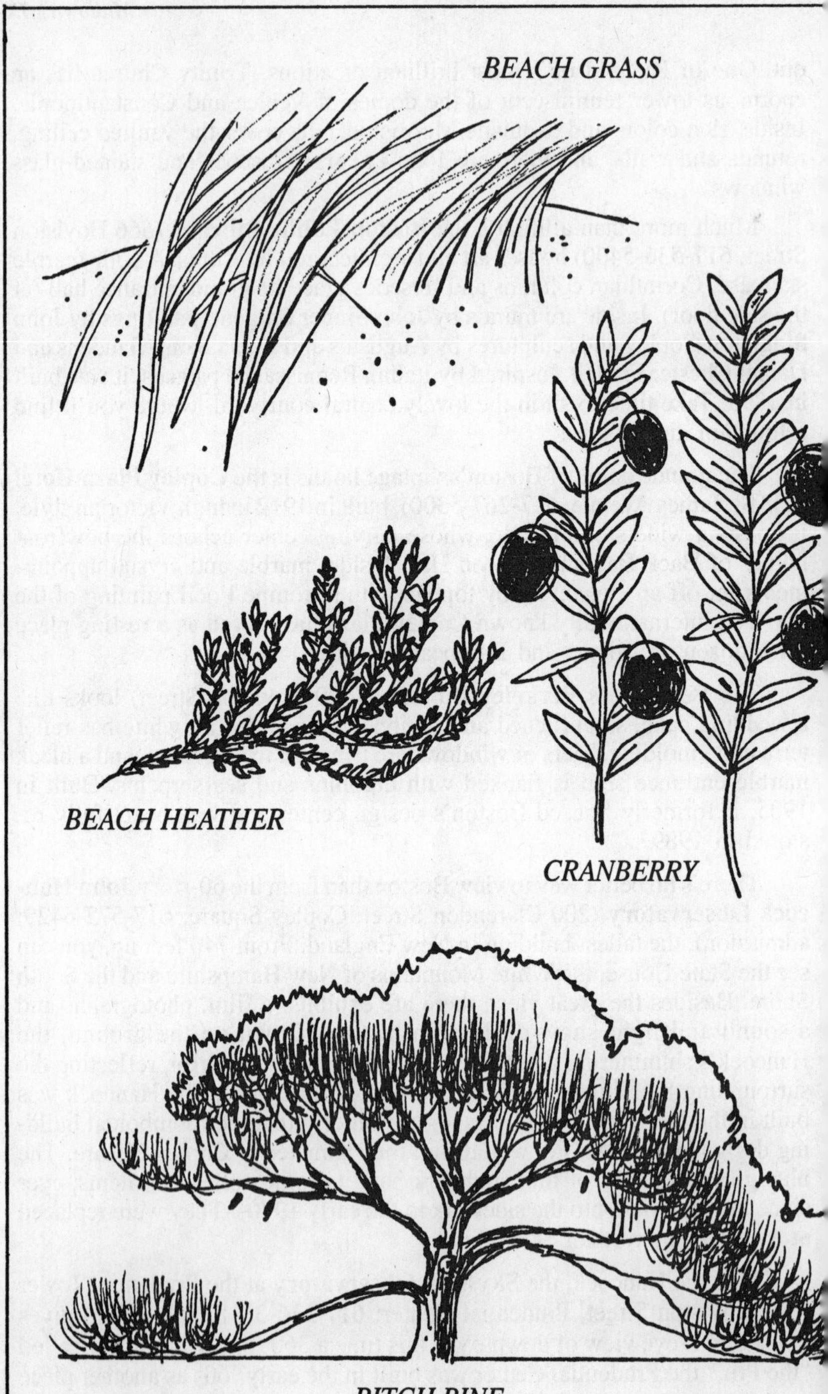

BEACH GRASS

BEACH HEATHER

CRANBERRY

PITCH PINE

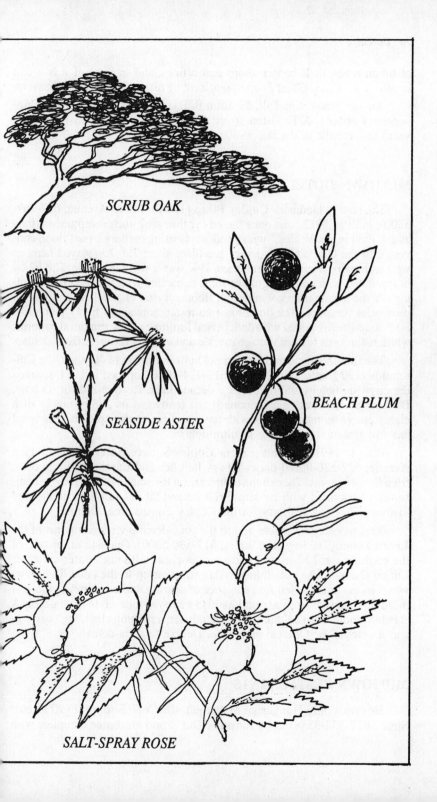

SCRUB OAK

SEASIDE ASTER

BEACH PLUM

SALT-SPRAY ROSE

of urban renewal. It houses shops and offices, and in front of it is a cast bronze statue called *Quest Eternal*, representing man reaching for the heavens.

A major convention hall, the **John B. Hynes Veterans Memorial Convention Center** (900 Boylston Street; 617-954-2000) was extensively renovated and rebuilt in the late 1980s.

MIDTOWN HOTELS

The stately landmark **Copley Plaza** (138 St. James Avenue; 617-267-5300), built in 1912, was once famed for throwing such sumptuous affairs as an "Evening in Venice," with gondolas floating on the parquet floor, converted to the Grand Canal. Every president since Taft has stayed here, as well as royalty from eight countries. JFK was a regular visitor. The lobby is appointed with coffered gold ceilings decorated with trompe l'oeil paintings of the sky, marble columns and floors, crystal chandeliers and French provincial furniture. The hotel has two restaurants and a lively piano bar. Bedrooms are decorated with dark period furniture and warm floral patterns, while bathrooms feature vintage marble and chrome fixtures. Ultra-deluxe.

The first independent luxury hotel built in Boston in 40 years, the **Colonnade** (120 Huntington Avenue; 617-424-7000), opened in 1971, sparked the citywide hotel building boom a decade later. Recognized for its bold, Bauhaus architecture, the Colonnade has renovated its 288 rooms in such classy colors as mauve walls with navy-and-pink print spreads. The hotel has two restaurants. Deluxe to ultra-deluxe.

Built in 1891, the vintage stone **Copley Square Hotel** (47 Huntington Avenue; 617-536-9000) draws lots of families and Europeans to its cozy, friendly 141 rooms. Though the rooms are on the smallish side, they're comfortably appointed with modern furniture and fabrics in blues, greens and mauves. This is a real buy for the Copley Square area. Deluxe.

Real working fireplaces add to the considerable vintage charms of the **Lenox Hotel** (710 Boylston Street; 617-536-5300). Opening at the turn of the century, the 220-room Lenox was popular with such entertainers as Enrico Caruso, who pulled his private streetcar up to the door. The lobby wears its original Gilded Age elegance of soaring white columns, gold-leaf moldings, marble fireplace and handsome royal-blue-and-white decor. A standard room has a colonial-style chandelier, a rocking chair, high ceilings and a colonial or Oriental ambience. Deluxe to ultra-deluxe.

MIDTOWN RESTAURANTS

Boston's only Hungarian restaurant, the **Café Budapest** (90 Exeter Street; 617-734-3388) has a romantic Old World ambience complete with strolling violinist, crystal chandeliers, leaded-glass windows and a coat of arms over the fireplace. Try the iced cherry soup or wild mushrooms in paprika sauce for appetizers, followed by an entrée of wienerschnitzel à la Holstein, sauerbraten, beef gulyas or beef stroganoff, and apple and cherry strudel desserts. Deluxe to ultra-deluxe.

The **Café Promenade** (120 Huntington Avenue in the Colonnade Hotel; 617-424-7000) has a light and airy feel to its wide-windowed dining room, with caneback chairs, green, rose and white decor and banks of fresh flowers. A continental cuisine of steaks, seafood and sandwiches is offered. Breakfast, lunch, dinner and Sunday brunch; moderate to deluxe.

MIDTOWN SHOPPING

The jewel of Midtown shopping is brass- and marble-bedecked **Copley Place** on upper Huntington Avenue, resplendent with indoor waterfalls and trees. The Copley Place complex also includes the Westin and Marriott hotels, and the shopping mall is in between the two, connected to both hotel lobbies. A glass pedestrian bridge carries shoppers over Huntington Avenue to the Prudential Center.

Opened in the mid-1980s, Copley Place holds 100 upscale stores, anchored by classy Dallas import **Neiman-Marcus** (617-536-3660). Copley Place also houses outlets of **Polo–Ralph Lauren** (617-266-4121), **Gucci** (617-247-3000), **Enrico Celli** (617-247-4881), **Bally of Switzerland** (617-437-1910) and **Louis Vuitton** (617-437-6519).

Copley Place's much older and dowdier cousin is the **Prudential Center**, anchored by **Saks Fifth Avenue** (800 Boylston Street; 617-262-8500) and **Lord & Taylor** (760 Boylston Street; 617-262-6000) but otherwise filled with uninspiring shops.

Bonwit Teller (500 Boylston Street; 617-267-1200) moved to palatial new headquarters in 1989, fronted by a columned courtyard.

MIDTOWN NIGHTLIFE

World-class pianists play in **The Plaza Bar** (Copley Plaza Hotel, 138 St. James Avenue; 617-267-5300), which resembles a British officers' club in the era of the raj.

Diamond Jim's Piano Bar (710 Boylston Street, in the Lenox Hotel; 617-536-5300) is one of Boston's best piano bars, and a place where you're welcome to sing along.

South End

Boston's largest neighborhood is also the least known. Like the Back Bay, it was built on filled land, preceding Back Bay by more than a decade. Victorian brick row houses rose apace as residences for the middle class and well to do. Today, the South End is listed on the National Register of Historic Places as the largest concentration of such houses in the United States.

After the panic of 1873, banks foreclosed on the area, and those who could afford to moved to Back Bay. The area was carved up into rooming houses and factories and became an immigrant ghetto of more than 40 nationalities, notably black, Syrian, Hispanic and Lebanese.

The South End languished for decades, but when Boston's economy rebounded in the 1960s, so did this neighborhood. Since 1965, a new influx of middle-class professionals has renovated old row houses and partly gentrified the area. Not all of the South End has risen again, however, and there are still blighted, unsafe areas. But today the neighborhood is a vital center of artistic activity, and many artists live here. Fashionable shops, restaurants and nightclubs line the main thoroughfares of Columbus Avenue and Tremont Street.

The South End stretches hundreds of blocks, bounded roughly by the Southeast Expressway, Herald Street, the tracks of the MBTA's Orange Line and Huntington Avenue. Although the South End is a massive area to explore on foot, annual house tours are given by the **South End Historical Society** (532 Massachusetts Avenue; 617-536-4445).

If the South End reminds you of Beacon Hill, it's no wonder. The same hidden gardens and black iron grillwork decorate many facades. The oval-shaped **Union Park** resembles Beacon Hill's Louisburg Square. **West Rutland Square**, too, is a lovely little landscaped patch.

The **Boston Center for the Arts** (539 Tremont Street; 617-426-5000) is the center of South End arts activity. Built in 1884 to exhibit a huge circular painting, *The Battle of Gettysburg*, now in Pennsylvania, it's also where Albert Champion developed the spark plug. Its large rotunda hosts art exhibits, plays, festivals and an annual antique show.

Next door to the arts center is the **Mills Gallery** (549 Tremont Street; 617-426-7700), which specializes in exhibits by South End artists. These might include crafts, sculpture, oil paintings and gouache, and are always intriguing.

Once second in size only to the U.S. Capitol, the building that formerly housed the **Chickering Piano Factory** (★) (791 Tremont Street), now a craft guild, has been a Boston landmark since 1853. The pianos made here until 1929 were played not only in Victorian drawing rooms but in the concert halls of Europe and South America. Founder Jonas Chickering was said to be just like his pianos: "upright, grand and square." The building now serves as living, work and exhibition space for artists and musicians.

At the very northeast corner of the South End lies **Bay Village**, which used to be known as South Cove, bordered by Arlington, Tremont and Stuart streets and Charles Street South. This cluster of narrow little streets displays the most charmingly antique character in the area. Gaslights stand on the sidewalks outside these Victorian row houses decorated with black shutters and windowboxes, black iron grilled doorways and hidden, sunken gardens in backyards.

SOUTH END HOTELS

Although it has only three guest rooms, the **Terrace Townehouse** (★) (60 Chandler Street; 617-350-6520) is a hidden jewel. This 1870 townhouse has been richly redecorated, from its glowing salmon-painted hallway hung with 17th- and 18th-century French and English engravings, to individually themed rooms. The French Dining Room (formerly the house dining room, now a guest bedroom) is done entirely in French antiques, including an armoire, crystal chandelier and canopied bed. Breakfast is served in bed on antique china, and tea and sherry in the library at 4. Deluxe to ultra-deluxe.

Although not everything matches, the tub may be chipped and hallways are narrow and dark, the **Chandler Inn** (26 Chandler Street; 617-482-3450) offers 56 rooms priced closer to moderate than deluxe. Rooms are clean and appointed decently enough, in blues and greens and new oak furniture, with all the basic amenities. The hotel has a restaurant and a bar, which is a gay hangout.

The **Berkeley Residence/YWCA** (40 Berkeley Street; 617-482-8850) offers the most basic budget accommodations for women in the city. No men are allowed outside the public areas. Rooms have twin beds with chenille spreads and battered blond furniture, and bathrooms are down the hall. There are laundry facilities and a cafeteria.

SOUTH END RESTAURANTS

Ever since yuppies began moving into the South End in the 1970s and 1980s, restaurants have been springing up left and right, from small inexpensive cafés to upscale eateries.

Don't look for any silverware at **Addis Red Sea Ethiopian Restaurant** (★) (544 Tremont Street; 617-426-8727), the nation's first Ethiopian restaurant. A very African decor features authentic basketweave straw tables in a bright geometric pattern, low, carved wooden chairs, and paintings of

African villagers. Platters of food cover the entire table surface. Ethiopian *injera* bread is served with chicken, lamb, beef and vegetarian dishes. Budget to moderate.

A high-tech purple, black and gray decor with a black lattice ceiling dominates the noisy **St. Cloud** (557 Tremont Street; 617-353-0202). Fortunately, a lighter hand is taken with the international menu, which ranges from pheasant and grilled swordfish to pumpkin ravioli and shellfish minestrone. Deluxe to ultra-deluxe, but sandwiches, crostini and antipasti are available for more moderate prices.

Hamersley's Bistro (578 Tremont Street; 617-267-6068) embodies Paris, with a chic red, black and white dining room, bistro tables and chairs, and posters of Toulouse-Lautrec prints and the Côte D'Azur. You'll be tempted by the dressed-up versions of country fare like short ribs with mushrooms, bacon and red onion sauce; duck with a corn-bread stuffing; and halibut braised in cider with apples, capers and sage. Dinner only; deluxe.

Skipjack's Seafood Emporium (199 Clarendon Street; 617-536-3500) boasts one of the biggest and most varied seafood menus in Boston— over two dozen kinds of fresh fish daily, ranging from tuna, trout and salmon to lesser-known moonfish, parrot fish and opakapaka. The decor is far from traditional: glass block and glitzy red and blue neon, and changing exhibits of local artists. Moderate to deluxe.

SOUTH END SHOPPING

Some of the city's most fanciful and free-spirited boutiques lie on Tremont Street and Columbus Avenue.

Take, for instance, **Divine Decadence** (★) (535 Columbus Avenue; 617-266-1477), which boasts funky, fun household items from the past like vintage jukeboxes and art deco torchières, as well as contemporary neon paintings and sculptures.

Open since the '50s, **Skippy White's Records** (★) (410 Massachusetts Avenue; 617-266-1002) offers an impressive collection of gospel records, as well as reggae and rap.

SOUTH END NIGHTLIFE

The glitz of L.A. has come to Boston with the **Hard Rock Café** (131 Clarendon Street; 617-424-7625), a temple to rock history filled with such memorabilia as Elvis' white boots and Jimi Hendrix's jacket, and gold and platinum records from many groups. Elvis, Chuck Berry and Jerry Lee Lewis stare down from stained glass.

Club Café (209 Columbus Avenue; 617-536-0972), an avant-garde club, sponsors nationally known jazz musicians in a sophisticated art deco setting, attracting a gay and straight crowd. Cover.

South Boston

Not to be confused with the South End, South Boston lies directly east of it. Despite its name, South Boston juts farther east into the Atlantic than any other point in the city, cut off from Boston by the Southeast Expressway and the Fort Point Channel. Everyone here calls it "Southie," especially the Irish who call it home.

The Irish poured into South Boston in the early 19th century, attracted by the work opportunities of the glass, iron and shipping industries. They stayed, and today this is the most predominantly Irish community in Boston, evidenced by the riotous St. Patrick's Day parade. The Irish are fiercely proud of their L Street Brownies, a local swim club that has won national publicity for swimming every day, even in January.

Ideally positioned for shipping, the peninsula is lined with commercial fishing and shipping piers. The **Fish Piers**, near the World Trade Center and Jimmy's Harborside on Northern Avenue, are a lively scene at dawn, when the fishing boats return to port to unload their catch. The fresh catch is sold at auction right off the boats.

Three bridges link South Boston with downtown: the Summer Street Bridge, the Northern Avenue Bridge and the Congress Street Bridge, with its Chinese-lantern-style, wrought-iron lamps.

When you cross the Congress Street Bridge, you may not quite believe your eyes, but the first thing you'll see is a giant milk bottle. The 30-foot **Hood Milk Bottle** was a vintage lunch stand from the 1930s and sells snacks again today.

The Hood Milk Bottle signals the beginning of Museum Wharf, a mini-park of several museums. The Children's Museum and the Computer Museum are both housed in the same brick building, a former wool warehouse whose large windows and wool bays lend themselves nicely to exhibit spaces.

You don't have to be a kid to enjoy the **Children's Museum** (300 Congress Street; 617-426-6500; admission), a gigantic toy box filled with four floors of hands-on fun. Make giant bubbles, play instruments in a rock band, learn anatomy from a top-hatted skeleton. The exhibit on multiculturalism was the first of its kind.

As the world's only museum devoted solely to computers, the **Computer Museum** (300 Congress Street; 617-426-2800; admission) aptly dramatizes the swift pace of technology. Forty years of computing history are on display, starting with parts of an early Air Force vacuum-tube computer that occupied a four-story building. There are robots, animated films and a host of microcomputers to play with. To see how computers work, take a stroll through the giant Walk-Through Computer with its 25-foot keyboard and bumper-car-sized mouse.

The last member of Museum Wharf is the **Boston Tea Party Museum** (Congress Street Bridge; 617-338-1773; admission), a floating museum where you can board a two-masted brig and throw your own chest of tea into the harbor (it'll be retrieved by an attached rope for another visitor to heave). Displays here are lively and informative, explaining the events surrounding the 1773 dumping of 340 chests of tea overboard, a tax protest that was one of many spurs to the American Revolution.

A spanking white building with a flag-lined boulevard, the **World Trade Center** (Commonwealth Pier; 617-439-5000) replaced the drab old Commonwealth Exhibition Hall in the 1980s. It hosts many of Boston's biggest trade shows, including the New England Boat Show.

Four kinds of granite decorate the exterior of the **Boston Design Center** (1 Design Center Place; 617-338-5062), New England's major design center. Architects and designers come here from miles away to search out the latest and chic-est in interior designs. Outside the building stands an imposing cast of Auguste Rodin's sculpture *Cybèle*.

Commerce abandoned a good part of the Fort Point Channel area in droves by the 1950s. But today artists have happily moved into its old high-ceilinged, industrial buildings, and more artists live here than anywhere else in the city.

The work of painters, photographers, sculptors and others is on view at the **Fort Point Artists' Community Gallery** (249 A Street; 617-423-4299). Two other nearby galleries are **Alchemie** (286 Congress Street) and the **Laughlin/Winkler Gallery** (205 A Street, 7th floor; 617-269-1782). You can also visit individual artists' studios by appointment. Look for them along the 200 to 300 blocks on A Street.

Dorchester Heights National Historic Site (456 West 4th Street; 617-269-4212) is where George Washington set up his guns and forced the British to evacuate Boston in 1776, never to return. The British were astounded to see these guns, which had been dragged 300 miles by oxen from Fort Ticonderoga. A 215-foot marble tower marks the spot.

Out at the very tip of South Boston, **Castle Island** (William J. Day Boulevard) is a windswept place of green lawns and high granite ramparts, a fine spot for picnicking and exploring. A series of eight forts has stood here since 1634, making it the oldest continuously fortified site in North America. The island was held by the British during the Revolution until Washington forced them out, from his vantage point at Dorchester Heights. The current fort, the star-shaped **Fort Independence**, was built in 1851.

On a peninsula just south of South Boston lies Dorchester, once the home of the country's oldest chocolate manufacturer, the **Walter Baker**

Chocolate Factory, founded in 1780. Today Dorchester is a quiet, residential area known for its characteristic three-story houses called triple deckers.

Don't miss the **John F. Kennedy Library and Museum** (Columbia Point, Dorchester; 617-929-4523; admission), a stirring place to visit both inside and out. In a parklike setting by the ocean that JFK loved so well, the striking, glass-walled building was designed by I. M. Pei. The museum houses JFK's papers, photographs, letters and speeches, and personal memorabilia such as his desk and rocking chair.

The **Franklin Park Zoo** (Franklin Park, Blue Hill Avenue, Dorchester; 617-442-0991; admission), once rated one of the country's ten worst zoos by *Parade* magazine, has made some dramatic improvements. The most impressive is an African Tropical Forest that opened in 1989. Inside the 75-foot-high bubble live tropical birds, antelopes, a pygmy hippo and gorillas, among other tropical denizens.

SOUTH BOSTON RESTAURANTS

As you walk east on Northern Avenue, it becomes the Fish Pier, a crowded place of fish processing plants and wharves. Not surprisingly, the Fish Pier is home to a spate of seafood restaurants, some of them among the city's finest.

Here on the pier, two of Boston's most famous restaurants, **Jimmy's Harborside** (242 Northern Avenue; 617-423-1000) and **Anthony's Pier 4** (140 Northern Avenue; 617-482-6262), have waged a decades-long battle for supremacy in harborside seafood dining. Both offer a long list of fresh fishes, from Boston scrod to steamed, boiled or baked lobster, as well as floor-to-ceiling windows with smashing views of Boston Harbor.

Albanian immigrant Anthony Athanas started life in Boston as a shoeshine boy and built the reputation of his Pier 4 with backbreaking work. The smiling Anthony has posed with Liz Taylor, Red Skelton, Gregory Peck and Richard Nixon, whose photos gaze down from the walls. Despite its fame, Anthony's has its detractors, who say the seafood doesn't live up to its reputation, the massive dining halls process guests like a factory and the wait for a table is too long. Anthony's is filled with marine kitsch, from brass binnacles to a wooden footbridge leading over twin lobster pools. Waiters wear colonial garb, adding to the dated atmosphere. Still, Anthony's has the largest wine list in Boston, and there is outdoor seaside dining on yellow-awninged terraces. deluxe to ultra-deluxe.

We much prefer Jimmy's, founded in 1924 by Greek immigrant Jimmy Doulos, the "Chowder King," whose first customers were fishermen at a nine-stool cafeteria. Since then, JFK, Bobby Kennedy, Tip O'Neill and Bob Hope have dined here, leaving their autographed photos on the wall. There

(Text continued on page 86.)

Boston Beaches and Parks

Boston is certainly not all highrises and history. Even amid the twisting, brick-lined center of the city, a visitor can find respite on the green of Boston Common and the Public Garden (see the "Downtown" and "Back Bay" sections). But Boston also has other, lesser-known parks and beaches.

Boston Harbor Islands (★)—Some 30 islands lie in Boston Harbor, scattered along the coast from Boston south to Hull, with eight comprising a state park. The Puritans used these islands for pastureland and firewood, and there are tales of buried pirate treasure and ghosts haunting old Civil War forts. Each island has a unique flavor. **Peddocks Island**, a 113-acre preserve of woodlands, salt marsh, rocky beaches and open fields, has a turn-of-the-century fort, a wildlife sanctuary and an old cottage community. Peaceful and primitive **Lovells Island** is characterized by long beaches and diverse wildlife, rocky tidepools and sand dunes. The smaller **Georges Island**, the most developed in the park, is dominated by Fort Warren, a National Historic Landmark built between 1833 and 1869.

Facilities: Picnic areas, restrooms, park rangers, nature trails, fort tours, historical programs, boat docks, concession stand on Georges Island. Information: Peddocks and Lovells Islands, 617-727-5290; others, 617-740-1605. *Camping:* Permitted on Peddocks, Lovells, Grape, Calf, Great Brewster and Bumpkin Islands (permit required). *Swimming:* Permitted on Lovells Island only. *Fishing:* Good on all the islands except Peddocks; lots of flounder, cod, haddock, and striped bass.

Getting there: Georges Island serves as the entrance to the park and provides free interisland water taxis from Memorial Day to Labor Day; for information, call 617-740-1605. The islands are also accessible by ferry and cruise lines, including Boston Harbor Cruises (1 Long Wharf; 617-227-4321), Bay State Cruise Company (67 Long Wharf; 617-723-7800) and Massachusetts Bay Lines (60 Rowes Wharf; 617-542-8000). The **Friends of the Boston Harbor Islands** sponsors boat trips and tours; call 617-523-8386.

Belle Isle Marsh (★)—This preserve holds 152 acres of the largest remaining salt marsh in Boston, typical of the wetlands that once lined the shores of the Massachusetts Bay Colony. It's a special place, where you can see lots of wildlife and salt marsh plants rare in an urban area.

Facilities: Nature trails, observation tower, guided tours; information, 617-727-5350.

Getting there: Located at 146 Bennington Street, East Boston.

Nantasket Beach—Once a classy mid-19th-century resort with grand hotels rivaling those in Newport, this area later declined into a tacky strip of bars
and Skeeball arcades. Still, this three-and-a-half-mile barrier beach is one of the
nicest in the area, with clean white sand and a wide open vista of the Atlantic
Ocean.

Facilities: Picnic areas, restrooms, bathhouses, lifeguards, shade pavil-
ions, boardwalk, restaurants and snack stands; information: 617-727-5215. *Swimming:* Always good.

Getting there: Located on Nantasket Avenue, at the terminus of Route
228 in Hull.

Wollaston Beach—Come high tide, the beach virtually disappears, so narrow is this two-mile stretch of sand. The beach is backed by a wide seawall and
parking strip. Here people sunbathe in lawn chairs or draped across the hoods
of their cars, and walk their dogs, giving this beach a distinctly urban feel. The
sand is gravelly, but the beach does have a splendid view of the Boston skyline.

Facilities: Picnic areas, restrooms, bathhouses, playground; snack bars
and restaurants across the street with great fried clams; information, 617-727-5293.

Getting there: Located on Quincy Shore Drive, south on Route 3A from
Neponset Circle, Quincy.

Blue Hills Reservation—This 6500-acre park is the largest open space
within 35 miles of Boston and site of Great Blue Hill, the highest point on the
coast of eastern Massachusetts. The reservation comprises dozens of hills, forested land and several lakes and wetlands, as well as 500 miles of hiking, ski
touring and bridle trails. A natural history museum has live animals and exhibits,
and there are 16 historic sites, including a 1795 farmhouse.

Facilities: Picnic areas, restrooms, lifeguards, snack bar, tennis courts,
golf course, small downhill ski run with ski rentals, ballfields, bike trails, nature
programs; information, 617-698-1802. *Camping:* The Appalachian Mountain
Club operates 20 huts in the reservation on Ponkapoag Pond (617-963-9856). Reserve well ahead. *Swimming:* Houghton's Pond, with its calm waters and sandy
bottom, offers good swimming for children. *Fishing:* Ponds are stocked with
trout, bass, bullhead, perch and sunfish.

Getting there: Reservation headquarters are located at 695 Hillside Street,
Milton, where maps are available.

could not be anything but seafood here, and plenty of it, served in a nautical decor where the bar is a boat and waiters wear gold-braided blue jackets. Moderate to deluxe.

The Daily Catch (261 Northern Avenue; 617-338-3093) helped pioneer the open kitchen. Its Sicilian menu offers more than a dozen fresh New England fishes and shellfish, as well as black pastas made with squid ink. Bare wood tables and paper placemats suit the Fish Pier's working-class ambience. The restaurant also has a location in the North End. Moderate to deluxe.

Largely undiscovered, the **International Food Pavilion** (★) upstairs at the World Trade Center (midway out Commonwealth Pier; 617-439-5000) is one of the cheapest places to eat with a view in Boston. It serves cafeteria-style Chinese, Italian and American food at white tables overlooking the harbor. Breakfast and lunch; budget.

The **No-Name Restaurant** (15½ Fish Pier; 617-338-7539) not only has no name, it has no decor either. Famed for the freshness of its fish bought right off the boats, the No-Name always has long lines. Budget to moderate.

SOUTH BOSTON NIGHTLIFE

A cavernous dance club, the **Channel** (25 Necco Street; 617-451-1050) books well-known local and national acts with wild diversity. Cover.

Sailing from Commonwealth Pier next to the World Trade Center, **Water Music** (12 Arrow Street, Cambridge; 617-876-8742) sponsors cabaret cruises of Boston Harbor in the summer—popularly known as "booze cruises"—featuring top jazz and blues.

The Sporting Life

SAILING

Sailing the blue waters of the Charles on a breezy day with views of both the Boston and Cambridge skylines is a moment to be savored. **Community Boating** (21 Embankment Road; 617-523-1038) rents boats to visitors who pass a test and buy a seven-day membership. You can also rent boats, with a captain, at the **Boston Sailing Center** (54 Lewis Wharf; 617-227-4198) and the **Boston Harbor Sailing Club** (72 East India Row; 617-523-2619).

WHALE WATCHING

Boston is within easy reach of Stellwagen Bank, a major feeding ground for whales. You can go whale watching with the **New England Aquarium** (Central Wharf; 617-973-5277), **Bay State Provincetown Cruises** (67 Long Wharf; 617-723-7800) and **A. C. Cruise Line** (28 Northern Avenue; 617-426-8419).

JOGGING

Jogging is very big in Boston, where half the population seems to be in training for the Boston Marathon. The most popular running paths are along both sides of the green strips paralleling the Charles River, which run more than 17 miles. For information call the **New England Athletics Congress** (617-566-7600). Another safe place to jog is the three-mile trail in the **Breakheart Reservation** (177 Forest Street, Saugus; 617-233-0834).

GOLF

You can tee up at numerous public golf courses, including the **George Wright Golf Course** (420 West Street, Hyde Park; 617-361-8313), the **Presidents Golf Course** (357 West Squantum Street, Quincy; 617-328-3444), **Braintree Municipal Golf Course** (101 Jefferson Street, Braintree; 617-843-9781), **Newton Commonwealth Golf Course** (212 Kenrick Street, Newton; 617-244-4763), **Stow Acres** (58 Randall Road, Stow; 508-568-1100) and the **Colonial Country Club** (Audubon Road, Lynnfield; 617-245-9300).

TENNIS

The **Metropolitan District Commission** (MDC) (20 Somerset Street; 617-727-9547) maintains 45 courts throughout the city and Greater Boston, first-come, first-served. Cambridge, too, has public courts (for information, call 617-349-6233). There are numerous private clubs; one open to the public is the **Sportsmen's Tennis Club** (Franklin Field Tennis Center, 950 Blue Hill Avenue, Dorchester; 617-288-9092).

ICE-SKATING

Skaters have been rounding the curves of the lagoon in the Public Garden and the Boston Common Frog Pond for more than a hundred years. The Charles River is almost never frozen enough for skating, but the **MDC** (20 Somerset Street; 617-727-9547) maintains 22 public indoor rinks, some with rentals available. The **Boston Parks and Recreation Department** also has rinks (for information, call 617-725-4505). The **Skating Club of Boston**

(1240 Soldier's Field Road, Brighton; 617-782-5900) offers public skating and has rentals available.

CROSS-COUNTRY SKIING

The **Weston Ski Track** (Park Road, Weston; 617-891-6575) has gently sloping trails that run over a golf course; lessons and rentals are available. The **Lincoln Guide Service** (Conservation Trail, Lincoln; 617-259-9204) also offers lessons and rentals. The **Middlesex Fells Reservation** (1 Woodland Road, Stoneham; 617-662-5214) has a free six-mile trail with trail maps, suiting a variety of skill levels. **Wompatuck State Park** (Union Street, Hingham; 617-749-7160) has relatively easy trails, with free trail maps at park headquarters.

BICYCLING

Biking is popular around Boston's scenic waterways, including the Charles River, although we wouldn't recommend it in the narrow, congested downtown streets. The Charles River Esplanade on the Boston side of the Charles River has a well-marked 18-mile route named the **Dr. Paul Dudley White Bike Path**, which goes from Science Park, through Boston, Cambridge and Newton, ending in Watertown. The scenic **Greenbelt Bikeway** covers seven miles from the Boston Common to Franklin Park, via the Fens and the Arnold Arboretum. The **Stony Brook Reservation Bike Path** runs four miles through forests and fields in Dedham (Turtle Pond Parkway, West Roxbury, Hyde Park; 617-698-1802). The **Mystic River Reservation** also has a nice short bike path, 3.5 miles long, that runs from the Wellington Bridge in Somerville along the Mystic River to beyond the Wellington Bridge in Everett.

If you're up for a really challenging route, try the 135-mile **Claire Saltonstall Bikeway**, the first segment of which runs from Boston to Bourne at the entrance to Cape Cod. Continuing segments follow the Cape Cod Rail Trail all the way to Provincetown at the tip of the Cape.

For information on area biking, contact the **Boston Area Bicycle Coalition** (P.O. Box 1015, Kendall Square Branch, Cambridge; 617-491-7433) or the **Charles River Wheelmen** (1 Belnap Road, Hyde Park; 617-325-2453).

BIKE RENTALS   To rent a bike in the Boston area, contact the **Community Bike Shop** (490 Tremont Street; 617-542-8623), **Ferris Wheels Bicycle Shop** (64 South Street; Jamaica Plain; 617-522-7082) or **Surf 'n Cycle** (1771 Massachusetts Avenue, Cambridge; 617-661-7659).

Transportation

BY CAR

If you arrive in Boston by car, you'll have to watch closely for road markings; routes change numbers and names frequently. Also, roads will be tied up well into the mid-1990s by a major project designed to construct a third harbor tunnel and to depress the Central Artery underground. No one in his right mind would want to bring a car to downtown Boston, where narrow, confusing streets are ruled by legendarily homicidal drivers. Save the car for touring the suburbs of Greater Boston or outlying areas.

From the north, **Route 95** follows a curving, southwesterly path to Boston, changing to **Route 128** as it forms a beltway around the city. **Route 93** runs directly north-south through Boston; its downtown portion is called the Central Artery, and it's known as the John Fitzgerald Expressway and the Southeast Expressway between Boston and Route 128 in Braintree. **Route 90**, the Massachusetts Turnpike, heads into and through Boston from the west. From the south, you can reach Boston by **Route 95, Route 24** or **Route 3**.

BY AIR

Logan International Airport (617-561-1800), the busy and crowded main airport serving Boston, is located two miles north of the city in East Boston. Numerous domestic and international carriers fly in and out of Logan, including Aer Lingus, Air Atlantic, Ltd., Air Canada, Air France, Alitalia Airlines, American Airlines, British Airways, Continental Airlines, Delta Air Lines, El Al Israel Airlines, Lufthansa German Airlines, Midway Airlines, Northwest Air Lines, Pan Am Air Lines, Sabena Belgian World Airlines, Swissair, TAP Air Portugal, Trans World Airlines, Trump Shuttle, United Airlines and USAir.

Limousines and buses take visitors to numerous downtown locations, including **Airways Transportation** (617-267-2981), **Hudson Airporter** (800-367-3885), **Carey Limousine** (617-623-8700), **Commonwealth Limousine Service** (617-787-5575), **Greyhound/Trailways** (617-423-5810) and **Peter Pan Bus Lines** (617-426-7838). You can also take the subway from the airport, by taking a free Massport bus to the Blue Line stop. The slickest way to get downtown is to hop the **Airport Water Shuttle** (617-330-8680), bypassing traffic altogether for a scenic ten-minute ride across Boston Harbor.

BY BUS

Greyhound/Trailways has bus service to Boston from all over the country. The main downtown terminal is at 10 St. James Avenue (617-423-

5810). Other bus lines servicing Boston include **Peter Pan Bus Lines**, from New York, New Hampshire and Cape Cod, and **Concord Trailways**, from points in New Hampshire only (both at 555 Atlantic Avenue; 617-426-7838).

BY TRAIN

Amtrak (Summer Street at Atlantic Avenue; 617-482-3660) will bring you to Boston on board its California Zephyr from Chicago, originating in San Francisco. The Lakeshore Limited travels from Chicago to Boston. Amtrak trains leaving New York City for Boston include the Night Owl, Metroliner, Minuteman, Yankee Clipper, Mount Vernon, Ben Franklin and Merchants Limited.

CAR RENTALS

Parking grows scarcer and ever more expensive, and you can easily see Boston on foot, but if you must rent a car, you can do so in the airport terminal at **Avis Rent A Car** (617-561-3500), **Budget Rent A Car** (617-569-4000) and **Hertz Rent A Car** (617-569-7272).

Companies offering free airport pickup are **Alamo Rent A Car** (617-561-4100), **American International Rent A Car** (617-569-3550), **Dollar Rent A Car** (617-569-5300), **Payless Car Rental** (617-569-9044) and **USA Rent A Car** (617-561-6500).

Among the used-car rentals in the Boston area are **Rent A Wreck** (617-720-1136) and **Advantage Rent A Car** (617-783-3825).

PUBLIC TRANSPORTATION

Boston's subway system is operated by the **Massachusetts Bay Transportation Authority**, MBTA (617-722-3200), popularly called the "T." In the 1980s, the MBTA spent $2.5 billion to improve and expand the system, and there are sparkling new stations on both the Red and Orange Lines. The T has four lines, the Red, Blue, Green and Orange, which will get you almost anywhere you want to go quite handily. The basic fare is 75 cents. Special seven-day discount passes can be bought at many T stations and the visitor booths throughout the city.

The MBTA also operates a fleet of buses providing extensive coverage of Boston and Cambridge. Exact change is required for the 50-cent fare.

A great boon to getting around Boston is the **Walking Distance Locator** (617-439-9299), a computerized service housed in granite, phone-booth-sized obelisks. A touch screen points to historic sights, restaurants, hotels, cultural attractions, stores and services in more than 100 categories and prints out a minimap with the address and phone number. Kiosks are at the corner of Washington and School streets, 60 State Street and several other locations.

TAXIS

Several cab companies serve Logan Airport, including **Checker Cab** (617-497-1500), **Red and White Cab** (617-742-9090), **Town Taxi** (617-536-5000) and **Cambridge Taxi Company** (617-876-5000).

WALKING TOURS

Uncommon Boston (437 Boylston Street; 617-731-5854) customizes coach and walking tours for any group. Among its specialties are tours for ice cream and chocolate lovers, a literary tour of Beacon Hill, a Halloween tour of graveyards and a Victorian Christmas tour.

CHAPTER THREE

Outside Boston:
Cambridge, Lexington and Concord

Heady doses of history and higher education greet visitors to the small cities outside Boston. It's hard to exaggerate the importance to America of events that took place in Lexington and Concord on April 19, 1775. Although nobody knows who really pulled the trigger, "the shot heard 'round the world" was fired here that day to start the American Revolution. The two towns, where echoes of revolutionary battles can still be found beside bucolic fields, on village greens and in museums, lie within a half-hour's drive of Boston. Even closer, right across the Charles River from the city, stands Cambridge.

Everyone thinks of Cambridge and Boston together, as if they were two sides of the same coin. While Cambridge is actually a separate city, the lives of the two are very much entwined, linked by a series of foot and vehicular bridges.

Cambridge was founded in 1630, originally named New Towne, and was the colony's first capital. In 1638, two years after the founding of Harvard, the nation's oldest university, the city was renamed after the English university town where many Boston settlers had been educated. Contrasting with Harvard's ivy-covered brick eminence is the city's other major center of learning, the Massachusetts Institute of Technology, which moved across the river from Boston in 1916.

Today Cambridge remains very much an intellectual center, home to Nobel Prize winners, ground-breaking scientists and famous writers, among them John Kenneth Galbraith, David Mamet and Anne Bernays. It's a book-lover's paradise, with 25 bookstores in the Harvard Square area alone (see

93

"Boston Bookstores" in Chapter Two). And Cambridge continues to be known as a site of progressive political activism.

During the 1960s and 1970s, Cambridge became the heart of what came to be nicknamed "Silicon Valley East" when high-tech companies blossomed here, as well as in outlying towns scattered along the Route 128 beltway. These think tanks and computer companies fueled a boom in the Massachusetts economy and its population.

Originally, Cambridge held within its borders several villages, including the spot that's now Lexington. Along with nearby Concord, Lexington retains much of the rural flavor it had during the time of the Revolution. Surrounding the towns, cornfields lie across 17th- and 18th-century farms that are still intact. Nearby Walden Pond, although crowded with locals and tourists alike on hot summer days, reflects the spirit of Thoreau during its more peaceful moments.

But it's revolutionary history that draws most people to Lexington and Concord. Today you can visit Lexington Green, where the Minutemen gathered before the battle (when the captain commanded, "If they mean to have war, let it begin here"), and follow the path along Battle Road taken by the citizen-soldiers during that momentous day. Old stone walls, where Minutemen crouched and shelled the British with musket fire, still stand throughout the countryside.

The short journey from Boston to these now peaceful suburbs still pulls people back through the centuries, to the time of America's birth as an independent nation. Visiting them is well worth a day's sidetrip.

Cambridge

A university town since shortly after its 1630 founding, site of the only college in the Americas until nearly the eighteenth century, Cambridge remains a revered seat of learning worldwide. Nearly half its 95,000 citizens are connected in some way to Harvard, MIT or the number of smaller colleges that dot the city.

But not all of Cambridge is serious or intellectual. It's given life and vitality by throngs of young students, protesters handing out leaflets, cult followers and street musicians.

The heartbeat of Cambridge is **Harvard Square**, where life revolves around the many bookstores, coffeeshops, boutiques and newsstands. In the very center stands the **Out of Town News and Ticket Agency** (617-354-7777) kiosk, a Harvard Square landmark for many years, famous for its thousands of national and foreign periodicals. Right next to it you'll find the **Cambridge Discovery Information Booth** (617-497-1630), which dispenses tourist information and walking maps.

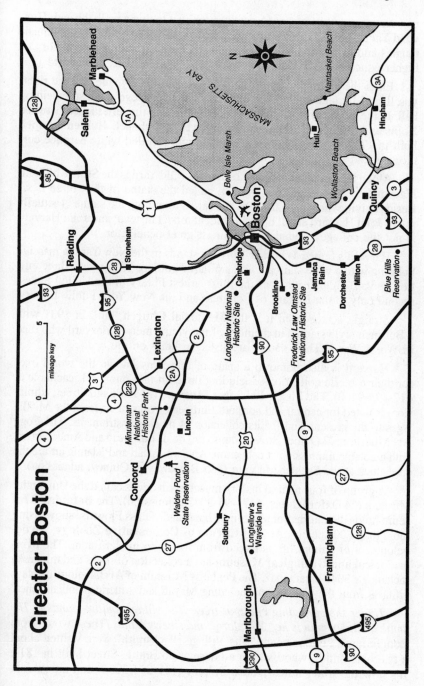

Greater Boston

No one would come to Cambridge without taking a walk through **Harvard Yard**. A stroll of the yard's winding paths, stately trees, grassy quadrangles and handsome brick buildings is a walk through a long history of higher education. Six U.S. presidents have graduated from Harvard.

Enter the main gate by crossing Massachusetts Avenue. On the right, you'll see **Massachusetts Hall**, built in 1718, the college's oldest remaining hall. In the quadrangle of the historic Old Yard, on the left, tucked between Hollis and Stoughton Halls, is a little jewel of a chapel. **Holden Chapel,** built in 1742, has blue gables decorated with scrolled white baroque cornices, ahead of its time in its ornateness.

Along the diagonal path that cuts across Old Yard is the **Statue of John Harvard** by Daniel Chester French, called the statue of the "three lies." Besides giving the wrong date for Harvard's founding, the statue is actually not of John Harvard at all, but of a student model instead; and John Harvard is not the college's founder but its first great benefactor.

Harvard's famed **Widener Library** stands in the New Yard, a massive building with a wide staircase and a pillared portico. With nearly three million books, Widener ranks as the third largest library in the United States, second only to the Library of Congress and the New York Public Library.

Straight across from it is the **Memorial Church**, built in 1931 with a Bulfinch-style steeple in memory of the young men of Harvard who died in World War I. Their names are listed in brass on the walls.

Harvard is also home to a spate of museums known the world over for their esoteric collections, including three art museums (all reachable at 617-495-9400). The **Busch-Reisinger Museum** (24 Kirkland Street; admission) is noted for central and northern European works of art from the Middle Ages to the present, and for its collection of musical instruments. The **Fogg Art Museum** (32 Quincy Street; admission) holds European and American art, with a notable impressionist collection. Ancient, Asian and Islamic art are the specialties at the Sackler Museum (485 Broadway at Quincy; admission).

A group of four natural history museums in one is called the University Museum (24 Oxford Street; 617-495-3045; admission). The **Botanical Museum** holds the internationally famed handmade Glass Flowers, showcasing more than 700 species. At the **Museum of Comparative Zoology**, the development of animal life is traced from fossils to modern man. The **Mineralogical and Geological Museum** has a collection of rocks and minerals, including a 3040-carat topaz. The **Peabody Museum of Archaeology** displays artifacts from the world over, including Mayan and American Indian relics.

Under the spreading chestnut tree/ The village smithy stands;/ The smith a mighty man is he/ With large and sinewy hands. These words from Longfellow's famous poem "The Village Blacksmith" were written about a real blacksmith, who lived in a house at 56 Brattle Street built in 1811. It's now the **Blacksmith House Bakery** (617-354-3036) and an outdoor café in warm weather. Old World pastries and cakes are made here the same way they have been for decades.

Harvard Lampoon Castle (57 Mt. Auburn Street at Bow Street), a funny-looking building with a round brick turret and a door painted bright red, yellow and purple, befits its occupants: the publishers of Harvard's longstanding satirical magazine, the *Harvard Lampoon.*

Christ Church Episcopal (Zero Garden Street; 617-876-0200), a simple gray-and-white structure with a squat steeple, is Cambridge's oldest church. George and Martha Washington worshipped here on New Year's Eve 1775.

Under an elm tree on the grassy **Cambridge Common** (Massachusetts Avenue and Garden Street), General Washington took command of the Continental Army in 1775. A plaque and monument to Washington mark this spot. Nearby it are three old black cannons, abandoned by the British at Fort Independence when they evacuated in 1776.

The **Longfellow National Historic Site** (105 Brattle Street; 617-876-4491; admission) is where poet Henry Wadsworth Longfellow lived for 45 years and wrote most of his famous works. Painted a cheery yellow and accented with black shutters, the house was built in 1759 for a well-to-do Tory and years later was used by Washington as his headquarters during the siege of Boston. The house has many fine Victorian furnishings, among them Longfellow's desk, quill pen and inkstand.

A handsome, slate-blue Georgian house with black shutters, the **Hooper-Lee-Nichols House** (159 Brattle Street; 617-547-4252; admission) was built by a physician named Richard Hooper. Later it was the home of Joseph Lee, a founder of Christ Church, and then the home of George Nichols.

The western end of Brattle Street is called **Tory Row** because of the lovely homes built there by wealthy Tories in the 18th century. A fine example is at Number 175, the **Ruggles Fayerweather House**, first the home of Tory George Ruggles, later of patriot Thomas Fayerweather. The house served as an American hospital after the Battle of Bunker Hill.

Just down the street sits **Radcliffe College**, once a women's branch of Harvard but now fully integrated into the university. The gates to **Radcliffe Yard** are entered off Brattle Street, between James Street and Appian Way. As you walk the path, the four graceful brick main buildings of the campus will be in a semicircle to your right. First is **Fay House**, a mansion built in 1807, the administrative center. Next you'll find **Hemenway Gymnasium**, which houses a research society that studies women in society. Third is **Agassiz House**, fronted by white classical pillars, which holds a theater, ballroom and arts office. Last is the college's renowned **Schlesinger Library**, which contains an outstanding collection of books and manuscripts on the history of women in America, including papers of Susan B. Anthony, Julia Ward Howe and Elizabeth Cady Stanton.

Who says taking the subway has to be grim? The newest Red Line stations, opened in the 1980s, showcase major works of art in the country's first and largest program of its kind, **Arts on the Line**. Artworks range from stained-glass walls and bronze sculptures to a bright red windmill sculpture, a shimmering mobile and a whimsical mural of black-and-white cows. A favored piece is *Lost Gloves*, immortalized in bronze along an escalator railing. People inevitably reach out to touch these gloves as they ride. Look for some 20 artworks at Harvard, Porter, Davis and Alewife stations.

A few miles east of Harvard Square lies Cambridge's other famous university, the **Massachusetts Institute of Technology** (M.I.T.). Offering a premier education in engineering and technology since 1865, M.I.T. draws students from all over the world, including China, Japan and Vietnam. In distinct contrast to the hallowed ways of Harvard, M.I.T. students are famed for their witty irreverence and stage contests to outdo each other in intellectual pranks. One of their episodes involved placing a car on top of a campus building. Fittingly, the campus looks modern and high tech, with geometrical buildings designed by Eero Saarinen.

CAMBRIDGE HOTELS

Set in an office tower and shopping complex, the 296-room **Charles Hotel** (1 Bennett Street at Eliot Street; 617-864-1200) is just steps away from Harvard Square. Rooms are styled in grays and blues, with a Windsor bed, upholstered loveseat and armchair, and new oak armoire. The gray-tiled bath has a second phone and television and pink-and-gray marble counters. There are two restaurants and one of the city's best jazz bars, as well as a health spa with steam room, sauna and whirlpool. Ultra-deluxe.

The stepped, pyramidal walls of the **Hyatt Regency Cambridge** (575 Memorial Drive; 617-492-1234) sit right on the banks of the Charles River, offering splendid views of the Boston skyline from many rooms. A 14-story atrium lobby has a semitropical feeling, from the Australian finches in a glass cage to a large fountain and towering potted plants and trees. Lighted glass elevators whoosh you up through the atrium, past a trompe l'oeil mural of an Italian villa and a 100-foot-high glass wall. The 469-room hotel has three restaurants, a lap pool and a health club with sauna, whirlpool and steam bath. The fair-sized rooms have rose-colored contemporary furnishings and carpeting, plus marble vanities in the bathroom. Ultra-deluxe.

A relatively inexpensive but still convenient place to stay in Cambridge is the **Harvard Manor House** (110 Mount Auburn Street; 617-864-5200). Although some rooms are on the smallish side, this 72-room private hotel offers nicely appointed digs with contemporary furniture and floral spreads. Deluxe.

Some of the cheapest accommodations are to be had at the **Irving House** (24 Irving Street; 617-354-8249) near Harvard Square. This wood-frame walkup offers 44 plain but clean rooms at budget prices (moderate

Hiking Boston's Backroads

Scant miles outside the urban clatter of downtown Boston, Massachusetts turns to rolling green hills, river valleys and pine and hardwood forests. A surprising number of parks and wildlife sanctuaries are to be found in these rural country towns, where you can hike scenic trails, short or long.

The **Quincy Quarries Footpath** (2.5 miles) leads past steep quarry walls, the first commercial railway in America and an 1898 turning mill, used to cut and polish the Quincy granite columns and slabs that went into many famous buildings in America.

The main path at **World's End** (★) (4 miles) winds uphill and down over a little peninsula extending north from Hingham into Massachusetts Bay. Its beautifully landscaped, gently curving roads were laid out by famed landscape architect Frederick Law Olmsted for a housing development that was never built. The wide, grassy path meanders through meadows and marshland, past rocky, glacial drumlins, through avenues of English oaks, pine and red cedars, and up a steep knoll, where your reward is a knockout view of the Boston skyline, one of the best on the South Shore.

The **Ponkapoag Trail** (3.5 miles) in the Blue Hills Reservation circles Ponkapoag Pond, passing through wetlands and a golf course. From it, the Ponkapoag Log Boardwalk crosses a floating bog, filled with highbush blueberries, blue flag iris and Atlantic white cedar.

Little-known and little-used, Stony Brook Reservation allows you to walk in solitude among peaceful woods along the **Bearberry Hill Road** trail (3 miles). For part of the way, the trail joins an asphalt bicycle path. It takes you past Turtle Pond, a swampy thicket and a golf course.

The **Skyline Trail** (7.4 miles) in the Middlesex Fells Reservation is a rugged trail that climbs many rocky knobs running between two observation towers. Scenery varies considerably along the way, from a pond with water lilies and frogs, to volcanic-rock-covered hills, wild hardwood forests, an old soapbox derby track, carpets of Canada mayflower and swampy areas.

Although you will do so with crowds of others, you can walk the shores Thoreau walked at **Walden Pond** in Concord. A 1.7-mile circuit trail winds through woods along the crystal clear waters of the pond. At the cabin site where Thoreau lived for two years, travelers from all corners of the globe have piled up stones in memoriam.

with private bath). Your best bets are the top-floor units featuring skylights, private baths and wall-to-wall carpets.

Although it's quite a way from Harvard Square, **A Cambridge House** (★) (2218 Massachusetts Avenue; 617-491-6300) is a special place to stay. A private home built in 1892 with a wide pillared porch, it's listed on the National Historic Register. Beautifully restored and richly furnished with floral print fabrics, patterned wallpapers, period antiques and Oriental rugs, the living room, den and dining room offer guests luxurious spaces. Each of the 26 guest rooms is individually decorated with antiques. The room we saw had a canopied bed with a white lace duvet and a working fireplace. A full breakfast is complimentary; moderate to ultra-deluxe.

CAMBRIDGE RESTAURANTS

East Cambridge is a treasure chest of colorful and ethnic restaurants, particularly along Cambridge Street.

A retrofit, '50s-style decor of diner stools, neon and a black-and-white-tiled floor enlivens the **East Coast Grill** (1271 Cambridge Street; 617-491-6568). The moderately priced southern grilled ribs, pork and chicken are served with coleslaw, baked beans, corn bread and watermelon, and hot drinks to match: blue, green and gold margaritas. Appetizers are equally muscular, notably the "sausage from hell." Leave room for pudding cake. Dinner only. Next door, East Coast Grill operates a take-out stand, **Jake & Earl's Dixie Barbecue** (1273 Cambridge Street; 617-491-7427), serving the same menu at budget prices. *People* magazine hailed it as one of America's ten best barbecue joints, and who are we to argue? Presided over by a plastic bust of Elvis, Jake and Earl's hews to such "barbecue rules to live by" as, "If it ain't got smoke, it's a joke!"

What's a Cajun restaurant doing in Yankee land? It's doing the bayou cuisine proud, at the **Cajun Yankee** (1193 Cambridge Street; 617-576-1971), starting with appetizers of seafood gumbo, Cajun popcorn and shrimp rémoulade. The moderate-to-deluxe menu features blackened tuna, pan-fried catfish and sausage jambalaya and desserts of sweet potato pecan pie and praline parfait, all served up in a rustic decor with Spanish overtones. Dinner only.

It would be hard to find a friendlier place than the **Casa Portugal** (1200 Cambridge Street; 617-491-8880), one of only a handful of Boston Portuguese restaurants. Imbibe the Latin mood set by black iron lanterns, red-vested waiters and folk art murals of bullfights and musicians. *Chourico* arrives in a small, flaming grill, followed by spicy dinners of marinated pork cubes with potatoes or mussels, linguica and onions, and squid stew, all served with thickly cut Portuguese french fries. There's a good selection of Portuguese wines and beers, and espresso and cappuccino to top it all off. Moderate.

The family-owned **La Groceria** (853 Main Street; 617-876-4162) looks like an Italian trattoria, with its striped awning, lattice ceiling and exposed brick wall. Famed for its hot antipasti and homemade pasta, La Groceria does old-style Northern Italian dishes such as lasagna, pizzas, eggplant parmigiana and a seafood marinara that must be eaten to be believed. Its splendid dessert case offers cannoli, *tartufo* and *zuppa inglese*. Ask for the Godfather Family room, a beaded alcove, if it's available. Moderate to deluxe.

Brick, wood-fired ovens line the wall at **Bertucci's Brick Oven Pizzeria** (799 Main Street; 617-661-8356), where you can watch your pizza lifted out with wooden paddles. Outstanding deep-crust pizzas come with 20 toppings, including artichoke hearts, prosciutto and cream sauce, and there are also hearty soups, calzones and pastas. Budget to moderate.

African folk art hangs on the walls of the red, black and white dining room of **Asmara** (714 Massachusetts Avenue; 617-864-7447), yet another Ethiopian eatery in Greater Boston. Chicken, lamb, beef and vegetarian entrées are to be eaten without silverware, in the Ethiopian manner. Budget.

The owners of **The Harvest** (44 Brattle Street; 617-492-1115) researched European cafés to come up with their decor mixing brightly patterned upholstered banquettes with wooden shutters and tables and a Parisian bar. The clientele is ultra-Cambridge—you'll sit next to architects and psychiatrists. The menu changes every day and features American game and seafood entrées. Deluxe to ultra-deluxe.

Upstairs at the Pudding (10 Holyoke Street; 617-864-1933) is located at the home of a Harvard institution, the Hasty Pudding Dramatic Society. The stairway and dining room walls are plastered with old theatrical posters from Pudding productions dating to the 1800s. Despite its emerald green walls and pink tablecloths, the dining room has the casual feel of a college dining hall. While the fixed-price menu is tabbed ultra-deluxe, it offers one of the top dining experiences in Greater Boston, mixing Northern Italian cuisine with exotic ingredients from seven continents.

The **Coffee Connection** (The Garage, 36 John F. Kennedy Street; 617-492-4881) serves the best coffee in Greater Boston, and the most varieties of it. There are also teas, cocoas and European pastries. Small and intimate, the Coffee Connection is permeated with the thick aroma of fresh-roasted beans. A breakfast and lunch menu includes muffins, quiches, salads and sandwiches. There's almost always a wait at this popular, budget restaurant.

The **Algiers Coffeehouse** (40 Brattle Street; 617-492-1557) is one of Cambridge's most Bohemian eateries. Entered through a little alleyway next to the Cambridge Center for Adult Education, it's down a flight of steps into a dark little basement dotted with battered café tables and chairs. The budget-priced menu has a Middle Eastern flavor, with lentil, falafel and *baba ganoosh*. There are 16 kinds of coffees and hot drinks, teas, iced drinks and Arabic pastries.

Troyka (★) (1154 Massachusetts Avenue; 617-864-7476) is a real Russian restaurant. Even if its interior has the unfortunate look of a gulag dining hall, its hearty peasant fare includes borscht, piroshki, meat-potato pie and Russian dumplings. Russian cakes and meringues appear on the dessert list. Budget.

Shades of the Southwest pervade the **Cottonwood Café** (1815 Massachusetts Avenue; 617-661-7440), decorated in green-and-purple neon and spiky cactus plants. A southwestern-style menu includes desert pizza, made with chicken, cheese, olives and jalapeños served on a deep-fried tortilla; enchiladas; chicken or steak diablo; Rocky Mountain lamb; and Hill Country mixed grill. Moderate to deluxe.

CAMBRIDGE SHOPPING

The **Out of Town Newspapers** (0 Harvard Square; 617-354-7777) kiosk has been declared a National Historic Landmark. Set right in the middle of Harvard Square and surrounded by traffic, the kiosk carries more than 3000 newspapers and magazines from all over the world.

Harvard Square offers a wealth of shopping, from eclectic boutiques to upscale chain stores. Most notable in this intellectual bastion are the many bookshops surrounding the square. (See "Boston Bookstores" in Chapter Two.)

Yet another Harvard institution is the **Harvard Coop** (1400 Massachusetts Avenue; 617-492-1000), formed in 1882 by several Harvard students as a cost-saving measure. The Coop holds three floors of men's and women's clothing, housewares, gifts, computers and calculators, games and toys, and an astonishing selection of records, art prints, posters and books.

Colonial Drug (49 Brattle Street; 617-864-2222) is like a European perfume shop, with more than 500 kinds of fragrances.

The creativity of Cambridge-area artists is for sale at the **Cambridge Artists Cooperative** (★) (59-A Church Street; 617-868-4434), a treasure trove of whimsical and beautiful things: handmade paper face masks, fiber animals, Raku bowls, handmade quilts and hand-painted silk scarves.

Little Russia (★) (99 Mt. Auburn Street; 617-661-4928) sells authentic Russian lacquered boxes and nesting dolls, jewelry, illustrated Russian fairy tales and pins of Lenin, Stalin and Trotsky.

CAMBRIDGE NIGHTLIFE

The **Plough and Stars** (912 Massachusetts Avenue; 617-492-9653) is that rare thing, an uncorrupted working-class bar where habitués are logo-capped, burly types who belly up for live, boisterous entertainment. Black-and-white caricatures of neighborhood regulars line a whole wall.

Native son Pat Metheny occasionally stops in to jam at **Ryle's** (212 Hampshire Street; 617-876-9330), which features nightly jazz, rhythm-and-blues, Latin music and swing in a casual atmosphere. Cover.

One of the best jazz showcases in Greater Boston, the **Regattabar** (1 Bennett Street, in the Charles Hotel; 617-661-5000) offers an intimate jazz experience in a sophisticated club environment. The Regattabar regularly features such headliners as Miles Davis, Wynton Marsalis, Ahmad Jamal and Stephane Grapelli. Cover.

Nightstage (823 Main Street; 617-497-8200), one of the Boston area's best nightclubs, showcases headliners like Wynton Marsalis, Jesse Colin Young, Semenya McCord and Simply Red. Concerts range from jazz, blues

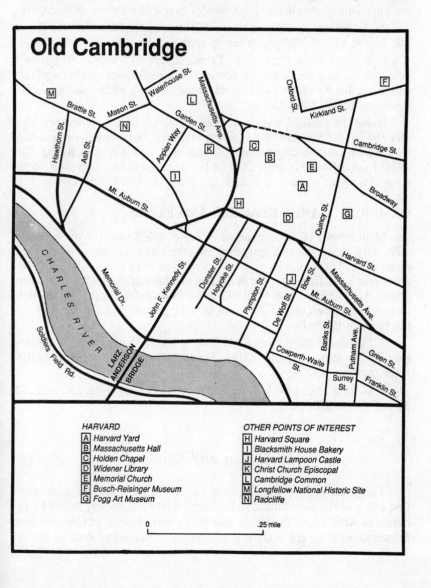

Old Cambridge

HARVARD

- A Harvard Yard
- B Massachusetts Hall
- C Holden Chapel
- D Widener Library
- E Memorial Church
- F Busch-Reisinger Museum
- G Fogg Art Museum

OTHER POINTS OF INTEREST

- H Harvard Square
- I Blacksmith House Bakery
- J Harvard Lampoon Castle
- K Christ Church Episcopal
- L Cambridge Common
- M Longfellow National Historic Site
- N Radcliffe

0   .25 mile

and rock, to funk, country-and-western and Brazilian dance bands, and the audience ranges from suits to shorts. Cover.

Cantares (15 Springfield Street; 617-547-6300) offers reggae, African, Latin and blues sounds in a Cambridge-casual setting. You never know what you'll hear on open mike nights at the **Cantab Lounge** (738 Massachusetts Avenue; 617-354-2685), but the rest of the time it's soulful rhythm-and-blues bands in a let-it-all-hang-out playpen. Cover at both places.

At the **Mystery Café** (1667 Massachusetts Avenue; 617-262-1826), the audience participates in solving a murder over a four-course dinner. Cover.

An art gallery cum bar with retro '50s atmosphere, **Man Ray** (21 Brookline Street; 617-864-0400) serves up rock and funk for dancing. Cover.

Ever since 1969, **Passim** (47 Palmer Street; 617-492-7679) has been going strong as a showcase for acoustic folk performers, including Tracy Chapman, Jimmy Buffett and David Bromberg, in a clean-cut, no-alcohol basement coffeehouse. Cover.

Harvard's professional theater company, **American Repertory Theatre** (64 Brattle Street; 617-547-8300) produces world premieres and classical works, often taking a nontraditional approach. **Catch a Rising Star** (30-B John F. Kennedy Street; 617-661-9887) showcases rising young comics seven nights a week in a dark and cozy basement club. Cover.

CAMBRIDGE AREA BEACHES AND PARKS

Middlesex Fells Reservation—"Fells" is a Scottish word meaning wild, hilly country, which aptly describes the 2000-plus-acre terrain of this reservation. These rugged highlands were first explored in 1632 by Governor Winthrop, first governor of the Massachusetts Bay Colony. They were acquired as public parkland in 1893, and a 19th-century trolley line brought in droves of picnickers. Fifty miles of hiking trails and old woods roads run through the Fells.

Facilities: Picnic areas, ski touring trails, skating rink, swimming pool; information, 617-662-5214. *Fishing:* Ponds hold sunfish, catfish, perch, pickerel and bass.

Getting there: Located five miles north of Cambridge, off exits 32, 33 and 34 from Route 93.

Lexington and Concord

The green and wooded towns of Lexington and Concord, sites of the first battle of the Revolutionary War, are forever historically linked by the events of April 19, 1775. The British planned to advance on Concord from Boston to seize the colonials' military supplies. Warned by Paul Revere the

Lexington and Concord

LEXINGTON

A	Lexington Green
B	Visitor's Center
C	Minuteman Statue
D	Buckman Tavern

LEXINGTON TO CONCORD

E	Hancock-Clarke House
F	Munroe Tavern
G	Museum of Our National Heritage
H	Walden Pond State Reservation

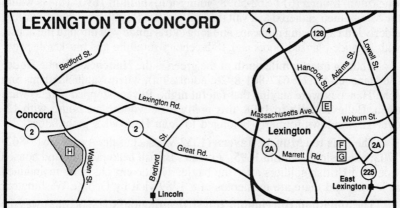

LEXINGTON TO CONCORD

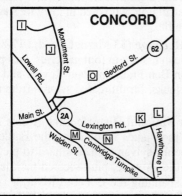

CONCORD

CONCORD

I	Minuteman National Historic Park
J	Old Manse
K	Orchard House
L	The Wayside
M	Emerson House
N	Concord Museum
O	Sleepy Hollow Cemetery

night before, farmer-soldier Minutemen had mustered early before dawn on the Lexington Green.

About 77 men at Lexington Green, and hundreds more at Concord, fought off 700 highly trained British regulars. With heavy casualties, the British retreated back to Boston, and the Revolution had begun.

When you arrive in Lexington, a few miles north of Lincoln off Route 128, stop first at the **Lexington Visitors' Center** (Lexington Green, 1875 Massachusetts Avenue; 617-862-1450) for maps and brochures, and to see a diorama of the battle.

Across from Lexington Green, in the center of town, stands the **Minuteman Statue** (Battle Green, intersection of Massachusetts Avenue, Harrington Road and Hancocks and Bedford streets), a simple bareheaded farmer holding a musket. The statue's rough, fieldstone base was made of stone taken from the walls the American militia stood behind as they shot at the British. This statue has become symbolic of Lexington history.

On the green next to the Visitors' Center is the yellow, woodframe **Buckman Tavern** (617-862-5598; admission), built in 1690. This is where the Minutemen gathered to await the British after Revere's warning. Smiling elderly ladies wearing mobcaps and long skirts guide you through the house, with its wide-planked floors and 18th-century furniture and musket displays.

About a quarter mile north of the green is the **Hancock-Clarke House** (36 Hancock Street; 617-861-8928; admission), where Samuel Adams and John Hancock were staying that fateful night. Revere stopped here to warn them. Believed built in 1698, this pretty little woodframe house with 12-over-12 windows formerly belonged to John Hancock's grandfather.

The little red **Munroe Tavern** (1332 Massachusetts Avenue; 617-862-1703; admission), built in 1695, served as British headquarters, and housed wounded British soldiers after the battle. The tavern has been maintained as it was, and there are mementos of a 1789 visit by George Washington.

The **Jonathan Harrington House** (Harrington Road; private) was the home of Minuteman fifer Jonathan Harrington, who died in his wife's arms after being fatally wounded in the battle.

The **Museum of Our National Heritage** (33 Marrett Road; 617-861-6560) has changing exhibits on American history in four galleries. Past programs have included retrospectives on Ben Franklin, Paul Revere and the *U.S.S. Constitution*, plus exhibits of clocks, furniture and swords from different periods.

Within the 750-acre **Minuteman National Historic Park** (Route 2A, Concord; 508-369-6944) are several more sites involved in the Battle of Lexington and Concord. In this peaceful, sylvan spot, it's hard to picture the bloody carnage of the historic battle. A wide, pine-scented path leads to the site of the **Old North Bridge** spanning the Concord River, a 1956 replica of the bridge where Concord Minutemen held off the British. Another

Minuteman Memorial stands across the river, made of melted 1776 cannon, designed by Daniel Chester French. This one shows a farmer with gun and plow in hand. At the **Visitor Center** (174 Liberty Street) are a film and exhibits.

Concord is also famed as the home of four great literary figures of the 19th century: Nathaniel Hawthorne, Ralph Waldo Emerson, Henry David Thoreau and Louisa May Alcott.

The **Old Manse** (Monument Road near North Bridge; 508-369-3909; admission) was home not only to Emerson but also to Hawthorne, who lived there with his wife for two years, while writing *Mosses from an Old Manse*. The restored house is filled with Emerson and Hawthorne memorabilia.

The Alcott family lived at **Orchard House** (399 Lexington Road; 508-369-4118; admission) for almost 20 years. Here Louisa May Alcott wrote her most famous novels, *Little Women* and *Little Men*.

The Alcotts and Hawthorne also lived at **The Wayside** (455 Lexington Road; 508-369-6975; admission). The Alcotts lived here for several years while Louisa May was a girl. Hawthorne bought the house in 1852 and wrote his biography of Franklin Pierce here.

Emerson House (28 Cambridge Turnpike; 508-369-2236; admission) is where Emerson lived for almost 50 years, with Thoreau, Hawthorne and the Alcotts as his frequent guests. Almost all furnishings are original.

The **Concord Museum** (200 Lexington Road; 508-369-9609; admission) contains Revolutionary War artifacts, literary relics and other historic items associated with Concord. Emerson's library was reconstructed and moved here, and the Thoreau Room holds the simple furniture Thoreau made for his cabin at Walden Pond.

At the **Thoreau Lyceum** (156 Belknap Street; 508-369-5912; admission) is a replica of the cabin Thoreau built on Walden Pond. Headquarters of the Thoreau Society, the lyceum has a research library and sponsors lectures about the writer.

Few places have been more indelibly stamped by the presence of one individual than **Walden Pond State Reservation** (915 Walden Street; 508-369-3254; admission). "I went to the woods because I wished to live deliberately, to front the essential facts of life, and see if I could not learn what it had to teach, and not, when I came to die, discover that I had not lived," wrote Thoreau in his famous account of his two years spent in a little cabin in these woods, beginning in 1845. Thoreau occupied himself studying nature, fishing and hoeing his bean crop. Today, Walden Pond offers less solitude—it's almost always crowded. But you can swim or fish in the pond, or perhaps try a little boating. Nature trails wind around the pond, and there are picnic tables. You can also visit the little cairn of stones that marks the cabin site.

Concord is also known for **Concord grapes**, developed and cultivated here by Ephraim Wales Bull.

(Text continued on page 110.)

Exploring Boston's Outreaches

Although many tourists never leave the bounds of Boston and Cambridge—except perhaps to see Lexington and Concord—there is much of interest in the surrounding towns, many holding rich colonial histories.

Due east of the city and bordering the Fenway, Brookline is one of the more prestigious and wealthy residential surrounding towns. The architect of Boston's Emerald Necklace—parks and other green spaces that dot the city—lived and worked in a quiet neighborhood here. At the **Frederick Law Olmsted National Historic Site** (★) (99 Warren Street; 617-566-1689; admission), you can tour the house and grounds and see many of his landscape plans, memorabilia and photographs.

President John F. Kennedy was born in Brookline in 1917, in a little house now restored to its period appearance as the **John F. Kennedy National Historic Site** (83 Beals Street; 617-566-7937; admission). The house holds much JFK memorabilia, including his crib and some of his toys.

South of Brookline lies Jamaica Plain, technically part of Boston. Its star is the **Arnold Arboretum of Harvard University** (125 Arborway; 617-524-1718), a remarkable green strand. The 265-acre preserve was established in 1872, and growing here are more than 7000 kinds of trees and plants from around the world, plus one of the largest lilac collections in North America, 200-year-old bonsai trees and rare specimens from China. A two-mile walk offers serene and secluded vistas of these special collections.

To the southeast, the working-class city of Quincy may look uninteresting, but it happens to be the "City of the Presidents"—birthplace of John Adams and his son John Quincy Adams, the second and sixth U.S. presidents. There are several sights surrounding the Adams family history.

At the **Adams National Historic Site** (135 Adams Street, in Quincy Center; 617-773-1177; admission) stands an elegant gray colonial house built in 1730, home to four generations of Adamses. The house is on several acres strikingly set off with formal gardens. Inside are many original furnishings, including portraits of George and Martha Washington and Louis XV furniture. The National Park Service gives excellent tours.

Nearby are the **John Adams** and **John Quincy Adams Birthplaces** (133 and 141 Franklin Street; 617-773-1177; admission), a pair of simple salt box houses where the two presidents were born, built in 1663 and 1681. East of there lies the **Quincy Homestead** (1010 Hancock Street; 617-472-5117; admission), home to four generations of Edmund Quincys, the family of Abigail Adams.

A colonial-style herb garden and authentic period furnishings embellish the 1686 house, and one of John Hancock's coaches is displayed.

Dominating downtown Quincy Square is a beautiful granite church, **United First Parish Church** (1306 Hancock Street), built in 1828. The church crypt holds the remains of John Adams, John Quincy Adams and their wives.

Across the street is the 1844 Greek Revival **City Hall**, and nearby is the **Hancock Cemetery**, dating to about 1640, resting place for Hancocks, Quincys and Adamses.

Besides history, Quincy is home to the spot that won *Boston* magazine's "Best Mexican Restaurant" award six years running, **La Paloma** (195 Newport Avenue; 617-773-0512). It serves first-rate (budget-to-moderate priced) fare, including beef and chicken fajitas, vegetarian grilled tacos and *gorditos* (fried tortillas topped with homemade sausage and sour cream).

Surrounding the Route 128 beltway are several more towns of interest to the traveler. A large and urbanized town about 20 miles west of Boston, Framingham offers a lovely respite within the **Garden in the Woods** (★) (Hemenway Road; 508-877-7630; admission), the largest collection of native plants in the Northeast. You can meander 45 acres of woodland trails, planted with some 1500 varieties of flora.

A few miles north of Framingham lie the endearing green colonial towns of Sudbury and Lincoln, still quite rural in character. Just off the historic Old Post Road, **Longfellow's Wayside Inn** (Route 20, Sudbury; 508-443-8846) is a wonderful place to visit, stay or dine. Built about 1700, the inn was made famous by Longfellow's cycle of poems, *Tales of a Wayside Inn*, which includes "Paul Revere's Ride." Several other historic structures have been moved to the site, including an 18th-century grist mill and a little red schoolhouse. Restored in 1923, it's a fully functioning (moderate-to-deluxe priced) inn and (moderate) restaurant, serving hearty, traditional country fare.

Walter Gropius, founder of the Bauhaus school of art and architecture in Germany, built his family home in the rolling green hills of Lincoln when he moved here in 1937. **Gropius House** (68 Baker Bridge Road; admission) embodies the Bauhaus principles of function and simplicity. The house has works of art and Bauhaus furnishings.

Set in a wooded green 30-acre park, the **DeCordova and Dana Museum** (Sandy Pond Road; 617-259-8355; admission) has a collection of 20th-century American art, including paintings, sculpture, graphics and photography. In the summer, its amphitheater plays host to outdoor concerts ranging from jazz to rock to modern dance to folk music.

LEXINGTON AND CONCORD HOTELS

Built at the turn of the century, the **John David House** (★) (1963 Massachusetts Avenue, Lexington; 617-861-7376) opened as a bed and breakfast inn in late 1989 after a loving restoration. The foyer is a visual feast of twin white-balustered staircases, set off by rich, jewel-like wallpaper in red tones. Common areas, spacious and furnished with period antiques, include a sitting room and formal dining and living rooms. Four guest rooms all have private baths and are furnished with four-poster brass-and-mahogany beds and white eyelet spreads and pillow shams. Bathrooms are gorgeously new with Italian tile, pedestal sinks and pastel colors. Rooms, several of which overlook the Lexington Battle Green, include afternoon tea and continental breakfast. Moderate to deluxe.

If you're looking for an inexpensive place to stay right in the middle of Lexington, you might stop at the **Battle Green Motor Inn** (1720 Massachusetts Avenue; 617-862-6100). The 96 rooms at this L-shaped motel surround two courtyards graced with tropical plants and a heated swimming pool. Inside, guest rooms sport blond furniture and a colonial decor. Moderate.

Concord is greener and more rural than Lexington, making it a more restful place to stay. You can't stay there without stumbling over history.

The **Hawthorne Inn** (462 Lexington Road, Concord; 508-369-5610), built around 1870, is situated on land that once belonged to Emerson, the Alcotts and Hawthorne, and stands right across the street from the Hawthorne and Alcott houses. The homey inn has seven rooms, three furnished with canopied, antique four-poster beds covered with handmade quilts, as well as colonial-patterned wallpapers and Oriental rugs. The private baths are large and nicely redone. Moderate to ultra-deluxe.

Right on the town green, the **Colonial Inn** (48 Monument Square, Concord; 508-369-9200) dates to 1716. The original part of the house was owned by Thoreau's grandfather. Although the inn has 60 rooms, few are in the historic old inn. Some 30 rooms are in a newer wing added in 1961 and are comfortable but bland. Fifteen similar rooms are in a nearby annex. The 15 rooms in the original part of the house are larger and have a more historic ambience, with wide-planked floors, hand-hewn beams and four-poster beds. The inn has a restaurant with five dining rooms, and two taverns. Moderate to deluxe.

LEXINGTON AND CONCORD RESTAURANTS

For a quick bite and a break from sightseeing, stop for an excellent coffee and pastry at **One Meriam Street** (1 Meriam Street, Lexington; 617-862-3006), a cozy and casual café-style eatery. They also serve pancakes, omelettes, sandwiches, burgers and salads. Budget.

For elegant dining in Lexington, try **Le Bellecour** (10 Muzzey Street; 617-861-9400). A Parisian ambience is imparted by pink walls and tablecloths, Breuer chairs, brass torchières and paintings of the French countryside. The French continental menu features such traditional dishes as *poulet braisé au chou frisée* and *escalopes de veau Normandie*, at deluxe to ultra-deluxe prices. There are also wonderful desserts and an extensive wine list. Lighter fare—sandwiches, soups and salads—is available at the moderately priced café.

Yangtze River Restaurant (21-25 Depot Square, Lexington; 617-861-6030) specializes in Polynesian cuisine, as well as Szechuan and Cantonese favorites. The dining room is noisy and casual, with a jungle of greenery and exposed brick walls. Budget to moderate.

Not everyone will appreciate **The Willow Pond Kitchen** (745 Lexington Road, Concord; 508-369-6529), but we do. Its ma-and-pa, down-home atmosphere hasn't changed since the 1930s, with decor that features moth-eaten stuffed fish, wildcats and opossum, plus tacky formica tables and battered wooden booths. Paradoxically, good food is served here, on paper plates and at budget to moderate prices, including cheeseburgers, lobster rolls and lobster pie, steamed clams and a fine roster of beer and ale. Budget to moderate.

Located upstairs in an old railroad depot turned shopping arcade, **A Different Drummer** (86 Thoreau Street, Concord; 508-369-8700) offers a little bit of everything in an airy, simple dining room with white café chairs and tables, overlooking the tracks. A second dining room overlooks gift shops. Moderately priced items include lots of seafood, pasta and stir-fried and vegetarian entrées. They have the best Sunday brunch in town.

For some traditional Yankee fare in a historic setting, try the **Colonial Inn** (48 Monument Square, Concord; 508-369-9200). Built in 1716, the original part of the house was owned by Thoreau's grandfather. There are five dining rooms, each with its own colonially inspired decor. The moderate-to-deluxe-priced menu includes prime rib, steak, scrod, scallops and lobster.

The Sporting Life

For information on participatory sports in the areas around Boston, see Chapter Two.

Transportation

Visitors generally come to Cambridge, Lexington and Concord via Boston. See Chapter Two for information on air, bus and train transportation as well as rental cars.

CHAPTER FOUR

Cape Cod and the Islands

Every year starting in June, close to 3.5 million people invade a foot-shaped peninsula jutting out into the Atlantic south of Boston, grappling with horrendous traffic and crowded beaches just to be on their beloved Cape Cod. It's easy to understand why.

The Cape has it all: silver gray saltbox cottages, historic villages, sports, seafood, art, first-rate theater and more. But those attributes aren't the real reason people come here. It's the land itself. With its ethereal light, comforting woodlands and 300 miles of majestic, untamed shoreline, Cape Cod reaches deep into the soul. Formed 12,000 years ago from an enormous glacier that left in its wake a unique and magical landscape of sand dunes, moors, salt marsh and ocean vistas, the Cape has a staggering number of utterly beautiful beaches and natural parks.

Linked to the Cape in the minds of many travelers (although definitely *not* in the minds of residents) are the nearby islands of Martha's Vineyard and Nantucket, wealthy enclaves where celebrities find retreat and make their homes along quiet or dramatic seascapes, beside purple heath or in museum-perfect villages dotted with historic buildings. Following in the footsteps of Lillian Hellman and Dashiell Hammett, folks like Jackie Onassis, William Styron and Walter Cronkite have moved to Martha's Vineyard. Smaller Nantucket has one lovely town filled with museums, galleries and history, plus great wild beaches and backroads. Everyone calls Nantucket and Martha's Vineyard "the Islands"—except the people who live there. Don't even *suggest* that the "islanders" are connected to the Cape unless you want to start a row.

The Cape's first visitors were the Pilgrims, who landed near Province-town just long enough to write the Mayflower Compact before heading off to Plymouth. As Massachusetts thrived after the Revolution, Nantucket and Martha's Vineyard joined other coastal areas as major whaling ports.

In the 1800s, artists and writers such as Henry David Thoreau discovered the Cape, while Emily Dickinson made her home on Martha's Vineyard. Tourists were soon to follow, and these once-isolated fishing communities were never the same again.

Tourism has taken its toll. The Cape has a commercial side, complete with tired-looking shopping malls, pizza parlors, video arcades, tract houses and ugly motels. But it's easy to avoid all that if you know where to go.

The 70-mile-long Cape projects out into the ocean in an east-west direction for about 35 miles, then becomes narrower and turns northward. Practically everything worth seeing here lies along the shore, so an ideal way to explore is to follow the northern coast along Cape Cod Bay to the tip in Provincetown, then go back down along Nantucket Sound to Falmouth and Woods Hole. This is the route we will take.

We have labeled the first segment the North Cape, which follows scenic Route 6A along the north shore past some of the Cape's most charming historic villages. Route 6A eventually joins with busy Route 6 and soon arrives at Eastham. Here begins the Outer Cape, the region known for sand dunes, rolling moors, impressive beaches and the bohemian and tourist enclave of Provincetown. Route 28 runs back along the South Cape past a couple of attractive villages and some of the region's less-scenic commercial areas (including Hyannis, home to the Kennedy clan). This section ends at the scientific community of Woods Hole, noted for its oceanographic institute. We then journey to those two pearls off the Cape's southern coast, Martha's Vineyard and Nantucket.

Touring this area, perhaps you'll understand what inspired Thoreau to write *Cape Cod*. There's something here, though, that can't be put into words, a special chemistry and charisma that draw people back year after year, generation after generation.

The North Cape

Hugging Cape Cod Bay along Route 6A are the beautiful historic villages of Sandwich, Barnstable, Yarmouth, Dennis and Brewster. Once known as Olde Kings Highway, Route 6A is a tree-lined road that dips and turns past lovely old homes, sweeping lawns, stone walls, duck ponds, museums, elegant restaurants and antique stores.

Sandwich, the first town we reach, is very green, woodsy and English looking. It dates back to 1639 and has a 17th-century grist mill. Sandwich has more sights than any town on the Cape except Brewster. Maps are available at the **Cape Cod Canal Chamber of Commerce** (70 Main Street, Buzzard's Bay; 508-759-3122).

Near the heart of the village stands **Hoxie House** (Water Street, Route 130; 508-888-1173; admission), the oldest house in Sandwich. Built around 1637, this modest saltbox structure has furnishings that are impressive in their simplicity and ingenuity. A 1701 chest is decorated with soot and herb dye to give it a grained look; chairs turn into tables and beds into benches.

A few doors down is the **Thornton W. Burgess Museum,** (4 Water Street, 508-888-4668; admission), the former home of the author of *Old Mother West Wind* and *Peter Cotton Tail*. This homey little cottage overlooking an idyllic, willow-lined duck pond contains a large collection of books by Burgess, beautiful old book illustrations and a gift shop with children's books.

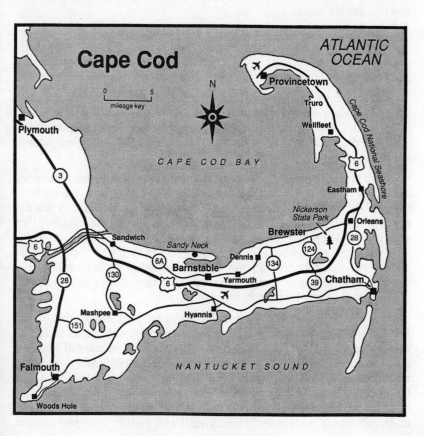

Heritage Plantation (Pine and Grove streets, 508-888-3300; admission) has a 1912 carousel, an antique car collection (including a stunning Dusenburg once owned by Gary Cooper), a military museum and an arts and crafts museum. If cars, folk art or military history interest you, you'll be impressed. The military museum has 2000 hand-painted miniatures and all sorts of colorful old uniforms and firearms. The crafts museum includes an impressive collection of antique weathervanes, Early American primitive and western art including many Currier and Ives lithographs, and animated cigar-store carved figures. The plantation's 76 acres of gardens are so perfectly manicured they look artificial.

In the heart of Sandwich village is the **Sandwich Glass Museum** (Town Hall Square; 508-888-0251; admission). In 1825 Deming Jarves, a Bostonian, built a glass factory in Sandwich because of its many ponds (water is crucial to the process of blowing glass) and because he thought his employees wouldn't squander their money on city temptations, as they had in Boston. His formula worked, and in no time Sandwich became renowned for its glass.

The museum's collection includes everything from jars, nursing bottles and tableware to saucers, vases and candlesticks. A lot of the glass is displayed on shelves in front of large picture windows. Sun illuminates the glass, and it lights up the museum in a kaleidoscope of sparkling colors.

A few steps away from the Glass Museum you'll find **Yesteryears Doll Museum** (Main and River streets; 508-888-1711; admission), two floors packed with every antique doll and accessory imaginable—princesses, nurses, Indians, doll furniture, houses, paper dolls, baby buggies, parasols and much more.

The **Green Briar Jam Kitchen** and the **Old Briar Patch Conservation Area** (6 Discovery Hill Road; 508-888-6870) are east of the center of town. "'Tis a wonderful thing to sweeten the world which is in a jam and needs preserving," wrote Thornton W. Burgess to Ida Putnam. As a boy Burgess roamed the woods around Ida's jam kitchen. Today, the Burgess Society produces natural jams, pickles and jellies from Ida's recipes. Nestled deep in the woods next to a pond, the old-fashioned kitchen looks like an illustration from one of Burgess' books. Peter Cotton Tail and his animal friends would have loved it here.

East of Sandwich lies the popular resort town of **Barnstable**, where some of the Cape's most beautiful inns and tempting restaurants and shops are located. Here, too, you'll find the **Donald Trayser Memorial Museum** (Route 6A; 508-362-2092), a brick structure built in 1856, which was once a custom house, then a post office. Named after a local patriot and historian, the museum includes a potpourri of artifacts related to Cape Cod life and history, such as Indian tools and ships in bottles. Next to the museum stands an old jail whose wooden walls are covered with graffiti written by seamen.

Farther along Route 6A, Yarmouthport is the site of two historic homes with impressive antiques. A white Greek Revival home with black shutters, **Captain Bangs Hallet House** (★) (11 Strawberry Lane; 508-362-3021) is furnished with elegant settees, tables and chairs, and many classic old toys such as a rocking horse with real animal hide and hair.

The 1780 **Winslow Crocker House** (Route 6A, Yarmouthport; 508-227-3956), a shingled Georgian with handsome wood paneling and an impressive walk-in fireplace, has a rare 17th-century wooden cradle and blanket chest, a Windsor writing chair and many more valuable antiques.

Brewster has a number of sights for children and history buffs. **Cape Cod Aquarium** (Main Street, Route 6A; 508-385-9252; admission) offers a dolphin pool, touch tanks and aquariums. The **New England Fire and History Museum** (Main Street, Route 6A; 508-896-5711; admission) displays hand- and horse-drawn fire equipment that makes you wonder how they ever put out fires. Kids like all the bells and fire alarms that are constantly sounding off here. The **Cape Cod Museum of Natural History** (Main Street, Route 6A; 508-896-3867; admission) has a working beehive and a weather station, and a curator gives guided walks through salt marshes.

Through the use of enormous oil paintings, special effects and life-sized mannequins, the **Drummer Boy Museum** (787 Main Street, Route 6A, Brewster; 508-896-3823; admission) depicts 21 scenes and events from American history including the Boston Tea Party and Washington crossing the Delaware.

NORTH CAPE HOTELS

Located in the heart of Sandwich village, **The Village Inn** (★) (4 Jarves Street; 800-922-9989) is a renovated 1830s Federal-style house. Without sacrificing historic details, the owners have made everything look fresh and new. The six soothing, uncluttered guest rooms, decorated in shades of raspberry and moss, have Colonial armoires and pickled four-poster beds. All of the wood furniture is made by the owner and sold in a shop in the inn. A wraparound front porch is a good spot for people watching. Moderate.

Six Water Street (6 Water Street, Sandwich; 508-888-6808), an 1845 bed and breakfast next to the Thornton W. Burgess Museum, overlooks picture-perfect Shawme Pond. Guests enjoy rowing or simply sitting on the lawn that spills down to the water. Geese and swans enhance the scenery. The inn has only three rooms, each impeccably decorated in spring colors such as lavender and mint. Furnishings include brass beds, sleigh beds, clawfoot bathtubs, willow branch chairs and wicker pieces. Located within walking distance of Sandwich village. Deluxe.

The Daniel Webster Inn (149 Main Street, Sandwich; 508-888-3622) is one of the few full-service hotels on historic Route 6A. The Federal-style,

47-room hotel is so much bigger than the other buildings in Sandwich, it looks a little out of whack. But the inside is very warm and cozy. Guest rooms in shades of gold and raspberry or smoke and rose are decorated with reproduction Colonial furniture and wing-back chairs; some beds have canopies. Brick paths lead through graceful flower gardens to a gazebo and pool area. The hotel has three restaurants. Rates available with or without breakfast and dinner; deluxe to ultra-deluxe.

The **Beechwood** (2839 Main Street, Barnstable Village; 508-362-6618) is one of the prettiest inns on Route 6A. An ancient weeping beech tree shades a good portion of this buttery yellow, gabled Queen Anne Victorian and its lovely wraparound porch. The entire house is furnished with fine antiques. In the Cottage room you'll find a rare 1860 hand-painted bedroom set, in the Marble room a graceful marble fireplace and 19th-century brass bed. The Garret room on the third floor has steeply angled walls and a half-moon window overlooking Cape Cod Bay. It doesn't matter where you stay —all six guest rooms are wonderful. A full breakfast is served in the wood-paneled dining room and tea on the porch. Deluxe to ultra-deluxe.

Built in 1812, the **Wedgewood Inn** (Route 6A, Yarmouthport; 508-362-5157) sits on a little hill overlooking historic Route 6A. Surrounded by stately elm trees and stone walls, the Colonial inn makes a lasting impression. Guest rooms sport handcrafted cherry wood pencil post beds, antique quilts and wideboard floors and fireplaces. The decor is an elegant interpretation of Early American styles. Ultra-deluxe.

A rambling white 1881 Victorian close to the beach, the **Four Chimneys Inn** (946 Main Street, Dennis; 508-385-6317) is the kind of place where you can plop down on the living room couch in front of the fire and settle in for a good read selected from the library. Homey and low-key, the nine guest rooms (some with shared bath) are large, white and airy with high ceilings and chenille bedspreads. A large yard surrounds the house, which sits well back from the road. Budget to moderate with shared bath; moderate with private bath.

The **Isaiah Clark House** (1187 Main Street, Brewster; 508-896-2223), an 18th-century sea captain's home, is surrounded by five acres of gardens, fruit trees and wild berry patches. Impeccably appointed with Shaker and Colonial antiques, many of the guest rooms have stenciled walls, canopy beds, sloping pine floors and fireplaces. Breakfast is served in an appealing room with an enormous fireplace—guests linger here all morning long. Pre-dinner get-togethers and a full breakfast are included. Moderate to deluxe.

A large turn-of-century gray-and-white house, the **Old Sea Pines Inn** (2553 Main Street, Brewster; 508-896-6114) used to be a girls' school. The spacious public and 21 guest rooms are comfortably furnished with antique brown wicker, slip-covered chairs and sofas. A wraparound porch with rockers, perfect for reading or snoozing, overlooks a yard shaded by pine and oak trees. A full breakfast is served in a bright renovated dining area with many skylights. Budget to deluxe.

You get a lot for your money at **The Poore House** (Route 6A, Brewster; 508-896-2094), one of the few bargains on Route 6A. A charming old inn with dark green shutters, the place offers bright and cheery guest rooms with painted yellow floors and some antique furnishings. A full breakfast is served in a cozy living room. Behind the inn stands an attractive garden shop and nursery. Potted flowers and plants arranged along the stone driveway create a profusion of color. (Since you're saving so much money here, consider dining at Chillingsworth [see "North Cape Restaurants"], one of the Cape's most elegant and expensive restaurants. It's within walking distance.) Budget.

NORTH CAPE RESTAURANTS

The **Daniel Webster Inn** (149 Main Street, Sandwich; 508-888-3622) is so Colonial looking, you expect it to serve traditional New England fare, but the menu is rather diversified. Lunch includes chicken pot pie, pizza, lobster cakes, sandwiches and salads. Dinner entrées range from veal Oscar, baked scrod and filet mignon to changing specials such as baked swordfish rolled with shrimp and basil stuffing, grilled salmon with rosemary-sherry butter and roast quail over wild rice. Meals are served in a formal dining room with peach walls, mahogany chairs and brass chandeliers or in a greenhouse room overlooking a garden. Breakfast is also available. Moderate to deluxe.

Barnstable Tavern (3176 Main Street, Barnstable; 508-362-2355) serves traditional lunch and dinner fare such as steak au poivre, mussels marinara, shrimp scampi, pasta and spinach salad. Located in a small complex of shops, the restaurant creates a pleasant country-style feeling with Windsor chairs, folk art, brass light fixtures and blond wood floors. The friendly bar is a good place for a drink, and different varieties of wine are served by the glass. Moderate to deluxe.

The food's hearty and predictable, the service fast and friendly at **Marshside Restaurant** (★) (28 Bridge Street, East Dennis; 508-385-4010), a glorified coffee shop popular with locals. Omelettes, bagels, pancakes and french toast are some of the breakfast offerings. Lunch items include lobster salad, quesadillas and fried clams. At dinner it's fried clams, stuffed shrimp, steak, chicken picatta and daily specials. The decor is kitchen-cute with fake Tiffany lamps, bentwood chairs and ruffled curtains. The back room has a spectacular view of a salt marsh meadow. Moderate.

Don't be fooled by the name. Although cozy little **Margarite's Restaurant** (★) (Route 6A, Dennis; 508-385-3279) is a perfect spot for sinfully good desserts and a cappuccino, they also serve breakfast, lunch and dinner.

Located in a small, Colonial-style shopping complex, it resembles a country tea room with ruffled curtains, cranberry tablecloths and an antique wood-burning stove. The traditional menu features quiche, french toast and eggs for breakfast; sandwiches, salads and chowder for lunch; prime rib, stuffed shrimp, veal marsala and pasta for dinner. Desserts change daily. One popular offering is the Hot Fudge Pie. A cross between chocolate fudge and cake, it's very thick, gooey and good. Moderate to deluxe.

Gina's By The Sea (★) (134 Taunton Avenue, Dennis; 508-385-3213), a sweet little white clapboard restaurant within walking distance of Chapin Beach, is far more sophisticated than it looks. The predominately seafood menu changes daily and includes entrées like mussel soup, grilled Muscovy duck and red snapper with champagne sauce. Ruffled curtains, white tablecloths and plain wooden chairs create a casual formality. Moderate.

You might find yourself sitting near a well-known actor at the **Playhouse Restaurant** (Route 6A, Dennis; 508-385-8000), located on the grounds of the Cape Playhouse. Banks of windows on three sides of the attractive peach-colored restaurant overlook sweeping lawns and flower gardens. The continental menu includes a host of fish, chicken and steak dishes. Moderate.

Cranberry Moose (Route 6A, Yarmouthport; 508-362-3501) serves new American cuisine in an 18th-century Cape Cod cottage on one of the prettiest stretches of historic Route 6A. A good spot for a special lunch or dinner, the restaurant has an imaginative, seasonally changing menu. Dishes have included seafood terrine, game salad with sage–pine nut vinaigrette and bouillabaisse with fennel, saffron, pernod and orange zest. Cozy yet sophisticated, it has a number of small dining rooms with low ceilings, Windsor chairs and white tablecloths. Deluxe.

With its blond-wood floors, green tablecloths, small library and New Age music, the **Brewster Fish House Restaurant** (★) (Route 6A, Brewster; 508-896-7867) feels more like a café than a fish house. Its small, creative menu features dishes such as chilled grilled scallops with an herb vinaigrette, salmon stuffed with sole mousse and calamari with aioli. Moderate.

Elegant and expensive, **Chillingsworth** (Route 6A, Brewster; 508-896-3640) has been repeatedly praised by the *New York Times* and *Esquire*. The menu changes daily, utilizing seasonal and fresh ingredients. The food is strictly nouvelle, with dishes such as loin of veal with sun-dried tomatoes, risotto and sage, and free-range chicken with greens, chili brown sauce and sweet potato chips. Located in a 300-year-old, tree-shaded Colonial house, the restaurant has dining areas combining modern and traditional decorative touches such as contemporary artwork, antique mirrors and white tablecloths. Lunch and brunch are served in the greenhouse and garden. After lunch, browse in the restaurant's antique and pastry shop. The seven-course dinner is served at two seatings, and reservations are mandatory. Ultra-deluxe.

The **Bramble Inn** (Route 6A, Brewster; 508-896-7644) is one of those restaurants people always rave about. Housed in a Greek Revival farmhouse on scenic Route 6A, the place offers a prix-fixe menu that changes daily. Dinner is served in four small dining rooms complete with Queen Anne chairs, fresh flowers, antiques and china blue walls. Innovative dishes have included grilled seafood in curry sauce, smoked bluefish pâté, and rack of lamb with garlic and rosemary. Ultra-deluxe.

NORTH CAPE SHOPPING

Some of the Cape's best shopping is along Route 6A, which is lined with antique stores and artists studios selling pottery, weavings, handcrafted furniture and more.

With its sloping wood floors and wainscotting, **The Brown Jug** (155 Main Street, Sandwich; 508-833-1088) looks like an old general store. But it sells fine quality, hand-blown antique glass. Many of the pieces were made in Sandwich in the 19th century.

The Blacks (597 Route 6A, West Barnstable; 508-362-3955) has beautiful handwoven blankets, throws, place mats, hats, gloves and wallhangings in lush colors—rich navy and cream, dusty lavender and gray, russet and forest green. The store is in a large barn-shaped room where you can watch owners/designers Bob and Gabrielle Black working at one of the many looms.

Even if you don't intend to buy a weathervane, stop by **Salt and Chestnut** (Route 6A, West Barnstable; 508-362-6085). It's like a weathervane museum. The shop sells new and antique hand-hammered copper weathervanes in a myriad of styles—a witch on a broom, mermaid, lobster, sailboats, dogs, elephants, deer and more.

One of the nicest sights on Route 6A is the vibrant display of fresh produce and flowers at **Tobey Farm Country Store** (Route 6A, Dennis; 508-385-2930). Stop here in the summer for peaches and plums and in the fall for pumpkins and apples. The white clapboard farm also sells reasonably priced dried wreaths made from German statice, rose hips, lavender, yarrow, dried pink rosebuds, baby's breath purple statice and eucalyptus.

Design Works (159 Main Street, Yarmouthport; 508-362-9698) specializes in antique Scandinavian pine armoires, mirrors, chairs, settees and white linen and lace napkins, tablecloths and bed accessories.

Even if you can't afford anything at **Kingsland Manor Manor** (Route 6A, West Brewster; 508-385-9741), stop and browse through its labyrinth of beautiful rooms and gardens filled with exquisite American and European antiques.

Aptly named **Bird Watcher's General Store** (Route 6A, Orleans; 508-255-6974) sells anything having to do with birds—field guides, glasses, calling whistles, 50 kinds of birdbaths, bath heaters and carving kits. It's also got coffee mugs, T-shirts, stamps, floor mats and pot holders adorned with birds.

NORTH CAPE NIGHTLIFE

Heritage Plantation Concerts (Pine and Grove streets, Sandwich; 508-888-3300) offers a diverse program including jazz, ballet, banjo music, Scottish pipe bands, chorale groups and big bands.

Established in 1926 and America's oldest summer theater, **The Cape Playhouse** (Route 6A, Dennis; 508-385-3911) presents well-known plays and musicals such as *The Sound of Music, Ain't Misbehavin'* and *Betrayal*, performed by Hollywood and Broadway stars. Lana Turner, Gregory Peck and Henry Fonda have been on stage here. Nostalgic and romantic-looking, the Playhouse is in an 1810 meetinghouse surrounded by graceful lawns, gardens and a Victorian Gothic ticket booth.

The Cape Museum of Fine Arts' **Cinema Club** (Route 6A, Dennis; 508-385-4477), on the grounds of the Cape Playhouse, shows quality films, both new and old, such as *Henry V* with Laurence Olivier, *Ginger and Fred* and *House of Games.*

Barnstable Comedy Club (Route 6A, Barnstable Village; 508-362-6333), founded in 1922, is the oldest amateur theater group on the Cape. Throughout the year it gives major productions and workshops. Kurt Vonnegut, an alumni of the Club, acted in many of its earlier productions.

NORTH CAPE BEACHES AND PARKS

North Cape beaches are on protected Cape Cod Bay. They tend to be quiet and calm, with gentle surf and scenic vistas of soft sand dunes and salt marsh.

Sandy Neck Beach and the **Great Marshes**—This area has all the ecological treasures for which the Cape is known. Very straight and long, beautiful Sandy Neck Beach offers a 360° view of the ocean and rippling sand dunes bordered by the Great Marshes, 3000 acres of protected land harboring many species of marine life and birds. The sand is ideal for beachcombing, and trails meander through the dunes and marsh.

Facilities: Restrooms, snack bar; groceries a short drive away in Sandwich. *Swimming:* Calm.

Getting there: Take Sandy Neck Road off Route 6A in Sandwich.

Grey's Beach—This small, quiet beach is perfect for children. But the main reason people come here is to stroll along the long, elevated walkway stretching across the marsh that skirts the beach. The walkway permits a close-up view of marsh flora and fauna, and from a distance it appears to be floating in grassy water. There's not much to do here, but this area is quite beautiful, especially at sunset.

Facilities: Picnic tables, restrooms, lifeguards; groceries nearby in Yarmouth. *Swimming:* Calm.

Getting there: Located off Route 6A on Centre Street in Yarmouth.

Chapin Beach—The sand-strewn road leading to Chapin Beach passes gentle sand dunes and small, unpretentious, summer cottages. A pleasant spot for walks along the shore, the thin, slightly curved, dune-backed beach has soft, white sand ideal for clean, comfortable sunbathing.

Facilities: Restrooms; groceries are found nearby in Dennis. *Swimming:* Calm.

Getting there: Located off Route 6A on Chapin Beach Road in Dennis.

Paine's Creek Beach (★)—There are better beaches nearby for sunning and swimming, but Paine's Creek is ideal for quiet walks through timeless scenery bathed in golden light. Weatherbeaten skiffs are moored along the shore, and Paine's Creek, a gentle slip of a stream, winds through a salt marsh meadow down to a narrow strip of soft beach surrounded by tiny coves and inlets.

Facilities: None; groceries are found nearby in West Brewster. *Swimming:* Calm.

Getting there: Located off Route 6A on Paine's Creek Road in West Brewster.

Nickerson State Park—This 1700-acre park looks more like the Berkshires than Cape Cod. Dense pine groves, meadows and jewel-like freshwater ponds with beaches are home to abundant wildlife including red foxes and white-tailed deer. There is so much to do here—hiking, biking, motor boating, canoeing—it gets very crowded in the summer. Quiet beaches and hiking trails can be found around Cliff Pond. In winter there's cross-country skiing and ice-skating on the ponds.

Facilities: Picnic areas, restrooms, showers, ranger station, interpretive programs; groceries a short drive away in Brewster; information: 508-896-3491. *Camping:* Permitted in 420 sites on a first come, first served basis. *Fishing:* Excellent at Higgins Pond, which is stocked annually with trout. *Swimming:* In freshwater ponds.

Getting there: Located off Route 6A on Crosby Road in Brewster.

The Outer Cape

Route 6A ends at Orleans, where it intersects with Route 6 and leads to Eastham. At this point the character of the landscape changes dramatically. The woods disappear and the sky opens up to reveal towering sand dunes, miles of silver marsh grass and windswept moors. At the very tip is Provincetown, one of the Cape's largest communities.

About 50 percent of the Outer Cape is under the jurisdiction of the Cape Cod National Seashore, a natural playground with miles of bicycle paths, hikes and the Cape's most dramatic beaches (see "Bicycling Cape Cod and the Islands" and "Hiking Cape Cod and the Islands" in this chapter).

Fort Hill (★) off Route 6 in Eastham offers a mesmerizing view overlooking Nauset Marsh that's so beautiful it doesn't seem real. Once productive farmland, the marsh today is laced with wavy ribbons of water that wind through downy, soft green-gold marsh grass past old farmhouses, stone walls and ponds complete with ducks. Trails meander through this area, which is a resting place for blue herons. Near the Fort Hill parking lot is the **Edward Penniman House** (★) (not open to the public), a fairy-tale-like, red-and-yellow French Empire house with an enormous archway of whale jaw bones at its gate. Built by an eccentric whaler in the 19th century, the whimsical structure contrasts dramatically with the Cape's simple saltbox homes.

After Eastham is **Wellfleet**, an unpretentious, wiggle-your-toes-in-the-sand kind of place with a surprising number of good art galleries and gourmet restaurants. On Saturday nights in the summer, many galleries have openings that feel like neighborhood block parties. Wellfleet has many year-round residents, and they all seem to know each other.

Before heading into town, stop at the **Wellfleet Chamber of Commerce** (Route 6; 508-349-2510) for a gallery guide. On the way to Wellfleet is **Uncle Tim's Bridge** (★), a low wooden boardwalk that goes over a field of silvery marsh grass to a small wooded hill. A dreamy sort of place shrouded in delicate mist in the morning and soft mellow light in the afternoon, it's perfect for a picnic or quiet walk.

North of Wellfleet lies magnificent **Truro**, a vast treeless plain of rolling moors surrounded by water and some of the state's most impressive sand dunes. Named after an area of Cornwall, England that's similar in appearance, Truro is a wonderful area for picture taking.

Provincetown, at the Cape's outer tip, is nestled on a hill overlooking the bay. Everything good and bad about Cape Cod can be found here: elegant sea captains' mansions, a honky-tonk wharf, dazzling beaches, first-rate museums, schlocky galleries, hamburger joints and gourmet restaurants.

The people are equally diverse. Provincetown has a large gay population, as well as artists and writers, Portuguese fishermen, aristocrats, beer-guzzling rabble-rousers and plenty of tourists. Of all the towns on the Cape, Provincetown has the most interesting history. The Pilgrims landed here in 1620 before going to Plymouth, and in the 18th and 19th centuries it was a prominent whaling and fishing port, attracting many Portuguese settlers who still fish the waters today.

Around the turn of the century, artists and writers, such as Eugene O'Neill, started moving to Provincetown, and it became one of America's most renowned artists colonies. A renaissance period flourished until about 1945, when tourism evolved and many artists scattered for quieter parts of the world.

To immerse yourself in Provincetown's artistic past, get a copy of *Walking Tours No. 2 and 3* from the **Provincetown Chamber of Commerce** (307 Commercial Street, MacMillan Wharf; 508-487-3424). These pamphlets list the name and address of every famous writer and artist who ever lived here. Their former homes aren't open to the public, but it's fun to walk by 577 Commercial Street and imagine what it was like when O'Neill rented a room there.

For a free directory of gay- or lesbian-owned hotels, restaurants, bars, shops and services, stop by the **Provincetown Business Guild** (115 Bradford Street; 508-487-2313). **Provincetown Heritage Museum** (Center and Commercial streets; 508-487-0666; admission) provides an overview of the town's historic and artistic past. The *Rose Dorothea*, the world's largest indoor model of a fishing schooner, fills up the entire second floor of the museum. Other exhibits include hand-painted furniture featuring seascapes, photographs of artists at the turn of the century and many paintings.

Walk east on Commercial Street, the main drag, to the **Provincetown Art Association and Museum** (460 Commercial Street; 508-487-1750; admission) for the best art on the Cape. The museum exhibits work by noted Provincetown artists such as impressionist painter Charles W. Hawthorne, who founded the Cape's first art school in 1899. Much of the work is figurative, depicting everyday Provincetown scenes such as a plumber at work, a schooner in Cape Cod Bay, a young girl sewing.

For a picture-postcard view of Provincetown and the surrounding seashore and sand dunes, visit the **Pilgrim Monument** and **Provincetown Museum** (High Pole Hill; 508-487-1310; admission). The 252-foot granite tower, with 30-foot arches and turrets, was copied from the Torre del Mangia tower in Siena, Italy. The museum houses an eclectic collection that includes everything from a model of a Thai temple, antique dolls, Wedgwood china, primitive portraits and scrimshaw to figureheads, a captain's cabin from a whaling ship and Provincetown's oldest fire engine.

(Text continued on page 125.)

Hiking Cape Cod and the Islands

Otherworldly sand dunes, heaths that recall those across the Atlantic, sheltering forests and salt marshes are just a few of the environments available to hikers on Cape Cod and the Islands. You can trek through wilderness areas or stick to spots close to town. For more information on hikes, contact the **Massachusetts Department of Environmental Management Trails Program** (225 Friend Street, Boston; 617-727-3160).

CAPE COD TRAILS

Talbot's Point Salt Marsh Trail (1.5 miles), off Old Country Road in Sandwich, offers excellent views of the Great Marsh. The trail winds through red pine forest, along the fern-filled marsh and past cranberry bogs and the state game farm, where thousands of quail and pheasant are raised.

Nauset Marsh Trail (1 mile) offers some of the Cape's lushest scenery. The trail starts at the Salt Pond Visitor's Center in North Eastham and goes past the shoreline of Salt Pond and Nauset Marsh, then rises through pastoral farmland filled with beach plums, bayberries and cedars.

A mesmerizing view of salt marsh and the ocean beyond greets you at **Goose Ponds Trail** (1.5 miles) in the Wellfleet Bay Wildlife Sanctuary. The path leads through forest down a slight grade past Spring Brook to marshlands covered with wild lupine. A wooden boardwalk leads to a secluded beach. Among the many species of bird life are white-bottomed tree swallows nesting in bird houses located throughout the sanctuary.

Great Island Trail (8.4 miles), a wind-bitten wilderness, is best in the morning when the sun isn't too intense. Located at the end of Kendrick Road in Wellfleet, the trail borders tidal flats, grassy dunes, pitch pine forest, the ocean

and meadows where purple marsh peas and fiddler crabs flourish. Great for solitary beachcombing, the trail offers a number of spectacular views.

Beech Forest Trail (1 mile) winds to the Cape's most monumental sand dunes. Most of the trail wanders through cool beech forests and past freshwater ponds, and at one point it opens up to reveal the desertlike sand dunes. It starts on Race Point Road in Provincetown.

MARTHA'S VINEYARD TRAILS

Felix Tree Neck Wildlife Sanctuary Trail (1.5 miles), off the Edgartown-West Tisbury Road, offers many opportunities to view ducks, swans, otters, muskrats, egrets, harrier hawks and other wildlife. The trail winds past waterfowl ponds, salt marsh, the end of a peninsula, wetland vegetation and oak forest. It ends at the sanctuary's exhibit building, which has aquariums, wildlife displays, a library and a naturalist gift shop.

NANTUCKET TRAILS

Nantucket doesn't have marked hiking trails. But the Nantucket Conservation Foundation owns parcels of wilderness the public can explore. For more on this, see "Nantucket Beaches and Parks" section in this chapter. Following are two of the most scenic areas in which to hike:

Tupancy Links, off Cliff Road immediately west of town, is laced with paths that overlook Nantucket Sound. A former golf course, today it is a big, open grassy field offering dramatic views.

Alter Rock off Polpis Road in the central moors is crisscrossed with unmarked paths and rutted dirt roads. Dotted with kettle hole ponds, rocks and scrub oak thicket, the scenery is classic heathland.

OUTER CAPE HOTELS

If you want to capture the essence of Wellfleet, stay at the **Holden Inn** (★) (Wellfleet Bay; 508-349-3450), a long, white farmhouse-style lodging. There's nothing fancy about the place, but like Wellfleet, it has an easy, casual feeling. Located on a shady country lane five minutes from the wharf, the inn offers well-kept guest rooms (some with shared bath) with ruffled white curtains and floral wallpaper or wood paneling. Budget to moderate.

With its dark wood shingles, sky-blue shutters and nursery-rhyme garden, the **Bradford Gardens Inn** (★) (178 Bradford Street, Provincetown; 508-487-1616) looks like an illustration from a Mother Goose book. One of the most inviting cottages in Provincetown, the Bradford has 11 guest rooms and apartments, many with working fireplaces. An apartment on the side of the house with its own entrance has a sitting room, Franklin stove and garden view. A full breakfast is served by the cozy fireplace. The inn is popular with both lesbians and straights. Deluxe.

The **Heritage House** (7 Center Street, Provincetown; 508-487-3692), a cheerful yellow clapboard bed and breakfast with colorful window boxes, is on a narrow side street one block from the beach. Small and extremely tidy, the blue-and-white living room is filled with fine antiques. The inn's jovial owner, Robert Kulesza, makes everyone feel welcome. Guest rooms are small and tastefully furnished with country-style antiques and neutral colors. A second floor porch offers a good view of the harbor. Moderate.

The **Asheton House** (3 Cook Street, Provincetown; 508-487-9966) makes an elegant first impression. A beautiful, curved two-sided stairway leads to the front door of this pristine white 1840 house surrounded by brick paths and an English boxwood garden. The seven guest rooms and one apartment are all decorated differently. The handsome Captains room (shared bath) has a four-poster bed, neutral color scheme and antiques. The Safari room is quite spacious, although its jungle print wallpaper seems more 1966 than 1840. Budget to moderate for room with shared bath; deluxe for private bath.

Built in 1820, the **Watership Inn** (7 Winthrop Street, Provincetown; 508-536-7289) is popular with gay men. Located on a quiet street yet close to everything, the inn features guest rooms with arched beamed ceilings and antiques. Some have private decks. Breakfast is served on an outdoor deck or in an attractive living room with vaulted ceilings and a bank of french doors leading out to a yard where volleyball is played in the summer. The inn offers terrific off-season bargains. Budget.

OUTER CAPE RESTAURANTS

The **Bayside Lobster Hutt** (Commercial Street, Wellfleet; 508-349-6333), a noisy, friendly place, is perfect after a day at the beach. Located on a country road leading to Wellfleet's galleries and wharf, it looks like an old white schoolhouse. On the roof, a fisherman statue hauls an enormous red lobster into a boat. Everyone sits at long tables covered with red-and-white-checked oil tablecloths. Buoys and fish nets decorate the walls. The menu features lobster, flounder, steamed clams, scallops and shrimp. There's a raw bar and a take-out window where you can order clambake picnics. Moderate.

A combination art gallery and restaurant, **Cielo** (East Main Street, Wellfleet; 508-349-2108) has all the warmth and charm of a European café, plus a five-course, fixed-price dinner. It's located in a 100-year-old saltbox overlooking salt marsh and ponds. The menu combines French and ethnic cooking and includes daily specials such as plum soup, cold Szechuan soy noodles with shrimp, salmon mousse and pork with sausage stuffing. The candle-lit dinner is served in the living room and gallery, appointed with antiques and contemporary art. Reservations a must. Ultra-deluxe.

The Lighthouse (Main Street; 508-349-3681) is a Wellfleet institution. If you want to mingle with the locals, come here in the morning for breakfast. The ambience is strictly coffee shop, as is the food, which includes french toast, bacon and eggs, fried seafood, sandwiches, hamburgers and the like. Located in the center of town, it has a kitschy miniature lighthouse on its roof that is impossible to miss. Budget.

Sweet Seasons (The Inn at Ducke Creeke, East Main Street, Wellfleet; 508-349-6535) is an exceptionally pretty restaurant overlooking an idyllic duck pond surrounded by flower gardens, flagstone paths, locust trees and woods. The pale gray and apricot restaurant serves dishes such as grilled swordfish, warm duck salad, grilled veal with wild mushroom sauce and lamb with rosemary sauce. Deluxe.

Located on a narrow side street, rustic, ivy-covered **Grand Central Café** (5 Masonic Place, Provincetown; 508-487-9116) looks like a cozy English tavern. The interior has dark, heavy wood, thick beams, stained-glass lamps and wrought-iron grillwork. In the many dining rooms or on the outdoor patio, you can choose from traditional and affordable fare—steaks, sole florentine, shrimp scampi or a "Southwestern" menu with fajitas, soft tacos and smoked prawns. Moderate.

The Red Inn (15 Commercial Street, Provincetown; 508-487-0050) is so close to the water, you can't see any land below the large picture windows that run the length of the restaurant. Built in 1805, the red-and-white inn serves traditional American fare, with a sprinkling of newer dishes—roast duckling, filet mignon, balsamic grilled chicken on a warm bed of spinach and mushrooms and lobster sautéed then vodka flambéed and served over fettucine. The bouillabaisse is a favorite. The beautiful bar has a magnificent old fireplace, antique chairs and large-paned windows with expansive views of the ocean. Moderate to deluxe.

Ciro & Sal's (4 Kiley Court; 508-487-0049) is one of Provincetown's most legendary restaurants. Established in 1951 as a coffeehouse for artists, it grew into a full-fledged restaurant serving classic Italian food. In 1959 Sal left and opened his own restaurant (described below). Dripping with atmosphere, the basement dining room resembles an Italian wine cellar with a low ceiling, slate floor and candle-lit tables. An upstairs dining room overlooks a garden. Popular dishes include fresh sardines with fennel, poached bass with clams and veal tenderloin with mozzarella and prosciutto. Tasty Italian bread is baked on the premises. Deluxe.

Sal's Place (99 Commercial Street, Provincetown; 508-487-1279) is cozy, dark, intimate and arty. In this seaside cottage with Italian ambience, Chianti bottles hang from the low-beamed ceiling, bay windows are draped with lace curtains and a Modigliani poster adorns a wall. The menu includes 12 kinds of pasta, veal dishes and inventive seafood entrées such as squid stuffed with pine nuts, flounder and shellfish. Moderate to deluxe.

The place to be on a sunny summer morning is the outdoor patio at **Pearl's Café** (★) (401½ Commercial Street, Provincetown; 508-487-2114), a turquoise-and-white oceanfront cottage. The menu covers the basics, and the portions are hearty, with items like granola with fruit, omelettes, pancakes and baked goods. Breakfast only; budget.

With its white-cloth-covered tables, black chairs and brick walls, **Gallerani's Café** (133 Commercial Street, Provincetown; 508-487-4433) looks a little bit like a New York City art-crowd restaurant. But that's where the similarity ends. The prices are a bargain, the food is down to earth and so is the crowd. The room is bright and airy, and the long bar in the back is a pleasant place for a drink. Open for breakfast, lunch and dinner, Gallerani's serves dishes such as fruit- and sausage-filled pancakes, homemade granola, chicken pot pie, seafood casserole and marinated grilled shrimp. Moderate.

Café Heaven (199 Commercial Street, Provincetown; 508-487-9639) is located on a part of Commercial Street away from the touristy hoopla. Housed in an old storefront with large picture windows, the restaurant is bright and uncluttered, with white wooden tables and pale gray carpeting. A colorful mural of tango dancers by nationally known artist John Grillo adorns one wall. The food is hearty and all American—bacon and eggs, waffles, omelettes, tasty muffins, lusty sandwiches on thick slabs of homemade bread and salads such as chicken tarragon. This popular hangout for gays and lesbians is open for breakfast and lunch only. Budget.

OUTER CAPE SHOPPING

Remembrances of Things Past (376 Commercial Street, Provincetown; 508-487-9443) is fun to explore even if you aren't in the mood to buy. It's full of nostalgic memorabilia from the '20s to the '50s—a jukebox, hilarious issues of *True Confessions* magazine, and vintage photographs of Elvis, Marilyn and Lucy.

Marine Specialties (235 Commercial Street, Provincetown; 508-477-1250) sounds like a straightforward place, but it's not. Housed in a barnlike room, this eclectic shop is jammed with all sorts of reasonably priced oddball nautical and military items such as antique brass buttons, old fashioned oars, bells, baskets, antique diving gear, fog horns, vintage shoe carts, Army and Navy clothing, flags, bicycle lights, shells and fishing nets. Even people who hate to shop love this place.

OUTER CAPE NIGHTLIFE

Provincetown has first-rate gay and lesbian entertainment—everything from afternoon tea dances, cabaret and ministage productions to piano bars, discos, you name it. Here are some of the most popular hot spots a few of which draw straights and gays alike:

Female impersonators bring to life such legends as Judy Garland and Pearl Bailey at the **Crown and Anchor** (247 Commercial Street; 508-487-1430), housed in a historic waterfront building. Reservations are a must. This place attracts gays, lesbians and straights. Cover.

The Post Office Café Cabaret (303 Commercial Street; 508-487-6400) is the spot for lesbians during the summer, when it presents noted female performers such as Teresa Trull. The café is open year-round and is a good place to hang out.

The **Pied Piper** (193A Commercial Street; 508-487-1527) was cited by *Time* magazine as "the best women's bar" in the country. Locals say the best time to go is after ten for the dancing.

During the summer the most popular activities for gays are the afternoon tea dances at **The Boatslip Beach Club** (161 Commercial Street; 508-487-1669), a full-service resort on the beach.

The hottest gay bar and disco in town is the **Atlantic House** (4-6 Masonic Place; 508-487-3821).

A popular spot for quality entertainment is the **Town House Restaurant** (291–293 Commercial Street, Provincetown; 508-487-0292). During the summer it offers a variety of acts—piano music, drag shows and comedians. Cover.

OUTER CAPE BEACHES AND PARKS

First Encounter Beach—This is where the Pilgrims first encountered the Wampanoag Indians, who were not exactly happy to see them. Six years earlier an English slave dealer had kidnapped some of them to sell in Spain. When the Pilgrims arrived a mild skirmish broke out, but no one was hurt and the Pilgrims made a hasty retreat. Sandy paths lead through dense green grass to this striking beach bordered by a vast marsh meadow and brilliant sky. The long, wide beach attracts a relatively quiet crowd in the summer.

Facilities: Restrooms, groceries a short drive away in Eastham. *Swimming:* Calm.

Getting there: Take Samoset Road off Route 6 in Eastham.

The Cape Cod National Seashore—This 27,000-acre ecological wonderland includes endless stretches of unbelievably beautiful beaches, 60-foot sand dunes, steep cliffs, wind-bitten moors, salt marsh, freshwater ponds and woodlands. Undisturbed and undeveloped, the area runs from Chatham to Provincetown and is laced with some of the Cape's finest hiking and bicycle trails (see "Bicycling Cape Cod and the Islands" and "Hiking Cape Cod and the Islands" in this chapter).

What follows are some of the National Seashore's most renowned beaches and ponds. For more information visit the **Salt Pond Visitor Center** (Route 6, Eastham; 508-255-3421) or the **Cape Cod National Seashore Headquarters** (Route 6, South Wellfleet; 508-349-3785).

Coast Guard Beach—"On its solitary dune my house faced the four walls of the world," wrote Henry Beston of the place he built in 1927 on this extraordinary beach. In 1972 the house washed away in a storm, but Beston's experiences are chronicled in a wonderful book, *The Outermost House*, available at most Cape Cod bookstores. Rugged and wild Coast Guard Beach goes on for as far as the eye can see. Bordered by cliffs, marsh grass and tributaries, a red-and-white coast guard station sits on a bluff overlooking the beach. The beach is ideal for long walks, sunbathing, swimming and surfing.

Facilities: Restrooms, lifeguards; groceries nearby in Eastham. *Swimming:* Good, but can be rough at times. *Surfing:* Good; waves break at high tide.

Getting there: Take Doane Road off Route 6 near Eastham.

Nauset Light Beach and **Marconi Beach**—These impressive beaches —bordered by towering, shrub-covered cliffs—are right next to each other. Long, steep wooden stairways descend to the clean, white sand beaches. The imposing cliffs and expansive vistas make you feel very small and in awe of it all. Walk north along the shore for a quiet spot in the summer, when the beaches get crowded. On the road to Nauset Beach is **Nauset Light**, a classic red-and-white lighthouse, one of the most photographed sights on Cape Cod.

Facilities: Restrooms, showers (at Marconi only), lifeguards; groceries in Eastham or Wellfleet. *Swimming:* Excellent, but watch undertow.

Getting there: Nauset Light is located off Route 6 at the end of Cable Road and along Nauset Light Beach Road in Eastham. Marconi is located off Route 6 on Marconi Beach Road in Wellfleet.

Great Pond and **Long Pond** (★)—Wellfleet has some of the most idyllic freshwater ponds on the Cape. Less than a mile from wild-looking shoreline, these two offer a completely different nature experience. Densely wooded and pine-scented, they look like mountain ponds. The sparkling water is fresh and invigorating. Long Pond has a lovely shaded grassy area with picnic tables, a small sand beach and a float in the water. Great Pond is approached via wooden steps leading down from the parking lot overlooking the pond. It has a pretty sandy beach. Half-hidden houses lie along some of the shoreline.

Facilities: Picnic tables; groceries are found nearby in Wellfleet. *Swimming:* Calm.

Getting there: To reach Great Pond, take Calhoon Hollow Road off Route 6 in Wellfleet; for Long Pond, take Long Pond Road off Route 6 in Wellfleet.

Race Point Beach and **Herring Cove Beach**—"Here a man may stand, and put all America behind him," wrote Thoreau in his book *Cape Cod*. Located at the end of the Cape, both beaches have magnificent 360° views of brilliant sky, ocean, dunes and a silver sea of beach grass. On cloudy days, the winds shift, the colors change and a minimalist environment unfolds. When the sun shines, everything shimmers. Both beaches offer long stretches of clean white sand surrounded by acres of untouched land. Bicycle paths and hiking trails are everywhere.

Facilities: Restrooms, showers, lifeguards, snack bar (Herring Cove only); groceries nearby in Provincetown. *Swimming:* Good.

Getting there: To reach Race Point, take Race Point Road off Route 6 in Provincetown; for Herring Cove, take Province Land Road in Provincetown.

The South Cape

This part of the Cape is a hodgepodge of scenic villages, inexpensive motels, mini-malls and gas stations. To explore it from Provincetown, head back on Route 6 to Route 28 in Orleans, a pleasant yet unassuming residential area. At Chatham, Route 28 swings around to the west and runs along the south shore of the Cape along Nantucket Sound.

Chatham, one of the most stylish towns on the Cape, has exquisite inns, good restaurants and beautiful shops. It's a very Ralph Lauren kind of place where everyone looks as though they play tennis.

Chatham's **Information Booth** (533 Main Street; 508-945-0342) is in the middle of town. At the end of Main Street, you run into **Shore Road,**

(Text continued on page 136.)

FROG

RABBIT

DUCKS

MUSKRAT

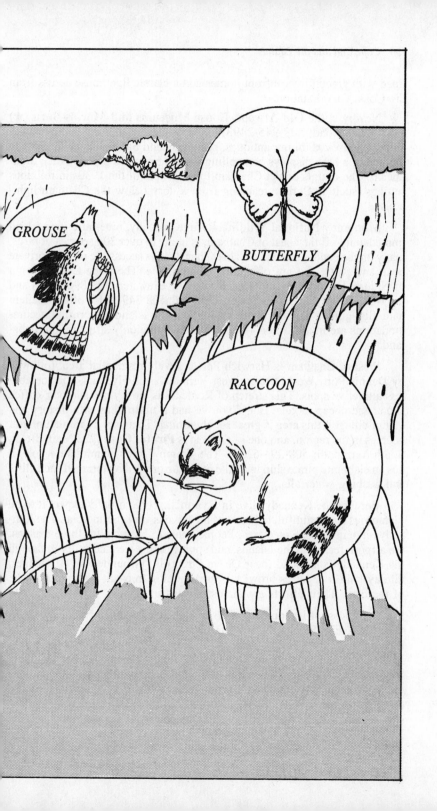

lined with graceful oceanfront homes and a classic lighthouse across from the Coast Guard station.

Nearby is the **Old Atwood House Museums and Murals Barn** (★) (347 Stage Road; 508-945-2493), an unassuming-looking 1752 brown-shingle house exhibiting antiques, sea shells and Sandwich glass. Next to the house, a barn displays compelling murals by realist painter Alice Stall-knecht. The murals depict Chatham townspeople of the 1930s in religious settings, such as Christ preaching from a dory below the Chatham light-house.

Monomoy National Wildlife Refuge, a sandy, nine-mile-long island immediately off the coast of Chatham, is home to over 300 species of birds, many on the endangered species list. The island is accessible only by private boat, and parts of it are off limits to the public. The Cape Cod Museum of Natural History (Main Street, Route 6A, Brewster; 508-896-3867) and the Wellfleet Bay Audubon Society (Route 6; 508-349-2615) offer excellent naturalist-guided day and weekend tours of the island. Overnight accommodations are in a restored 1825 lighthouse—the only structure on the island.

West of Chatham is Harwich Port, a lovely residential area, followed by Dennis Port, West Dennis, West Yarmouth and Hyannis, considerably less attractive spots. This stretch of Route 28 is mostly gas stations, coffee shops and cheap motels. But if you've had it up to here with history and quaint villages, this area is great for slumming. There are 11 miniature golf courses in the region, and one of the best is **Pirates Cove** (728 Main Street, South Yarmouth; 508-394-6200). The Trump Tower of miniature golf, it has an elaborate pirate ship in a fake pond surrounded by terraced rock cliffs and gushing waterfalls.

Because the Kennedys live in **Hyannis**, people usually expect it to be glamorous and beautiful, but most of the town is very commercial. The Kennedys live in the one nice area. People come to Hyannis for three reasons: the airport, ferries to the Islands, and spying on the Kennedys. Even though the Kennedy compound (near Ocean Street) is surrounded by tall hedges, all day long tour buses prowl this area, hoping to catch a glimpse of one of the clan. Their efforts are almost always in vain.

Southwest of Hyannis is the **New Alchemy Institute** (★) (237 Hatch-ville Road, East Falmouth; 508-564-6301), a nonprofit center that explores new and ancient methods of organic farming, landscape design, greenhouse horticulture and composting. If you're the least bit interested in gardening, this place is a great find. Visitors can wander around the grounds on their own or take a guided tour. There's a compost greenhouse, a geodesic greenhouse dome, vegetable gardens utilizing natural pesticides and striking flower gardens such as an all white one that looks like an enormous wedding bouquet.

At the western end of the South Cape is **Falmouth**, a large and bustling town with a beautiful village green surrounded by some of the Cape's loveliest historic homes. One of these, which houses the **Falmouth Historical Society** (Village Green, Palmer Street), is a creamy yellow, hip-roofed 1790 Colonial building with a widow's walk. Close by is the **Katherine Lee Bates House** (16 West Main Street; 508-548-4857; admission), the former home of the author of "America The Beautiful." Now a small museum, it has books about the author and poet.

The rest of downtown Falmouth isn't as scenic, but it does have a number of beautiful, high-quality clothing and home furnishing stores. The **Falmouth Chamber of Commerce** (Academy Lane; 508-548-8500) is right off Main Street.

Immediately south of Falmouth is **Woods Hole**, a small, deeply wooded, hilly village that's home to the **Woods Hole Oceanographic Institute**. The Institute isn't open to the public; it's strictly a research facility ranked in stature alongside Scripps Institute of Oceanography in California. However, the nearby **National Marine Fisheries Service Aquarium** (Water Street; 508-548-7684) is open to the public in the summer. Its sole function is to preserve regional species, hence everything in its 16 display tanks is native to the area: cod, lobster, flounder. The aquarium also has a seal tank.

Woods Hole is a scientific community, and it looks and feels like a small university town, with a good bookstore, craft galleries and cafés. This is also where you can catch a ferry for the Islands—Martha's Vineyard and Nantucket.

SOUTH CAPE HOTELS

A romantic, dark brown 1807 farmhouse, the **Nauset House Inn** (Beach Road, East Orleans; 508-255-2195) is within walking distance of beautiful beaches. One of the inn's most memorable features is a magnificent 1907 conservatory with white wicker furniture, exotic plants and grapevines. Most of the 14 guest rooms have tiny floral-print wallpaper, stenciling and antiques such as a hand-painted Victorian cottage bed. Guest rooms in the main house share baths; those in an adjacent carriage house have private baths. Moderate.

Chatham Bars Inn (Shore Road, Chatham; 800-527-4884), one of Cape Cod's most luxurious grand resorts, looks like the kind of place where everyone should be wearing white linen and playing croquet. Built in 1904 as a hunting lodge, the horseshoe-shaped gray-shingled inn sits high on a gentle hill overlooking Pleasant Bay. An expansive brick veranda runs the length of the inn. The inviting lobby has white wicker chairs with chintz cushions, potted palms and shiny hardwood floors. The 44 guest rooms and 26 cottages are decorated with lace curtains, English pine antiques and wicker. The 80-acre resort has a private beach, swimming pool, tennis courts, fishing, sailing, windsurfing, golf and two restaurants. Ultra-deluxe; breakfast and dinner included.

Chatham Village Inn (★) (207 Main Street, Chatham; 945-0792) is located one block away from the historic Chatham lighthouse. The small, attractive inn stands in an exclusive residential neighborhood of winding streets and impeccably restored oceanfront homes. Chatham village is about a ten-minute walk. The inn's guest rooms are decorated with Early American touches such as wall stenciling and antique furnishings. The Tavern restaurant is located in front of the inn. Deluxe.

Most of Chatham's hotels are expensive, but not the **Bow Roof House** (59 Queen Anne Road; 508-945-1346), a real bargain. Located in the heart of the high-rent district, five minutes from the beach, this cozy 200-year-old sea captain's house feels comfortable and casual. A brick patio overlooking a scenic, winding road makes an ideal spot for tea or cocktails in the afternoon. Guest rooms are appointed with Colonial bedspreads and nondescript furniture, but they're far apart and private. Budget.

Motels aren't known for beautiful landscaping, but **Pleasant Bay Village** (Route 28, Chatham Port; 508-945-1133) is a welcome exception. Located across from salt marsh, ponds and ocean, Pleasant Bay boasts impeccably maintained rock and flower gardens that are so lush you hardly notice the 58 nondescript guest rooms and apartments. Deluxe to ultra-deluxe.

Accommodations in Harwich Port are limited and expensive, but Harbor Walk (★) (6 Freeman Street; 508-432-1675) is a refreshing exception. The white 1880 bed and breakfast with gingerbread trim is within walking distance of the town's exclusive beaches. Six guest rooms (three with shared bath) are decorated with a mix of new and antique furnishings. A porch runs the length of this house overlooking the yard. Budget.

Augustus Snow House (528 Main Street, Harwich Port; 508-430-0528) is one of the most beautiful inns in New England. Every inch of this magnificent Queen Anne Victorian is flawless. It's known for its fabulous wallpapers—some have ceiling borders of antique roses or clusters of fall flowers that look hand painted. Then there are the unbelievable bathrooms—one has an antique Victorian mahogany sink, another a black-and-white diamond tile floor and claw-footed tub. The dazzling public rooms are appointed with thick oak and mahogany paneling, moreen drapes, etched-glass french doors and period antiques. Located in a quiet, affluent town, the inn has five guest rooms and serves a full breakfast. Ultra-deluxe.

Route 28 from Dennis Port to Hyannis is dotted with one indistinguishable motel after another. However, if you head south toward the beach you'll find some nice surprises, like **The Lighthouse Inn** (★) (Lighthouse Road, West Dennis; 508-398-2244). This sprawling, 61-room, Old World resort is remarkably affordable for Cape Cod. Located on the ocean, the inn is formed around a lighthouse that stood at nearby Bass River during the 19th century. The ambience is friendly and unpretentious. Activities include shuffleboard, horseshoes, miniature golf, hiking in nearby woods, swimming in the pool or ocean and nightly entertainment. A children's director provides day and evening babysitting. Guest rooms in the main inn are simply furnished, and separate cottages are also available. Rates include breakfast and dinner. Ultra-deluxe.

Located in elegant Hyannis Port, the **Simmons Homestead Inn** (288 Scudder Avenue; 508-778-4999) was once a country estate. Built in 1820, this gracious inn is furnished with quality antiques, canopy beds, white wicker and brass. Sweeping porches overlook gardens leading down to Simmons Pond. Unlike those in most old inns, the ten guest rooms here are fairly large. Deluxe to ultra-deluxe.

Tucked away on a tree-lined street in elegant Centerville is **The Inn at Fernbrook** (★) (481 Main Street; 508-775-4334), a large, graceful Victorian with wraparound porches, gables and turrets. The understated decor doesn't compete with the dramatic house. The six guest rooms and cottage are beautiful and unusual. The Spellman Room, named after Cardinal Francis Spellman, a former owner of the house, has a pyramid-shaped ceiling, stained-glass windows, tiled fireplace and enormous Victorian canopy bed. Not surprisingly, it resembles a church. For all its grandeur, there's something serene and unaffected about Fernbrook. It's a good place for collecting one's thoughts. Deluxe to ultra-deluxe.

Horizons Inn (★) (2 Wyoming Avenue, Falmouth Heights; 508-548-3619) is in a magical little neighborhood of turn-of-the-century, dairy-barn-shaped houses with turrets, gables and gingerbread. Hidden from tourists, the inn sits on a bluff overlooking the ocean. Its Craftsman-style public rooms have dark oak paneling and bookshelves. Comfortable guest rooms are simply furnished. Moderate.

The **Village Green Inn** (40 West Main Street, Falmouth; 508-548-5621), a white clapboard house with green shutters and a picket fence, is typical of many of the homes in Falmouth's historic district. Guest rooms are decorated with antiques and four of the five rooms have fireplaces. One room has impressive wood inlay floors, another thick, luxurious carpeting. Deluxe.

In 1849 Captain Albert Nye built **Mostly Hall** (27 Main Street, Falmouth; 508-548-3786) for his New Orleans bride, who refused to live in a traditional Cape Cod house. Typical of houses in New Orleans' garden district, this striking, raised Greek Revival mansion has ten-foot windows, louvered shutters, a wraparound veranda, wrought-iron fence and a 35-foot center hall—which is why it's called Mostly Hall. Only steps away from Falmouth's historic village green, this elegant inn is set well back from the road and hidden from view by a large hedge. The six guest rooms are spacious and airy, furnished with antiques, including four-poster beds. Full breakfast included. Deluxe.

SOUTH CAPE RESTAURANTS

The Mad Hatter might have enjoyed **The Arbor** (Route 28 and 6A, Orleans; 508-255-4847). Fanciful and eclectic, it has a front yard filled with goofy junk—a bear riding a bicycle, a big wagon wheel. The inside is a hodgepodge of antique clutter—old bottles, vintage photos, tinware, colored pitchers. Tables are set with mismatched china. Somehow it all comes together in a magical way. The menu is as varied as the decor. Many dishes are elaborate and rich—saltimbocca, veal marsala, sweetbread with ham and mushroom caps. Behind the restaurant, the Binnacle Tavern (508-255-7901) is a cozy spot for a drink and light entrées. Moderate.

Kadee's Lobster and Clam Bar (Beach Road, Orleans; 508-255-6184) is a colorful, inexpensive sea shanty draped with lobster traps and buoys. The menu includes steamers, lobster, corn-on-the-cob, kale soup and chowder. An outdoor patio shaded by umbrellas is the perfect spot for beer and fried clams after a day at the beach. Moderate.

A popular local hangout, especially on Saturday nights, **Land Ho** (Route 6A and Cove Road, Orleans; 508-255-5165) is a fish and chips place. The new white clapboard restaurant has red-and-white checked tablecloths, dark wood walls and nautical decorative touches. The menu offers classic Cape Cod fare—fried and broiled seafood, hearty salads, fries and burgers. The bar is a friendly watering hole. Budget.

On their days off, chefs from the Cape's most noted restaurants often dine at **Nauset Beach Club** (★) (221 Main Street, East Orleans; 508-255-8547), on the road to beautiful Nauset Beach. The small gray-shingle restaurant, with indoor and outdoor dining, offers consistently good, reasonably priced Northern Italian fare such as saltimbocca, caesar salad, veal scallopine, a wide range of seafood dishes such as gnocchi and scallops, grilled shrimp scampi and a host of creative pasta dishes. Moderate.

The **Impudent Oyster** (15 Chatham Bars Avenue, Chatham; 508-945-3545) is the place to go for traditional or exotic seafood in an informal setting next to a park. The lunch and dinner menus change with the seasons. Many of the dishes have Chinese, Mexican or Vietnamese touches—mussels with sake, ginger and Szechuan peppers; or shrimp, Chinese noodles and vegetables in a Hunan sauce. There are also excellent non-seafood items, such as succulent Sicilian veal roast, fragrant with rosemary, oregano, thyme, basil, prosciutto and wine. The cheerful restaurant has skylights, a cathedral ceiling and stained-glass panels. Moderate.

In historic Chatham village, **Christian's** (443 Main Street; 508-945-3362) draws an attractive tennis and yachting crowd. The bar does as much business as the two restaurants. A formal dining room on the ground floor, appointed with Oriental rugs, dark wood floors and lace tablecloths, serves dishes such as codfish with champagne hollandaise sauce, seafood sauté, veal chops and lobster ragoût, and boneless split duck. An informal, wood-paneled restaurant and bar on the second floor serve quiche, hamburgers and sandwiches. Ultra-deluxe downstairs; moderate upstairs.

The **Chatham Bars Inn** (Shore Road, Chatham; 508-945-0096), one of the Cape's most luxurious resorts, also has an excellent restaurant. The food, service and location are superb, the crowd elegant old money. The large dining room overlooking the water is decorated in soothing shades of beige, cream and green. In the summer the restaurant offers a menu of healthful, low-calorie dishes such as steamed halibut, venison carpaccio and raspberry torte, plus a regular dinner menu—roast loin of hare with plum sauce, sea scallops Provençal, chilled cucumber soup, salmon soufflé. Reservations are mandatory if you aren't a guest at the inn. Ultra-deluxe.

Very pretty and very French, **Café Elizabeth** (31 Sea Street, Harwich Port; 508-432-1147) bills itself as a French country restaurant, but the sophisticated food, flawless service, hushed atmosphere and prices feel more big-city than country quaint. Housed in a former sea captain's home, the restaurant has small, intimate dining rooms with lace curtains and linen tablecloths in soft shades of blue and cream. Specialties of the house include lobster, veal, lamb and beef medallions with different sauces, chicken curry and shrimp sautéed in cognac. The deserts are truly memorable. Try the chocolate truffles laced with Grand Marnier, whipped cream and chocolate sauce. Ultra-deluxe.

The **Cape Half House** (★) (Route 28, West Harwich; 508-432-1964) looks like just another surf-and-turf restaurant, but the food is surprisingly inventive and reasonably priced. Dishes range from salmon with lobster over fettucine and filet mignon with green peppercorn sauce to fisherman's stew and clam cakes. Diners sit in captains chairs at wood tables, and the rough wood walls are adorned with antique boating tools. Moderate.

It looks like something out of a Popeye cartoon. Half of **The Lobster Boat** (681 Main Street, West Yarmouth; 508-775-0486) is a gray-shingled Cape Cod cottage with cheerful red window boxes, and the other half is an enormous red, white and blue lobster boat that seems to have grown out of the restaurant's side. The dining room overlooks a small harbor, and the decor is very yo-ho-ho with captains chairs, dark wood and rope. The atmosphere is free and easy, with lobster prices to match, plus a traditional menu featuring a variety of fried, sautéed and broiled seafood. Moderate.

Penguins Go Pasta (331 Main Street, Hyannis; 508-775-2023) sounds casual, but it's a formal restaurant serving traditional and nouvelle Italian cuisine such as roasted peppers and eggplant, tricolored pasta, braised rabbit with polenta and osso bucco. Exposed brick walls, potted palms, burgundy tablecloths and waiters in black tie contribute to the sophisticated ambience. Deluxe.

An attractive, reasonably priced nouvelle Italian restaurant, **The Hot Tomato** (Route 28, Mashpee; 508-477-8100) is in Mashpee Commons, an upscale outdoor mall that resembles an old-fashioned Cape Cod village. The clapboard restaurant has lofty ceilings, cream-colored walls, honey-warm wood and terra cotta floors. Fare includes thin-crusted focaccia pizza, pasta, grilled swordfish with basil butter, and veal chop with marsala and rosemary. A take-out counter sells desserts, pasta, salads, sandwiches and espresso. Moderate.

Set in an 18th-century, red-and-white inn on the edge of a duck pond, the **Coonamesset Inn** (Jones Road and Gifford Street, Falmouth; 508-548-2300) serves lobster pie, oysters on the half shell, quahog chowder, Indian pudding and other classic New England dishes. The Cahoon Room, one of three dining rooms serving breakfast, lunch and dinner, features primitive paintings by artist Ralph Cahoon depicting life on Cape Cod. The inn and restaurant are tastefully decorated with Shaker and Colonial furnishings. Moderate to deluxe.

Located on a winding country road, **Peach Tree Circle** (★) (Old Palmer Avenue, Falmouth; 508-548-2354) is the perfect place for lunch on a lazy summer day. A combination restaurant, farm stand and gourmet health food store and bakery, it is shaded by large graceful trees. Fresh flowers and vegetables are sold in front of the small gray building with nasturtiums climbing its walls. Lunch offerings include big, healthy sandwiches, quiche, chowder, salads, soups, desserts, fruit and cheese. Budget.

Locals come to **Fishmonger's Café** (56 Water Street; 508-548-9148) because it isn't as touristy as some other Woods Hole restaurants. The café serves California food—avocado tostada, tabouli, garden vegetable salad—and Cape Cod classics like fried clams, grilled fish and chowder. The atmosphere is casual, the decor salty dog. Paned windows overlook the harbor, and there's a counter where you can have lunch or a beer while you're waiting for the ferry. Budget to moderate.

SOUTH CAPE SHOPPING

For beautiful hand-painted dishes from all over the world and European kitchen utensils, visit **Chatham Cookware** (524 Main Street, Chatham; 508-945-1550), a white, pink and blue cottage-style store. Fresh and sweet, it also sells excellent bakery goods and coffee.

There are countless stores on Cape Cod selling nautical decorative items, but few are as classy as **The Regatta Shop** (582 Main Street, Chatham; 508-945-4999). Here you find silver dolphin bracelets, sleek hand-carved model boats, colorful fish-shaped magnets and a wide collection of museum-quality maritime posters.

The Spyglass (618 Main Street, Chatham; 508-945-9686) is a wonderful salty dog store filled to its dark brown rafters with antique telescopes, microscopes, opera glasses, barometers, nautical antiques, paintings and charts.

If you want your home to look as if it belongs in a magazine, **Marshmallow** (193 Main Street, Falmouth; 508-548-6506) has everything you need: hand-painted plates, shaker pine boxes, tables and armoires, blue-and-white striped couches and chairs, reproduction wicker, woven throws and cotton rugs.

SOUTH CAPE NIGHTLIFE

There's live entertainment nightly in the summer (weekends during the winter) at the **Chatham Wayside Inn** (512 Main Street; 508-945-1800). The music is blues and rock-and-roll. Cover.

Asa Bears (415 Main Street, Hyannis; 508-771-4131), a lounge and restaurant in a Victorian mansion, offers a little bit of everything—jazz, classical guitar, big bands, cabaret and more. Entertainment takes place in the attractive library lounge.

Musicals and comedies are presented at the **Academy Playhouse** (120 Main Street, Orleans; 508-255-1963), in a former town hall built in 1837.

Cape Cod Melody Tent (21 West Main Street Rotary, Hyannis; 508-775-5630), an enormous theater-in-the-round, hosts big names such as Willie Nelson, Tony Bennett, Kenny Rogers, Bob Newhart and Ray Charles.

Falmouth Playhouse (Theatre Drive, North Falmouth; 508-563-5922), on the shores of scenic Coonamesset Pond, stages Broadway musicals such as *Evita, Dream Girls* and *42nd Street*. Ranked in excellence alongside the Cape Playhouse, it has its own restaurant and lounge.

SOUTH CAPE BEACHES AND PARKS

South Cape beaches are usually big and wide with huge parking lots and ample facilities. Located in residential neighborhoods, they're popular with college students and families. Because this is the ocean side of the Cape, the water tends to be rougher than on the North Cape.

Hardings Beach—Big, straight and long, this popular beach attracts a gregarious crowd of kids. Expensive houses on a hill overlook Hardings, a spot good for swimming, sunning and hanging out with the neighbors. Modest little sand dunes with paths running through them lead down to the beach.

Facilities: Restrooms, showers, lifeguards, snack bar; groceries nearby in Chatham. *Swimming:* Good.

Getting there: Take Barn Hill Road off Route 28 to Hardings Beach Road in Chatham.

West Dennis Beach—The view at the end of this sprawling beach, where the Bass River empties into the Atlantic, is of old summer houses with green lawns spilling down toward docks dotted with boats. There's even a windmill. West Dennis Beach attracts big summer crowds; its parking lot can accommodate 1600 cars. Popular with surfers, families and teens, the beach is bordered by flat salt marsh laced with tributaries from the river.

Facilities: Restrooms, showers, lifeguards, swings, snack bar; groceries nearby in Dennis. *Swimming:* Good.

Getting there: Take School Street off Route 28 to Lighthouse Road in West Dennis.

Ashumet Holly Reservation and Wildlife Sanctuary (★)—A treat for birdwatchers and botany enthusiasts, this 45-acre reserve abounds with many varieties of holly grown by the late Wilfred Wheeler, who donated the land to the Audubon Society. You're definitely out in the wilds here, and nothing looks manicured or fussed over. An easy-to-maneuver trail goes past a pond, forest, dogwoods, rhododendrons and a grove of Franklinia, an unusual, fall flowering shrub discovered in Georgia in 1790. Wildlife includes catbirds, so named because they make a meowing sound, belted kingfishers and pond critters such as ribbon snakes, catfish and turtles with bright yellow heads and dark shells. Since 1935, a barn on the property has been a nesting site for swallows. Every spring up to 44 pairs arrive to nest, then depart in late summer.

Facilities: None; groceries are found nearby in Mashpee; information, 508-563-6390.

Getting there: Located at 286 Ashumet Road in East Falmouth.

Old Silver Beach—This spot, popular with a college-aged crowd, doesn't look like a typical Cape Cod beach. A large, modern resort is on the north end, and most of the beach houses in the immediate area are fairly new. A lovely cove to the south is protected by wooded cliffs jutting down to the shore. The beach itself is somewhat rocky.

Facilities: Restrooms, showers, lifeguards, snack bar; groceries nearby in Falmouth. *Swimming:* Calm; lessons are available.

Getting there: Located off Route 28A on Quaker Road in Falmouth.

Martha's Vineyard

With its museum-perfect villages, Gothic Victorians and scenery that mimics the coast of Ireland, it isn't any wonder this enchanting island swells from around 14,000 year-round residents to 80,000 in the summer.

Discovered in 1602 by the English explorer Batholomew Gosnold, it was named by him for its proliferation of wild grapes. Who Martha was is anybody's guess, but legend has it she may have been Gosnold's daughter or his mother.

An active whaling port in the 19th century, "the Vineyard," as it's often called, became a popular summer resort in the 20th century. Today it is a summer home to an impressive number of celebrities fiercely protected from ogling tourists by proud locals. Jackie Onassis, Carly Simon, James Taylor, Diana Ross, Beverly Sills, Walter Cronkite, Mike Wallace, William Styron and Art Buchwald have homes here.

One way not to impress the natives is to rent a moped. In the summer these noisy (but fun to drive) motorized bicycles sound like swarms of angry bees. They're considered a menace on the road, and bumperstickers that read "Outlaw Mopeds" are everywhere.

Only 20 miles long and 10 miles wide, the Vineyard can easily be toured in a day. Ferries dock at Oak Bluffs or Vineyard Haven, or you can fly in (see the "Transportation" section in this chapter). The Vineyard's three towns—Vineyard Haven, Oak Bluffs and Edgartown—are on the northeast side of the Island. The western end, known as "up-island," is comprised of bucolic farmland, moors and magnificent beaches.

In the '30s, Lillian Hellman and Dashiell Hammett spent their summers in **Vineyard Haven**, and ever since writers have been coming to this friendly, unpretentious town. Vineyard Haven has never attracted tourists like Edgartown, the island's main resort town, and therein lies its charm. It has the best bookstore (Bunch of Grapes), attractive shops, restaurants and a handful of wonderful inns. It's also home to the **Martha's Vineyard Chamber of Commerce** (Beach Road; 508-693-0085).

One historical sight of note here is the **Seaman's Bethel Museum and Chapel** (Union Street; 508-693-9317), built in 1893 to provide spiritual guidance to seamen and a refuge to shipwreck victims. Today it is part of a larger organization that still offers social services and ministry to seafarers. The bethel is open to the public, and the small museum houses a collection of seafaring artifacts.

Nearby stand the **Old Schoolhouse and Liberty Pole Museum** (110 Main Street). The schoolhouse, a sweet-looking, one-room, white-clapboard building with artifacts related to early island life, is right in the heart of town. The museum takes its name from a War of 1812 incident: British sailors tried to steal the Liberty Pole to replace a broken mast on their ship, but three young girls blew up the pole before the sailors could get their hands on it.

Oak Bluffs is only a couple of miles away. A must-see here is the **Camp Meeting Grounds** (also known as Cottage City), right off Circuit Avenue, the main drag through town. In 1835, Methodist church groups started holding annual summer meetings in Oak Bluffs, with hundreds of families living in tents for the occasion. Over time the tents were replaced by tiny whimsical cottages with Gothic windows, turrets, gables and eaves dripping with gingerbread and painted in a riot of colors—pink, green and white; peach, yellow and blue. Called "campground Gothic Revival," this is the only architecture native to the Vineyard. On Illumination Night in mid-August, in a custom dating back to 1870, hundreds of colorful glowing Oriental lanterns are strung up all over the cottages, creating a dazzling display of light.

With the exception of Cottage City and Ocean Park—a genteel neighborhood of Queen Anne Victorians overlooking the water on the road to Edgartown—most of Oak Bluffs is hamburger restaurants and T-shirt and souvenir shops. It has a funky, saltwater-taffy kind of charm. In the center of town is the **Flying Horses Carousel** (Circuit and Lake streets; 508-693-9481), an antique, hand-carved wooden carousel still in operation. In each horse's glass eye is a replica of a small animal.

Not far from Oak Bluffs is elegant **Edgartown**. With its narrow streets, brick sidewalks, graceful yachts and pristine Greek Revival and Federal-style architecture, it looks like a living museum. Prim, proper and perfect, Edgartown is a bit oppressive.

Edgartown has always been a town of considerable wealth and power. Prosperous whaling captains retired here, building magnificent homes along **North Water Street** that can still be seen today. Today's residents include many Boston Brahmin families. Life revolves around the formidable yacht club, where expert sailor Walter Cronkite reigns supreme.

The main thing to do in Edgartown is walk along its tree-lined streets window shopping and admiring the homes. The **Dukes County Historical Society** (Cooke and School streets; 508-627-4441; admission), tucked away on a beautiful side street, maintains a museum exhibiting scrimshaw, ship models, period costumes and whaling gear such as harpoons.

Right off the coast of Edgartown is **Chappaquiddick Island**. Called "Chappy" by locals, it is accessible by ferry (see the "Transportation" section in this chapter). There's not much to do here except go to the beach and take long walks. The island, of course, is noted for the tragic auto accident involving Senator Edward Kennedy that resulted in the death of a young woman. Chappaquiddick Road ends at Dyke Bridge, site of the mishap, which has now fallen apart and is off limits to cars and people. The island's only other road, Wasque Road, leads to Wasque Point, a beautiful natural area.

The up-island section of the Vineyard includes West Tisbury, Chilmark and Gay Head, bucolic rural areas with lush green farms, meadows and scenic harbors. To explore this area from Edgartown, take the Edgartown–West Tisbury Road. It cuts through the middle of the island.

About the only thing in West Tisbury is **Alley's General Store (★)**, where locals sit on the front porch drinking coffee and glaring at tourists. On Saturday mornings, the big social event is the outdoor produce market at **Agricultural Hall (★)**, down the road from Alley's. Don't be fooled by the casual way the locals are dressed. Look closely and you'll see Rolex watches, $600 cowboy boots and maybe, if you're lucky, James Taylor. This area of the island is where many accomplished writers, musicians and artists make their homes.

From West Tisbury, follow the road to **Chilmark**. There's nothing to do here except admire the scenery and try to guess which unmarked dirt road leads to Jackie Onassis' guarded mansion.

The road ends at **Gay Head Cliffs**, towering ocean cliffs laced with multicolored bands of rust, lavender, wheat and charcoal. A popular tourist attraction, the cliffs are approached by a path lined with chowder and gift

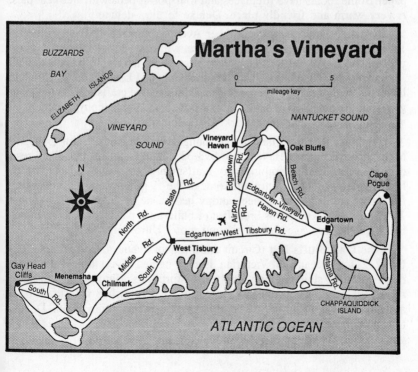

shops owned by the native Wampanoag Indians. (At the base of the cliffs on the beach, you can take a mud bath or swim in the nude—see "Martha's Vineyard Beaches and Parks".)

Leave Gay Head via Lighthouse Road and stop in peaceful **Menemsha**, a tiny fishing community that looks like a village on the coast of Ireland. Menemsha has a couple of restaurants, some good craft galleries and a scenic little **harbor** (★) that time forgot. From Menemsha head back to Vineyard Haven via North Road and State Road, which goes by **Chicama Vineyards** (★) (Stoney Hill Road, West Tisbury; 508-693-0309). The island's first and only winery, it offers guided tours and winetastings in an appealing shop that sells wine, homemade jam, mustard and herb vinegar.

MARTHA'S VINEYARD HOTELS

Upon entering the **Captain Dexter House** (100 Main Street, Vineyard Haven; 508-693-6564), you are greeted by the inviting aroma of cinnamon, cloves and warm bread. This meticulously restored 1843 white clapboard inn has sloping wood floors, Oriental rugs, fireplaces and many antiques. It's luxurious but not pretentious. The eight guest rooms are appointed with contemporary furnishings, Colonial antiques and period reproduction wallpaper. Some rooms have fireplaces and four-poster beds with lace canopies. A very warm and friendly place. Deluxe to ultra-deluxe.

Crocker House Inn (4 Crocker Avenue, Vineyard Haven; 508-693-1151) is tucked away on a quiet side street within walking distance of Vineyard Haven and the harbor. The eight guest rooms in this shingled Victorian are masterfully decorated. The octagonally shaped Lace Room is all white linen and lace; the Carpenter's Suite has impressive craftsman-style woodworking; the Sail Loft, a suite with harbor views and balcony, is decorated with ship models and brightwork. Ultra-deluxe.

A classic 1918 craftsman-style bungalow, **Thorncroft Inn** (★) (278 Main Street, Vineyard Haven; 508-693-3333) is on a quiet, tree-lined residential street. There's nothing very craftsman-like about the decor, which leans towards country Victorian. Some of the 19 guest rooms have working fireplaces and four-poster lace-canopy beds. One of the best things about Thorncroft is its enormous breakfast of buttermilk pancakes, bacon, french toast, quiche, sausage-cheese pie and more. Ultra-deluxe.

The **Oak Bluffs Inn** (Circuit and Pesquot avenues, Oak Bluffs; 508-693-7171), an oceanfront Victorian, is aptly named. Everything is made out of oak—walls, stairs, ceiling, cupboards, furniture. Many of the ten guest rooms are paneled entirely in wainscotting and furnished with brass beds and Oriental rugs. Continental breakfast is served on a sunny porch. Deluxe to ultra-deluxe.

With its elaborate windows and dormers, **The Victorian Inn** (24 South Water Street; 508-627-4784) looks formal from the outside, but it's an easygoing place located one block from Edgartown harbor. Guests enjoy the cool, private garden in the summer. The 14 guest rooms are sweet and tidy with canopy beds, floral bedspreads, antiques and some contemporary furnishings. Deluxe to ultra-deluxe.

The **Charlotte Inn** (South Summer Street, Edgartown; 508-627-4751) is one of the most elegant and luxurious inns in America. A sparkling white 1860 sea captain's house, it is nestled amid a profusion of flowers, lawns, wisteria and latticework. Guests check in at a gleaming English barrister's desk. Twenty-five meticulous guest rooms are appointed with fine English antiques, hand-painted china and equestrian prints. Suites, located in separate buildings, are quite extravagant—one has its own English cottage garden, another a bedroom balcony and palladium window. A continental breakfast is served in the inn's restaurant, L'Étoile, one of the finest dining establishments in New England and a favorite of Jackie Onassis. Ultra-deluxe.

The **Arbor** (222 Upper Main Street; 508-627-8137) is a quintessential New England cottage, fresh and white with a winsome vine-clad arbor, brick path and English garden. Located a couple of blocks from Edgartown's shopping district, the inn offers guest rooms simply but attractively appointed with antiques and fresh cut flowers. Tea is served in the old-fashioned formal parlor or in the garden. Moderate to deluxe.

Talk about off the beaten path. **Lambert's Cove Country Inn** (★) (Lambert's Cove Road, West Tisbury; 508-693-2298) is down a long country road deep in the woods. Surrounded by vine-covered stone walls, expansive lawns and apple orchards, the white clapboard inn is appointed with Shaker and Colonial-style antiques. Some of the 15 guest rooms have private decks, and one has a greenhouse sitting room. Guests have access to Lambert's Cove Beach, one of the Vineyard's most beautiful private beaches. On Sunday an elaborate, festive brunch is served. Deluxe.

One look at the **Captain R. Flander's House** (North Road, Chilmark; 508-645-3123) and you understand why it was featured in Martha Stewart's *Wedding Book*. The rambling, 18th-century farmhouse sits on a grassy knoll overlooking ancient stone walls, rolling meadows, grazing horses, a sparkling pond, ducks and woodlands. Chilmark is so peaceful and bucolic, it's no wonder the rich and famous have chosen to live here. The inn is simply furnished, but with scenery like this who needs decoration? Guest rooms (some with shared bath) are comfortable and sparsely appointed with antiques and country-style furnishings. Moderate to deluxe.

Breakfast at Tiasquam (★) (off Middle Road, Chilmark; 508-645-3685) lies on a slight hill overlooking rolling farmland, ponds and woods. This beautiful bed and breakfast is a tribute to fine 20th-century craftsmanship. Bathroom sinks are hand-thrown by local potter Robert Parrot, the exquisite cabinets are custom-made, doors are solid cherry, skylights are everywhere and some of the furnishings are by Thomas Moser, known for fine-crafted Shaker furniture. At breakfast, guests are served cinnamon french toast, corn-blueberry pancakes, freshly caught fish and more. Deluxe.

MARTHA'S VINEYARD RESTAURANTS

Only Edgartown and Oak Bluffs serve liquor, but you can bring your own when you dine in other towns.

A gray-shingled saltbox overlooking the harbor, rustic **Black Dog Tavern** (Beach Street Extension, Vineyard Haven; 508-693-9223) is a Vineyard institution popular with the yachting crowd. The best place to sit in the summer is an enclosed porch with beautiful ocean views. The fare is traditional—clams casino, baked scrod, roast duckling—with an emphasis on fresh seafood. Deluxe.

Café at the Tisbury Inn (Main Street, Vineyard Haven; 508-693-3416), a trendy establishment with cream-colored walls, deco light fixtures and gray industrial carpeting, attracts a young, stylish crowd. The menu includes grilled meat, poultry and seafood with different sauces such as Creole or rémoulade. Other dishes include lime chicken with pesto, seafood enchiladas and pastas. An awning-covered outdoor patio in front is a good spot for people watching in the summer. Moderate to deluxe.

Popular with locals, **Linden Street Café** (★) (72 Main Street, Vineyard Haven; 508-693-4480) looks like a coffee shop with old wooden booths and a long counter, but it serves one of the best budget dinners on the Vineyard. The traditional menu includes dishes such as stuffed sole, seafood lasagna, roast beef and more. Budget to moderate.

Papa's Pizza (158 Circuit Avenue, Oak Bluffs; 508-693-1400) isn't your average pizza parlor. This place has class. Located in a bright red, white and green storefront, it has an enormous dining room with a tin ceiling and walls, antique brass light fixtures and long wooden tables. The counter in back is solid granite—an elegant touch. Papa's serves lasagna, pizza, pasta and subs. The portions are healthy and hearty. Budget.

A high-profile watering hole and restaurant that resembles a French bistro, **The Oyster Bar** (162 Circuit Avenue, Oak Bluffs; 508-693-3300) attracts a chic, festive crowd. The green-and-yellow facade has rows of french doors that open to a cavernous dining room with tin ceilings, marbleized columns and an impressive 35-foot mahogany bar. People come here for oysters and champagne or a full meal. The menu includes dishes such as seafood pizza, wild smoked Scottish salmon appetizer and many grilled, sautéed and baked seafood and non-seafood dishes such as veal loin. Deluxe.

Small, white and bright, **Savoir Faire** (Post Office Square, Edgartown; 508-627-9864) is perfect for lunch. The cooking is done behind a counter piled high with delicious cakes and rich cookies baked on the premises. Dishes include oyster brie soup, caesar salad with grilled chicken, ceviche, goat cheese tart with sun-dried tomatoes, and roasted garlic. Takeout is available. Moderate.

With its salmon-colored walls, chintz banquettes and flower-bordered wallpaper, **Martha's Restaurant** (71 Main Street, Edgartown; 508-627-8316) is bright and feminine. Across the street from Edgartown's town hall, it serves a little bit of everything—stuffed sole, fettucine, enchiladas, steak Diane. There's even a sushi bar. At lunch, the restaurant attracts hordes of tourists; it's better to come for dinner. Moderate.

L'Étoile (27 Summer Street, Edgartown; 508-627-5187), in the Charlotte Inn, is perfect for a special occasion. An incredibly beautiful restaurant, it's in a 19th-century conservatory with skylights, bowed windows, a brick floor and lush plants adorned with twinkling Italian lights. In this romantic, fantasylike environment, contemporary French cuisine is served. The prix-fixe menu offers fresh game and seafood entrées. Sauces are light and aromatic, flavored with fresh herbs, exotic fruit, shiitake mushrooms and shallots. Ultra-deluxe.

On the way to Gay Head is **Feasts** (Bettlebung Corner, Chilmark; 508-645-3553), where you can have lunch and observe local artists or pick up picnic fixings and the *New York Times* while you have a cappuccino. The two-level restaurant and market has vaulted ceilings, white walls and a countrified high-tech look. An art gallery is on the mezzanine. The menu includes grilled tuna, fajitas, breast of duck salad and other nouvellish offerings. Moderate.

Even if you're not knocked out the by the surf-and-turf menu (steak, salad, lobster, etc.) at the **Home Port** (Basin Road, Chilmark; 508-645-2679), come here for the mesmerizing view. The rustic, brown-shingled restaurant overlooks sand dunes, rolling green pastures and idyllic Menemsha harbor. An outdoor patio is available for summer dining. Deluxe.

Small, exclusive **Beach Plum Inn** (North Road, Menemsha; 508-645-9454) is easy to miss. A tiny sign points the way down a dirt road to a building without a sign that looks like a private home with a terraced rock and flower garden. Once you've figured out where to go, you'll be glad you came. The intimate dining room has large picture windows overlooking Menemsha Harbor, a white grand piano and subtle mauve and green decorative touches. Diners have a choice of five prix-fixe dinner entrées that must be ordered in advance when making reservations. The creative cuisine features items such as steamed lobster, duck with honey-curry sauce and rack of lamb. Ultra-deluxe.

MARTHA'S VINEYARD SHOPPING

Bunch of Grapes Bookstore (Main Street, Vineyard Haven; 508-693-2291) is a writers hangout. The best bookstore on the island, it has shelves well-stocked with quality fiction and poetry. The store regularly hosts autograph parties.

Wicker and linen, pine antiques, knubby hand-knit sweaters and hand-painted coffee mugs can be found at **Bramhall & Dunn** (Main Street, Vineyard Haven; 508-693-6437).

Silver & Gold (64 Main Street, Vineyard Haven; 508-693-0243) is the best place on the island for beautiful jewelry. Many pieces artfully combine modern and antique styles.

Take It Easy Baby (142 Circuit Avenue, Oak Bluffs; 508-693-2864), a very hip used clothing store, sells World War II leather flying jackets, vintage Hawaiian shirts, stuffed armadillos and incredibly chic French and Canadian foul weather gear such as flannel-lined sou'westers. A fun store for the terminally cool.

Edgartown Wood Shop (55 Main Street, Edgartown; 508-627-9853), a cavernous red brick room, sells handsome hand-crafted wooden spoons, plates, bread platters, bowls, cutting boards, Christmas ornaments, tables and benches. Prices are reasonable, and the craftsmanship is superb.

MARTHA'S VINEYARD NIGHTLIFE

Throughout the year at the **Vineyard Playhouse** (Church Street, Vineyard Haven; 508-693-6450), local and equity actors star in Broadway plays such as *Noises Off*.

Island Theatre Workshop (P.O. Box 1893, Vineyard Haven; 508-693-4060) is the Vineyard's oldest theater group. Year-round it presents a wide range of plays and musicals performed by Vineyard actors. With no permanent home, it stages productions at different locations throughout the island.

Winton Marsalis, James Taylor and other musicians perform **Twilight Concerts** (The Tabernacle, Oak Bluffs; call WMVY radio station for schedule, 508-693-5000) in an open-air theater in scenic Cottage City.

Atlantic Connection (Circuit Avenue, Oak Bluffs; 508-693-7129), a hopping dance and music club, has live bands and entertainment by groups such as Taj Mahal, Leon Redbone and Queen Ida and her Zydeco Band. Cover.

Martha's Vineyard Performing Arts Center (Old Whaling Church, Main Street, Edgartown; 508-627-4440) offers cultural lectures, classic films, concerts and plays throughout the year. Located in an 1843 Greek Revival church, the center has featured stars such as Patricia Neal and Victor Borge.

Popular with the under-30 set, **Hot Tin Roof** (Martha's Vineyard Airport; 508-693-1137), formerly owned by Carly Simon, has live rock-and-roll bands and a jumping dance floor in the summer.

MARTHA'S VINEYARD BEACHES AND PARKS

Beaches in rural West Tisbury, Chilmark and Gay Head are dramatic, untamed and less crowded than beaches near the Vineyard's three towns. But the parking lots are for residents only, and in the summer guards check to see if cars have resident stickers. Nonresidents ride bikes to these beaches. Shore fishing is excellent from all south shore beaches.

Nantucket Sound Beaches—Strung together along protected Nantucket Sound are Oak Bluffs Town Beach, Joseph A. Sylvia State Beach, Bend-in-the-Road Beach and Lighthouse Beach. This is where the movie *Jaws* was filmed, but don't panic, this isn't shark country. The narrow, gently curved shoreline has clean sand and calm water. Swimming lessons are offered at some of the beaches, and bicycle paths run alongside the shore, which is bordered by ponds, salt marsh and summer homes. A stately lighthouse overlooks Lighthouse Beach.

Facilities: Lifeguards; groceries in Oak Bluffs or Edgartown. *Swimming:* Calm.

Getting there: Located along Beach Road between Oak Bluffs and Edgartown.

Cape Pogue Wildlife Refuge and **Wasque Reservation** (★)—If you want to get away from it all, take the two-minute car and passenger ferry from Edgartown to these wilderness areas on Chappaquiddick Island, an undeveloped peninsula of vast, empty beaches and moors. The refuge and reservation are adjacent to each other and form the northeastern tip of the Vineyard. Both offer an assortment of low dunes, ponds, tidal flats and cedar thickets. Wildlife abounds, including noisy least terns, piping plovers, common terns and American oystercatchers. East Beach, part of the Cape Pogue Wildlife Refuge, is the best spot for swimming.

Facilities: None; closest groceries in Edgartown; information, 508-693-3453. *Fishing:* East Beach is great for blue fish. *Swimming:* Good at East Beach, but sometimes rough.

Getting there: Cape Pogue is located at the end of Chappaquiddick Road on the other side of Dyke Bridge. At the time of this book's publication, the bridge had fallen apart and was unsafe, and plans to repair it were not yet final. Wasque Point is located at the end of Wasque Road.

South Beach—Also called Katama Beach, this popular, three-mile-long, Atlantic-facing beach is ideal for swimming and body surfing. Wide, expansive and flat, it is surrounded by heath dotted with 20th-century homes—a rare sight in Martha's Vineyard. In the summer the air is soft and warm from southeasterly winds.

Facilities: Restrooms, lifeguards; groceries nearby in Edgartown. *Fishing:* Excellent. *Swimming:* Excellent, but watch undertow.

Getting there: Located off Katama Road, south of Edgartown.

Manuel Correleus State Forest—Right in the center of the Vineyard lie 3900 acres of towering evergreens, scrubland, ponds and streams. Laced with bicycle paths, as well as hiking trails carpeted with soft, thick pine needles, the cool, hushed forest offers a peaceful respite from the Vineyard's wind-bitten moors and wide-open beaches.

Facilities: None; groceries in Edgartown or West Tisbury.

Getting there: Located between West Tisbury and Edgartown off Airport Road.

Long Point Wildlife Refuge (★)—A never-ending, loosen-your-teeth dirt road is the only way to get to this mystical, magical wildlife refuge. The road forks here and there; just stay on the widest part and eventually you come to a small parking lot. Shortly beyond lies an endless grass and huckleberry-covered heath that looks like a prairie with two enormous ponds. Tisbury Great Pond and Long Cove are home to black ducks, bluebills, ospreys, canvasbacks and swans. Beyond the ponds you'll discover a sea of silver beach grass and a white sand beach.

Facilities: None; groceries 15 minutes away in West Tisbury. *Fishing:* Excellent. *Swimming:* Good, but can get rough.

Getting there: This place is very difficult to find. It's one mile west of Martha's Vineyard Airport off Edgartown-West Tisbury Road on Deep Bottom Road, a deeply rutted dirt road without a sign. It's best to ask locals for directions.

Gay Head Clay Cliffs Beach—Nude swimming, mud baths and majestic scenery are just some of the reasons people break the law to come to this exceptional beach. Parking is limited to 20 minutes, and nudity is illegal, but that doesn't stop anyone from swimming in the buff or slurping around in silky, soft mud holes at the base of colorful Gay Head Cliffs. A beautiful spot for sunning, swimming and beachcombing.

Facilities: Restrooms, snack bars, groceries at top of cliffs. *Fishing:* Excellent. *Swimming:* Good, but can be a little rough.

Getting there: Located at the western tip of the Vineyard at the end of State Road, which is also called South Road in Gay Head.

Cedar Tree Neck Sanctuary (★)—The raucous chirping of king fishers, song sparrows and Carolina wrens is the first thing to greet you at this 200-acre preserve. This is their kingdom, and what a spectacular place it is. Follow one of two well-marked paths through hilly woods of beech, sassafras, red maple, hickory oak and bettlebung. Soon the sky opens up, and, out of nowhere, extraordinary vistas appear of deep ponds, rolling sand dunes and the ocean beyond. Paths lined with ferns, moss and mushrooms lead down through the woods to an elevated catwalk and the shore.

Facilities: None; groceries in West Tisbury. *Swimming:* Not permitted here.

Getting there: From State Road in West Tisbury, take Indian Hill Road to a dirt road with a Cedar Tree Neck sign. The road goes down a hill to the parking lot.

Nantucket

Located 30 miles out to sea from Cape Cod, this magical, fog-shrouded island is a study in contrasts. With its historic homes and cobblestone streets, it looks like storybook land, circa 1800. Yet it has sophisticated New York City/San Francisco-style restaurants and Madison Avenue shops. Outside of town, Nantucket is a bittersweet world of rolling moors, wild roses and windswept saltbox cottages that appear to have sprouted from the earth itself.

Nantucket was first sighted in 1602 by Captain Bartholomew Gosnold on his way to Martha's Vineyard. English settlers and Quakers farmed the land until the 1830s, when it was one of the busiest whaling ports in the world, a fact noted by Herman Melville in *Moby Dick*. In the 1870s, when kerosene started to replace whale oil as a fuel source and whales were becoming scarce, the industry started to decline and Nantucket lost 60 percent of its population. A depression followed, but around the turn of the century tourism blossomed and the island prospered once again.

Nantucket is so small and flat you can zip across it on a bicycle in about two hours or by car in 30 minutes. There are almost as many bicycle paths as roads, and bicycle rental shops abound on the wharf where the ferries dock. Like Martha's Vineyard, the only way to get here is by ferry or plane (see the "Transportation" section in this chapter).

There is only one town, Nantucket, but it can occupy you for hours or days if you enjoy historic homes, museums, fine restaurants, shopping and gallery hopping.

At the foot of Main Street and the wharf is the **Nantucket Chamber of Commerce** (Main Street; 508-228-1700). Benches are everywhere, so you can sit down and map out an itinerary or just people watch. Nantucket is a busy, colorful town inhabited by George and Barbara Bush types, yuppies and camera-toting tourists. Tail-wagging labradors wander about, and the local gentry stand on corners sipping coffee and chatting.

Nantucket has many historic homes, landmarks and museums. Not to be missed is the **Thomas Macy Warehouse** (Straight Wharf; 508-228-1700; admission), on the wharf where the ferries dock. In 1846 Thomas Macy (of Macy's Department store fame) built the two-story brick warehouse after a fire destroyed most of the town. Today it is a small, attractive brick and wood museum with historical, geological and art exhibits, including a 13-foot diorama of the waterfront before the great fire. A recorded voice tells the story of the fire.

The **Whaling Museum** (Broad Street; 508-228-1736; admission) is a couple of blocks north of the Chamber of Commerce. A former whale-oil refinery with enormous cross beams, this rustic old building is as fascinating as its exhibits, which include a whale skeleton, a lighthouse lens and a whaleboat.

The **Jethro Coffin House** (Sunset Hill and West Chester streets) is Nantucket's oldest house. Built in 1686, this classic saltbox is characteristic of late-17th-century Massachusetts Bay Colony homes.

If you walk up Main Street past the shops, you'll find many elegant mansions built during the heyday of whaling. Nearby stands the **Maria Mitchell Science Center** (Vestal and Milk streets; 508-228-9198). Mitchell, a Nantucket native, was the first person to discover a comet with a telescope, and the first female member of the American Academy of Arts and Sciences. The center, named in her honor, includes a natural science museum with an impressive insect collection, a library, aquarium, observatory and the house in which Mitchell was born. The center conducts summer field trips.

About a five-minute walk from here on Prospect Street stands the **Old Mill**, a classic red-and-gray-shingled windmill that's one of Nantucket's most photographed sights. In the summer when the mill is operating you can see the intricate wooden gears that used to grind corn.

For a heady dose of Nantucket country life, visit **Siasconset**, a dollsized hamlet of 17th-century pitched-roofed cod fisher shanties transformed into beguiling summer homes. In spring and early summer this endearing village looks as though it's been attacked by roses. Everywhere you look wild pink roses are climbing over fences, up sides of houses and over roofs, creating a dusty pink, gray and sage landscape.

Called "Sconset" by nearly everyone, the village lies seven and a half miles from Nantucket town on Milestone Road, which is bordered by a smooth, flat bicycle path. There isn't much to do here except enjoy the scenery and go to the beach. Sconset has a couple of restaurants, including renowned Chanticleer, and Summer House, one of Nantucket's prettiest inns.

On the way back to town, take scenic Polpis Road. It goes past **Sankaty Lighthouse** and **The Moors**, magnificent, wind-bitten low-lying land that resembles a Persian carpet in the fall. The road also passes the **Windswept Cranberry Bogs (★)**, where you can watch cranberries being harvested in the fall.

The rest of Nantucket is all huckleberry covered-heath dotted with houses surrounded by spectacular beaches (see "Nantucket Beaches and Parks").

NANTUCKET HOTELS

Nantucket has an astonishing number of inns and bed and breakfasts, but perhaps the best known is the **Jared Coffin House** (29 Broad Street;

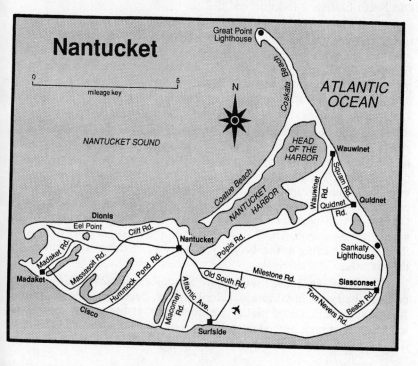

508-228-2400). Built in 1845 by wealthy shipowner Jared Coffin, it features guest and public rooms appointed with antiques, Oriental rugs, crystal chandeliers, period wallpaper, marble fireplaces and canopy beds. A busy, festive establishment, it feels like a big city hotel of the 19th-century. Sixty guest rooms span six different buildings. Deluxe to ultra-deluxe.

Right down the street from the Jared Coffin House is one of the island's few bargain spots, **The Nesbitt Inn** (21 Broad Street; 508-228-0156). The white Victorian was built in 1872 as an inn and has been operated by the Noblit family since 1914. Some of the original furniture still remains. One room has a wood-rimmed bath tub that accommodates two. There are 13 guest rooms, each with a sink and six with shared bath. The inn's front porch is a great place for people watching. Upon arrival, guests are greeted with a bottle of wine and flowers. Budget.

Anchor Inn (66 Centre Street; 508-228-0072), a narrow gray clapboard house with black shutters and window boxes, is typical of Nantucket's many bed and breakfasts. Old and quaint, with narrow halls and sloping wood floors, it offers 11 cozy guest rooms hidden under dormers and eaves in small irregular spaces. Once the home of the Gilbreth family of Frank Gilbreth's *Cheaper by the Dozen*, the Anchor is furnished with Colonial and Shaker-style antiques. A continental breakfast is served in a cheerful blue-and-white breakfast room, and a brick patio in back overlooks scenic Old North Church. Moderate and deluxe.

The Woodbox Inn (29 Fair Street; 508-228-0587) is one of Nantucket's oldest and most delightful inns. Built in 1709, it exudes New England charm, with low-beamed ceilings, wood-paneled walls and walk-in fireplaces. The three guest rooms and six suites are furnished entirely in period antiques. Located in a quiet part of town away from all the hoopla, it has an excellent restaurant that can get a little noisy on weekends. Deluxe to ultra-deluxe.

The Wauwinet (Wauwinet Road; 508-228-0145), a lavish resort outside of town, is decorated to the hilt with English pine antiques, green wicker, primitive folk art, Victorian carpet runners, white wainscotting and pickled floors. The 35 guest rooms sport gentle sea breeze colors like pale smoke, sage and cream. White wrought-iron furniture sits prim and proper on a vast lawn overlooking the ocean, and rockers line a wraparound porch. Guests are transported to and from town in an impeccably restored old woody station wagon. The Wauwinet is one of the most expensive inns on the island, attracting a well-heeled young crowd. There is a restaurant on the premises. Ultra-deluxe.

The Summer House (South Bluff, Siasconset; 508-257-9976), a rose-covered bed and breakfast overlooking the ocean, is quintessential Nantucket, the kind of place you dream about but rarely find. Not surprisingly, it once graced the cover of *New York* magazine. Quaint little low-slung,vine-clad cottages surrounding the main inn look as though they were designed by and for elves. But they're much bigger and lighter than they seem, and the decor blends just the right mix of rustic country charm. Rooms have features such as a fireplace, jacuzzi, rough-hewn beams, painted wood floor and rosebud wallpaper. There's a lively restaurant. Ultra-deluxe.

If you haven't stayed in a youth hostel since you gave up your back-pack, you might want to try it again when you see Nantucket's **Star of the Sea Youth Hostel** (★) (for reservations, write or call American Youth Hostels, Hostel Operators Dept., P.O. Box 37613, Washington, DC 20013; 202-783-6161). Located across from Surfside Beach, this historic wooden A-frame building looks like a cross between a Swiss chalet and a church. Originally a life-saving station, it today attracts a lot of young people, Europeans, senior citizens and cycling groups. Volleyball is played in a large yard in back bordered by sand dunes. The rows of twin beds inside remind most people of camp. As with most youth hostels, Star of the Sea is closed to guests during the day. Budget.

NANTUCKET RESTAURANTS

Among Nantucket's astonishing number of sophisticated restaurants, one of the best is **Le Languedoc** (24 Broad Street; 508-228-2552). Elegant and hushed, it has taupe walls, contemporary art and dark carpeting that are strictly big-city, yet its navy-and-white checked tablecloths and Windsor chairs add a touch of country. The menu includes poached halibut, black peppered salmon, veal chops and rack of lamb with a honey-mustard sauce. A lot of care goes into the presentation. Deluxe.

American Seasons (★) (80 Centre Street; 508-228-0397) serves nouvelle cuisine with Louisiana, Creole, Cajun and Mexican touches—blue corn tortillas with grilled shrimp and guacamole, pan-fried tuna with alligator fritters and red chili sauce, steak with bourbon gravy and straw potatoes. The restaurant is in a white cottage with window boxes spilling lush pink impatiens. The green-and-white interior is romantically lit with hurricane lamps, and New Age music plays softly in the background. The crowd is young, happy and casual. Deluxe.

People stand in line for **The Brotherhood** (23 Broad Street) because it serves reasonably priced basics—burgers, sandwiches and fried fish—in an 1840 whaling bar with a low ceiling, brick walls and weathered wooden tables. The Brotherhood is one of the few restaurants that serves until 12:30 a.m. Budget.

The Atlantic Café (15 South Water Street; 508-228-0570) is on a street that should be called Hamburger Row. Every restaurant on this block serves the same thing—burgers, beer and rock-and-roll. You can smell the fried food before you get here. In the day, the restaurant attracts families with small children, but at night it gets the college crowd. The Atlantic is a clean-looking establishment with white walls, wood beams and a bar in the middle surrounded by wooden chairs and tables. Moderate.

Espresso Café (40 Main Street; 508-228-6930) is good for a cappuccino and a designer brownie, picnic fixings or a casual lunch or dinner. It looks like an old-fashioned ice cream parlor with paddle fans, black-and-white tile floor, tin ceiling and ice-cream-parlor chairs. A tree-shaded brick patio is out in back. The food is trendy and hearty—cassoulet, soup, chili, pasta, thick pizza piled high with yuppie-loving ingredients such as sun-dried tomatoes and goat cheese. Budget.

One of Nantucket's most beautiful and versatile restaurants, the **Boarding House** (Federal and India streets; 508-228-9622) has a shady brick patio that's perfect for people watching and a lovely bar and café with floor-to-ceiling windows. (A woman could come to the bar alone and feel totally at ease.) A formal dinner is served in the cellar, a grottolike, candle-lit room with cream-colored arched walls. Dishes change with the seasons. Popular offerings, many served in both the café and dining room, include sautéed duck breast with fresh apples, sage and maple sauce, ravioli and wild mushrooms, free-range chicken and oysters with balsamic vinegar. Moderate to deluxe.

Le Chanticleer (40 New Street, Siasconset; 508-257-6231) is one of New England's most romantic restaurants. In spring, the many-windowed, gray-shingled house is covered with climbing roses, and the garden is a riot of pink, white and lavender flowers. The menu is creative to say the least—Muscovy duck with corn pancakes, foie gras with baked apple, fresh figs in sweet white wine and herbs, trout with salmon mousse and lobster ginger sauce. Many locals prefer the restaurant for lunch; dinner is a major production. Ultra-deluxe.

NANTUCKET SHOPPING

Hoorn Ashby Gallery (10 Federal Street; 508-228-9314), one of Nantucket's most beautiful galleries, sells contemporary paintings and still lifes, antique folk art such as a hand-painted blanket chests, blue and white pottery and more in a sun-filled room with wood-paneled walls, tall columns and floor-to-ceiling windows.

Many shops in Nantucket sell handwoven goods, but **Nantucket Looms'** (16 Main Street; 508-228-1908) blankets, throws and shawls are a cut above the rest. Popular designs include a voluminous, fluffy white blanket with thin navy stripes, and a pale pink shawl laced with foggy gray threads.

Nantucket Designs for Children (12 Orange Street; 508-228-2997) has sweet handmade clothes and furnishings that make grandmothers go weak at the knees: plaid school dresses, smocked sun dresses, chintz party dresses and little straw boaters.

Four Winds Craft Guild (Straight Wharf; 508-228-9623) specializes in the island's two oldest crafts: antique and new lightship baskets and scrimshaw. The former are tightly woven, bowl-shaped baskets used as purses or decorative items; scrimshaw are items decoratively carved from whale bone and teeth. Both crafts were created in the 18th century by lighthouse keepers and sailors with idle time on their hands. Lightship purses are a status symbol among the island's conservative ladies. The older the basket, the better.

19 Petticoat Row (19 Centre Street; 508-228-4144), one of the island's prettiest home furnishing and gift shops, sells French and English antique bed linens, hand towels, pillow shams, scented soap, potpourri, hand-painted dishes and many other temptations. During the whaling days, the street this shop is on was called Petticoat Row because of all the wives who ran stores here while their husbands were at sea.

NANTUCKET NIGHTLIFE

The **Nantucket Arts Council** (Box 554; 508-228-2227) presents classical music concerts in the Methodist church at the corner of Main and Centre streets. **Nantucket Musical Arts Society** (Box 897; 508-228-3735) gives classical concerts in the First Congregational Church on Centre Street.

Throughout the year, **The Theatre Workshop of Nantucket** (Bennett Hall, 62 Centre Street; 508-228-4305) stages plays such as *A Mid-Summer Night's Dream*, *Murder in the Cathedral* and *Alice in Wonderland*.

Actors Theatre of Nantucket (Folger Hotel, 89 Easton Street; 508-228-6325) has something for everyone: serious drama, light comedy (like Neil Simon's *I Ought To Be In Pictures*), musicals, modern dance, comedians and more. A children's matinee series features musicals, magicians and plays.

For cocktails and live entertainment in a comfortable old tavern, try the **Tap Room at Jared Coffin House** (29 Broad Street; 508-228-2400).

Fun, funky and informal, **The Chicken Box** (Daves Street; 508-228-9717), a bar with live entertainment, presents a variety of bands—rock-and-roll, reggae, rhythm-and-blues and others. Open year-round. Cover for bands.

NANTUCKET BEACHES AND PARKS

Bike paths go to Madaket, Dionis, Surfside and Siasconset Beaches, and fishing is great from those on the south shore. Nantucket doesn't have parks, per se, but the **Nantucket Conservation Foundation** (Larsen-Sanford Center, 118 Cliff Road; 508-228-2884) owns and manages more than 7700 acres of undeveloped land open to the public to explore. Foundation land is identified by roadside maroon posts topped with a wave and seagull logo. If you want to know more, stop in and talk to the foundation folks, a friendly group of people who are happy to discuss the island's flora and fauna.

Dionis Beach—If it weren't for a white rock on which the word Dionis is painted, you'd never find this beach, which is ideal for swimming, picnics and cookouts (fire permits available from the Nantucket fire station). Beyond the large dirt parking lot, a path leads through tall sand dunes to the beach. These are Nantucket's only dunes, and they are protected from natural erosion and people by a fence. The beach has some rocks and seaweed. During low tide, a sand bar stretches out into the water quite a distance.

Facilities: Lifeguards; groceries are found in downtown Nantucket. *Swimming:* Calm.

Getting there: Located three miles west of town off Eel Point Road in Dionis.

Madaket Beach—One of Nantucket's most beautiful bicycle paths ends at this spectacular western-facing beach. Everything about this long, wide beach is just right. The sand is white and clean, the surf fantastic, the sunsets the best on the island.

Facilities: Lifeguards, restaurant; groceries nearby in downtown Nantucket. *Fishing:* One of the best spots on the Vineyard. *Swimming:* Good, but can get rough.

Getting there: Located at the end of Madaket Road in Madaket.

Cisco Beach (★)—The road to this out-of-the-way beach goes past scenic Hummock Pond and rolling heathlands. The wide-open beach is a free and easy place where you can walk for miles on white sand. Popular with seasoned beach rats and young surfer types, it doesn't attract many families because the facilities are limited.

Facilities: Lifeguards; groceries in downtown Nantucket. *Fishing:* Excellent. *Swimming:* Excellent, but watch the undertow. *Surfing:* Good in the summer and fall. *Windsurfing:* Good, but choppy.

Getting there: Located at the end of Hummock Pond Road in Cisco, four miles southwest of town.

Surfside—Narrow sand paths lace the moors leading to this massive beach. Because Surfside is only three miles from town, it gets very crowded in the summer. But it's a great beach—big, long and wide with small rolling dunes to explore and the best surf on the island. Surfside attracts families and college students. To get away from the crowds, walk east along the shore toward Siasconset and soon you'll discover long stretches of blissfully empty beach.

Facilities: Restrooms, showers, lifeguards, snack bar, swings; groceries nearby on Surfside Road. *Fishing:* Excellent. *Swimming:* Good, but watch undertow. *Surfing:* Good. *Windsurfing:* Good but choppy.

Getting there: Located at the end of Surfside Road, three miles south of town.

Siasconset Beach—This lovely eastern-facing beach six miles from town is in the village of Siasconset. People make a day out of bicycling or driving here to explore the beach and the town. Part of the beach is surrounded by grassy cliffs and dunes, then the land dips and becomes flat. To the left of the beach is Sankaty Lighthouse and the summer community of Quidnet. Walk south along the beach for an empty spot. Because of the wind, seaweed can be a problem.

Facilities: Playground, lifeguards; groceries and restaurants a short walk away. *Swimming:* Good, but surf can be heavy.

Getting there: Located seven miles east of town at the end of Milestone Road in Siasconset.

Great Point, Coskata and **Coatue Beaches** (★)—If you really want to leave civilization, consider exploring this narrow stretch of uninhabited land that wraps around Nantucket Harbor. It's like one giant sand dune surrounded by water. Driving through this desertlike landscape is an adventure, and those who make the trek can swim in calm waters lapping a deserted white sand beach and view a nesting ground for eagles, clam and oyster ponds, the remains of a shipwreck and the Great Point Lighthouse. Driving in this area requires an expensive ($60) permit and a four-wheel-drive vehicle equipped with everything you need to dig yourself out of a deep sand rut. Permits are available from the Nantucket Conservation Foundation (Larsen-Sanford Center, 118 Cliff Road; 508-228-2884). Beach Excursions Ltd. (Jeff Irion; 508-228-3728) offers a three-hour Jeep ride and picnic in the area. (Other tours and fishing excursions are advertised in the local paper.)

Facilities: None. *Fishing:* Fantastic shore fishing at Great Point, the northernmost point of land. *Swimming:* Calm on Nantucket Sound; not recommended on the Atlantic side, where the current and undertow are rough.

Getting there: Located at the northeast end of the island at the end of Wauwinet Road off Polpis Road.

Sanford Farm (★)—Owned by the Nantucket Conservation Foundation, this former dairy farm consists of 767 acres of classic Nantucket countryside. A magical place for quiet walks and private picnics, it has 15 miles of trails meandering through rare maritime heathlands that look like Scotland. Follow the trail past long and winding Hummock Pond down to the empty beach. In spring and summer Sanford Farm is lush with wildflowers, but its most beautiful time is fall, when the land is a tapestry of burgundy, sage, rose, gold and ivory. Deer can be spotted early in the morning and at dusk. Rare short-eared owls nest on the ground in the grass, and turtles live in the pond.

Facilities: None; groceries are 15 minutes away in downtown Nantucket. *Swimming:* Good, but undertow can be dangerous.

Getting there: Located west of town off Madaket Road near the intersection of Cliff Road and Madaket.

The Sporting Life

Cape Cod, Martha's Vineyard and Nantucket offer a staggering number of opportunities for fishing, boating and other water sports, as well as cycling, golf, tennis and more.

SPORTFISHING

Blue fish, stripped bass, tuna, cod and flounder are abundant. No license is required to fish, and tackle shops are everywhere. For detailed information on what to catch when, where and how, call the Massachusetts Division of Marine Fisheries (100 Cambridge Street, Room 1901, Boston, MA 02202; 617-727-3193).

Among the hundreds of charter and party boat outfits on Cape Cod, some of the most reputable include **The Albatross** (Sesuit Harbor, East Dennis; 508-385-3244), **Naviator** (Wellfleet town pier; 508-349-6003) and **Teacher's Pet** (Hyannis Harbor; 508-362-4925).

Martha's Vineyard has **Ruddy Duck Marine** (Edgartown Harbor; 508-627-4709), and in Nantucket there's **Albacore** (Straight Wharf; 508-228-1439) and **Moonshadow Sportfishing** (Straight Wharf; 508-228-1512).

SAILING, SURFING AND WINDSURFING

Cape Cod abounds with marinas and harbors where you can rent sailboats, wind surfing equipment, canoes and more. Try these establishments: **Cape Water Sports** (Route 28, Harwich Port; 508-432-8407), **Cape Cod Boat Rentals** (Route 28, West Dennis; 508-394-9268), **Jack's Boat Rental**

(Route 6, Wellfleet, 508-349-9808; Gull Pond, Wellfleet, 508-349-7553; and Nickerson State Park, Brewster, 508-896-8556) and **Flyer's Boat Rental** (131-A Commercial Street, Provincetown; 508-487-0895).

For sailboat rentals and lessons on Martha's Vineyard, there's **Wind's Up** (Beach Road, Vineyard Haven, 508-693-4252). **Laissez Faire** (Owen Park, Vineyard Haven; 508-693-1646) and **Ayuthia Charters** (Coastwise Wharf, Vineyard Haven; 508-693-7245) offer half-day and evening harbor sunset sails on beautiful wooden yachts. **Harborside Inn** (South Water and Main streets, Edgartown; 508-627-4321) rents small sailboats such as Boston Whalers.

In Nantucket, **Indian Summer Sports** (6 Steamboat Wharf; 508-228-3632) rents surfboards, windsurfing equipment, waterskis and body boards.

GOLF

Three of Cape Cod's most scenic public courses, among many, include **Ocean Edge** (Brewster; 508-896-5911), **Highland Golf Club** (Highland Road, Truro; 508-487-9201), right near the Cape Cod National Seashore, and **Harwich Port Golf Club** (Harwich Port; 508-432-0250).

On Martha's Vineyard **Mink Meadows Golf Course** (Franklin Street, Vineyard Haven; 508-693-0600) and **Farm Neck Golf Course** (County Road, Oak Bluffs; 508-693-2504) offer beautiful scenery.

Nantucket has **Maicomet Golf Club** (West Somerset Road; 508-228-9764) and **Siasconset Golf Club** (Milestone Road, Siasconset; 508-257-6596).

TENNIS

Most Cape Cod towns have a number of municipal courts. For names and addresses in specific towns, call the **Cape Cod Chamber of Commerce** (508-362-3225). Two privately owned public courts include **Mid-Cape Racquet Club** (193 White's Path, South Yarmouth; 508-394-3511) and **Bissell Tennis Courts** (Bradford Street, Provincetown; 508-487-9512).

Tennis is very popular on Martha's Vineyard. Most courts are private, but one exception is the **Mattakesett Tennis Club** (270 Katama Road, Edgartown; 508-627-9506). Municipal courts are at Church Street in Vineyard Haven, Niantic Park in Oak Bluffs, Robinson Road in Edgartown, Old Country Road in West Tisbury and the Chilmark Community Center on South Road.

Nantucket's **Sea Cliff Tennis Club** (9 Tennis Club Road; 508-228-0030) has nine clay courts, and **Jetties Beach Public Tennis Courts** (North Beach Street; 508-228-7213) is right near town.

(Text continued on page 168.)

Bicycling Cape Cod and the Islands

Cape Cod, Martha's Vineyard and Nantucket are cyclists paradises. The flat landscape is laced with miles of smooth, paved bicycle paths that meander past sand dunes, salt marsh, woods and pastures. What follows is a modest sampling of some of the best rides.

Short Bike Rides, by Edwin Mullen and Jane Griffith (Globe Pequot Press) is a handy little book that describes 31 bike rides on Cape Cod, Nantucket and Martha's Vineyard.

The **Cape Cod Rail Trail**, an eight-foot-wide bicycle path, runs along the old Penn Central Railroad tracks from Route 134 in South Dennis to Locust Road in Eastham past classic Cape Cod scenery—ponds, forest, saltwater and freshwater marsh, cranberry bogs and harbors.

Head of the Meadow, a moderately hilly bicycle path in the Cape Cod National Seashore in Truro, traverses some of the Cape's most dramatic scenery, including The Highlands—vast expanses of grassy knolls. The path starts at Head of the Meadow Road off Route 6 and ends at High Head Road.

Talk about dramatic scenery. The **Province Lands Trail** dips and turns past towering sand dunes, silvery mounds of wavy beach grass, two magnificent beaches and the Province Lands Visitors Center. The path starts at Herring Cove Beach parking lot at the end of Route 6 and includes many places where you can stop and picnic.

The **Shining Sea** bicycle path between Falmouth and Woods Hole is popular with experienced cyclists because it's hilly in some areas and very scenic. The path runs along Palmer Avenue in Falmouth, then down a hill past deep woods and historic homes, and it ends at Woods Hole harbor.

The **Oak Bluffs–Edgartown–Katama Beach** bike path on Martha's Vineyard is smooth and easy, even though it's ten miles long. Departing from Oak Bluffs, the flat path runs along the shore past lovely old homes, beaches, ponds and salt marsh to historic Edgartown, then through heathland dotted with occasional houses to magnificent Katama Beach.

From Vineyard Haven, the hale and hearty bicycle to **Menemsha** and **Gay Head** via State Road to West Tisbury, then Middle Road to the end. The ride is hilly in parts, but the scenery is breathtaking. The beaches in this area have residents-only parking lots, so bicycling is the only way a nonresident can enjoy them.

Bicycling on Nantucket is a snap. Smooth, flat bike paths parallel the island's two main roads. The five-mile **Madaket** bicycle path is the most scenic, dipping and winding past moors and ending at Madaket Beach, the western tip of the island. The seven-mile **Siasconset** path is a straight, flat line that goes past barren scrub pine and sandy scenery, ending at the village of Siasconset on the eastern end of the island.

BIKE RENTALS   Practically every town on Cape Cod has a couple of bicycle rental shops; try **The Little Capistrano Bike Shop** (Route 6, Eastham; 508-255-6515), **Arnold's** (329 Commercial Street, Provincetown; 508-487-0844), **The Outdoor Shop** (50 Long Pond Drive, South Yarmouth; 508-394-3819) or **Holiday Cycles** (465 Grand Avenue, Falmouth Heights; 508-540-3549).

Rentals in Martha's Vineyard include **Anderson's Bike Rentals** (14 Saco Avenue, Oak Bluffs; 508-693-9346) and **R. W. Cutler Bike** (Edgartown; 508-627-4052).

Nantucket's wharf has many bicycle rental shops; one of the biggest outfits is **Young's Bicycle Shop** (Steamboat Wharf; 508-228-1151).

WHALE WATCHING

Among the many excursions departing from Cape Cod, try **Hyannis Whale Watcher Cruises** (Millway Marina, Barnstable Harbor, Hyannis; 508-775-1622) and **Dolphin Whale Watch** (MacMillan Wharf, Provincetown; 508-255-3857).

CANOEING AND SEA KAYAKING

According to the folks at **Atlantic Sea Kayak Company** (1025 Main Street, 6A, West Barnstable; 508-362-6896), Cape Cod resident, author and kayak enthusiast Paul Theroux has been largely responsible for the growing popularity of this sport. Atlantic will help guide you to the best spots such as Great Marsh Harbor.

SKINDIVING

In Cape Cod rentals and instructions are available at **Cape Cod Diver's** (815 Main Street, Harwich Port; 508-432-9035) and **East Coast Divers** (237 Falmouth Street, Hyannis; 508-775-1185).

HORSEBACK RIDING

Liability insurance has gotten so high, most stables won't rent horses, but a few still do. On the Cape there's **Deer Meadow Riding Stable** (Route 137, East Harwich; 508-432-6580). **Eastover Farm** (West Tisbury–Edgartown Road, Martha's Vineyard; 508-693-3770) has trails along the beach and through the forest.

Transportation

Special note: For up-to-the-minute information on every conceivable way to get to Martha's Vineyard, Nantucket and Cape Cod short of walking on water, call the **Massachusetts Office of Travel and Tourism** (100 Cambridge Street, Boston; 617-727-3201).

The **Cape Cod Information Booth** (Sagamore Rotary; 508-888-5555) is right off the Sagamore Bridge, the entranceway to the Cape from Boston. In addition, there are 17 other information booths throughout the Cape.

BY CAR

Route 6 cuts through the middle of Cape Cod, ending at Provincetown. **Route 6A** runs along the north side of the Cape, and **Route 28** runs along Nantucket Sound. Both routes connect with Route 6 in Orleans.

BY AIR

Five airports serve Cape Cod and the Islands: **Logan International Airport** in Boston (see Chapter Two), Barnstable Airport and Provincetown Municipal Airport on Cape Cod, Martha's Vineyard Airport and Nantucket Memorial Airport.

Barnstable Airport in Hyannis is served by Ace Air, Air Link, Continental Express, Delta Air Lines, Edgartown Air, Nantucket Airlines and Northwest Airlines.

Cape Air services **Provincetown Municipal Airport**.

Flying into **Martha's Vineyard Airport** are Continental Express, Delta Air Lines, Edgartown Air and Holiday Airlines.

Nantucket Airport is serviced by Ace Air, Continental Express, Delta Airlines, Express Air and Nantucket Airlines.

For ground transportation from Barnstable Airport to Logan Airport and areas throughout southern Massachusetts, contact **ABC Airport Coach** (508-747-6622), **Brewster Taxi** (508-255-3277) or **Nauset Taxi** (508-255-6965). Taxis and car rentals listed below provide ground transportation to all other airports except Logan.

BY FERRY AND BOAT

Ferries and boats between Boston, Cape Cod, Martha's Vineyard and Nantucket require reservations in the summer. Throughout the year, the **Steamship Authority** (157 Spring Bars Road, Falmouth, Cape Cod; 508-540-2022) transports cars and passengers between Woods Hole, Hyannis, Oak Bluffs, Vineyard Haven and Nantucket.

The following ferries and boats operate seasonally and do not transport cars: **Hy-Line** (Ocean Dock, Hyannis; 508-775-7185) takes passengers to and from Hyannis, Nantucket and Oak Bluffs on Martha's Vineyard. **Cape Island Express** (1494 East Rodney French Boulevard, Billy Woods Wharf, New Bedford; 508-997-1688) operates between New Bedford and Vineyard Haven on Martha's Vineyard. The **Island Queen** (Pier 45, Falmouth; 508-548-4800) goes between Falmouth and Oak Bluffs on Martha's Vineyard. The **On Time** (Edgartown, Martha's Vineyard; 508-627-9794) travels between Edgartown and Chappaquiddick Island.

BY BUS

Greyhound (617-292-4700) offers frequent service to Boston, Falmouth and Hyannis. **Bonanza** (17 Elm Street, Falmouth; 508-548-7588) runs buses to and from Logan Airport, Hyannis, Woods Hole, Falmouth, Bourne, New Bedford, Fall River, Connecticut, Rhode Island and New York. **Plymouth and Brockton Street Railway Company** (17 Elm Street, Hyannis; 508-775-5524) has year-round express service to and from Logan Airport and local service along Route 6 on Cape Cod from Sagamore to Provincetown and along Route 28 from Hyannis to Chatham. **Peter Pan Bus Lines** (Plymouth-Brockton Bus Terminal, 17 Elm Street, Hyannis; 508-775-5524) offers service to Hyannis from Mount Holyoke, Springfield, Newton, Worcester and Albany, New York.

BY TRAIN

Amtrak (800-872-7245) runs between Boston and Hyannis with summer bus connections to towns throughout Cape Cod. The Amtrak Cape Codder runs between New York and Hyannis from May to September.

CAR RENTALS

Car rental agencies at Barnstable Airport include **Avis Rent a Car** (508-775-2888), **Hertz Rent A Car** (508-775-5825) and **National Car Rental** (508-771-4353).

Budget Rent A Car (508-487-1539) serves Provincetown Municipal Airport.

Martha's Vineyard Airport has **Adventure Rentals** (508-693-1959), **All-Island Rent A Car** (508-693-6868), **Budget Rent A Car** (508-693-1911) and **Hertz Rent A Car** (508-627-4127).

Nantucket Airport agencies include **Budget Rent A Car** (508-228-5666), **Hertz Rent A Car** (508-228-9421), **Nantucket Windmill Auto Rental** (508-228-1227) and **National Car Rental** (508-228-0300).

PUBLIC TRANSPORTATION

Cape Cod Regional Transit Authority B-Bus Service (585 Main Street, Dennis; 508-385-8311) offers door-to-door minibus service (reservations required) and regular route service throughout the area. **Cape Cod Regional Transit Authority** (508-385-8311) makes five daily roundtrips along Route 28.

On Martha's Vineyard, from late May to mid-October, **Island Transport** (508-693-0058) runs shuttle buses between Vineyard Haven, Oak Bluffs and Edgartown. Less frequent service is available up-island; call the above number for schedules. Nantucket doesn't have public transportation. Most people get around with rental cars or bicycles.

TAXIS

Taxis serving airports in this area are as follows: Barnstable Airport, **All Points Taxi** (508-778-1400), **Hyannis Taxi** (508-775-0400) and **Town Taxi of Cape Cod** (508-771-5555); Provincetown Airport, **Martin's Taxi** (508-487-0243) and **Mercedes Cab** (508-487-9434); Martha's Vineyard Airport, **Hathaway's Taxi** (508-627-4462) and **Shaw's Taxi** (508-693-2828); Nantucket Airport, **All Points Taxi** (508-228-5779).

CHAPTER FIVE

Massachusetts Coast

Immortalized in the past by Herman Melville in *Moby Dick*, the Massachusetts coast today remains fertile territory for the imagination. This magnificent stretch of windswept coast abounds with historic seaside villages, vintage lighthouses, glorious beaches and history that reads like an adventure story complete with witches and pirates, authors and artists, Pilgrims and American natives, sea captains and Moby Dick.

An ethnic melting pot of Portuguese fishermen, Yankee blue bloods, old salts and the Irish (who seem to be everywhere), coast residents are very proud of where they live. North Shore loyalists wouldn't think of moving to Plymouth or New Bedford, and vice versa.

What unifies everyone is the sea. Rich and poor alike have miniweather stations on their roofs to determine wind direction, and everyone reads tide charts. Kids learn how to fish, sail and dig for clams when they're five years old.

That all-encompassing sea is, of course, what lured Europeans to these shores in the first place. One hundred years before the Pilgrims stepped foot on Plymouth Rock, English adventurers fished the waters around the Massachusetts coast. Between 1600 and 1610, explorers Samuel de Champlain and Bartholomew Gosnold sailed to Gloucester.

Aboard the *Mayflower*, 102 Pilgrims landed in Plymouth in 1620, establishing the first permanent settlement in New England. By 1640, about 2500 of the new settlers lived in eight communities. Although they came to America to seek religious freedom, the Pilgrims persecuted Quakers and anyone else who didn't adhere to their strict Puritan religion. Their intolerant thinking helped fuel one of the most infamous pieces of American colonial history—the Salem witch trials of 1692, in which 20 women were executed for practicing "witchcraft."

Fortunately by the 1700s the focus was more on commerce than religion. Salem sailing vessels had opened routes to the Orient, thus establishing the famous China trade and Salem's reputation as a major port. Shipbuilding and commercial fishing also flourished everywhere along the coast.

Evidence of the wealth gleaned during these years is apparent in the amazing number of 18th- and 19th-century mansions built by sea captains that dot the region. Impeccably restored by a people in love with the past, these coast homes make up an architectural feast bulging with Greek Revival, Federal, Queen Anne, Victorian Gothic, Colonial and classic saltbox structures. Historic villages and buildings throughout the area enable visitors to see the evolution of America's unique architectural style.

During the 1800s, artists and writers discovered the inspirational charms of the coast. Rudyard Kipling and Winslow Homer lived north of Boston in Rocky Neck, one of the country's oldest artist colonies. Nathaniel Hawthorne wrote about Salem, which he called home, in *The House of the Seven Gables*. Melville immortalized whaling in New Bedford.

To this day, creative people are drawn to the Massachusetts coast, now supported by light industry, fishing and a tourist industry that just keeps growing.

We have divided the coast into three geographic areas. The North Shore (everything above Boston to the New Hampshire border), the Plymouth area (from Boston south toward Cape Cod) and the New Bedford area, which includes Fall River.

The North Shore wears many faces. Immediately north of Boston are affluent commuter towns such as Marblehead, where prep schools, yachts and turn-of-the-century seaside mansions are a way of life. Nearby lies Salem, known for architecture, witches and maritime museums. Above Salem juts lovely Cape Ann, where Bostonians enjoy seaside minivacations without the hordes of travelers found on Cape Cod. Major spots on Cape Ann are the salty old fishing port of Gloucester and Rockport, an artist-colony-turned-resort. Along the northern coast above Cape Ann lies Newburyport, a scenic 19th-century town on the New Hampshire border.

Plymouth, of course, is "America's Home Town." In this area you find Pilgrim lore, historic villages, coastal pastures and fields of cranberries. New Bedford and Fall River combine factory outlets, whaling museums, scenic ports and a few lovely hidden beaches.

Whenever you choose to visit the Massachusetts coast, you're bound to be impressed. The scenery is unparalleled, the architecture magnificent, the seafood plentiful, the history fascinating. And you're sure to discover spots that seem untouched by the centuries, as welcoming now as they were to the first English explorers.

North Shore

The North Shore is a real sleeper. Unspoiled and relatively uncommercial, it's a place where you can still discover hidden inns, restaurants, beaches and parks. This vacation area and bedroom community to Boston

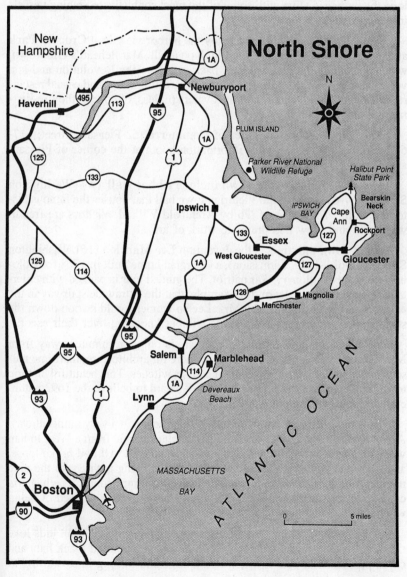

is populated by investment bankers, Yankee blue bloods, fishermen, artists and history buffs. An explorer's destination, it's perfect for people who like to go it on their own.

To explore this area from Boston, take the Callahan tunnel to Routes 1A and 129 north to Marblehead, a small village of clapboard houses, holly-hocks and cobblestone streets. Marblehead is sailboat country. All summer long the harbor is alive with some of the most sophisticated racing vessels in America.

A good place to picnic and enjoy the harbor view is at **Crocker Park** at the western end of Front Street, high on a hill. Marblehead's **Old Town**, which surrounds the harbor, dates back to before the Revolution and is a very pleasant place to stroll. It has many interesting shops and casual restaurants. Locals tend to ignore out-of-towners (unless, of course, they're first-rate sailors).

The **Marblehead Chamber of Commerce** (62 Pleasant Street; 617-631-2868) maintains a visitor information booth at the corner of Pleasant and Spring streets.

Historic sights in Old Town include **Abbot Hall** (★) (Washington Square; 617-631-0528), the Victorian town hall that houses the famous historic painting *The Spirit of '76* by Archibald Willard. Visitors are free to wander in and view this dramatic work of art.

Right down the street is the **Jeremiah Lee Mansion** (161 Washington Street; 617-631-1069; admission), a Georgian home built in 1768 for Colonel Lee, a Revolutionary War patriot. The guided tour is packed with entertaining anecdotes: we learn, for example, that the extrawide stairway in the entrance hall was designed by Mrs. Lee so women could swoop down the stairs in their enormous hoop skirts without knocking over their escorts.

Salem, the largest North Shore town, is only ten minutes away from Marblehead on Route 114. People come here for architecture, maritime museums, Nathaniel Hawthorne and, of course, witches. This beautiful historic town is so civilized and proper looking, it's hard to believe the 1692 witchcraft trials ever took place here.

This macabre piece of American history began in a very innocent way. A group of teenage girls, who had learned black magic from a West Indian woman named Tituba, were diagnosed as bewitched. All hell broke loose, and everyone started accusing everyone else of being a witch. In the nine months to follow, 20 women were hung and 150 imprisoned. The hysteria came to an end when the wives of prominent men were accused of being witches.

Salem's three witch exhibits are somewhat commercial, but kids love them. Every day in the summer, children wearing pointed black hats and capes purchased at nearby witch boutiques stand in long lines waiting to get in. The saving grace of the exhibits is that they are in historic build-ings—not re-creations of haunted houses.

Salem Witch Museum (19½ Washington Square North; 508-744-1692; admission) is a computerized sound-and-light show. **Witch House** (310 Essex Street; 508-744-0180; admission) is the restored 1642 home of witch trial judge Jonathan Corwin. **Witch Dungeon Museum** (16 Lynde Street; 508-744-9812; admission) re-enacts the witch trials.

Tourist information booths are at **Riley Plaza** (Washington and Margin streets) and the **Central Wharf Warehouse** (Derby Wharf). For more in-formation stop at the **Chamber of Commerce** (Old Town Hall, 32 Derby Square; 508-744-0004). An easy way to see historic sights is to follow **Salem's Heritage Trail,** a self-guided walking tour indicated by a red line painted on the street.

To understand the real story of Salem, which was a major port in the 18th and 19th centuries, visit the Peabody Museum and Essex Institute. The first-rate **Peabody Museum** (161 Essex Street; 508-745-9500; admission) houses a treasure trove of objects acquired during Salem's active China trade days, such as an elaborate, moon-shaped, hand-carved wooden Chi-nese bed.

Essex Institute Museum Neighborhood (132-34 Essex Street; 508-744-3390; admission) consists of a history and decorative arts museum and four impeccably restored homes and gardens dating from 1684 to 1818. The museum isn't as grand as the Peabody, but the houses are fascinating, espe-cially if toured in chronological order. The architecture and craftsmanship is superb. Anyone who has ever renovated an old house will appreciate a special exhibit about the painstaking efforts that go into museum restoration work. Since bright colors were a sign of wealth in the 17th century, the 1804 Gardner-Pingree House, a fine neoclassical building, holds a few surprises. The kitchen is deep salmon and green; one bedroom wears a vivid peacock blue hue, while another sports canary yellow.

Chestnut Street, one of the most architecturally significant avenues in America, is near Essex Institute. Many of its 17th-century mansions were designed by Salem's famed Federal-period architect and woodcarver, Sam-uel McIntire. These brick and wood houses are simple in their design, yet the overall effect is graceful and elegant.

Pickering Wharf, a short walk from Chestnut Street, is a new but made-to-look-old commercial development of tourist shops and chain res-taurants. About a block east stands **Derby Wharf**—a good area for strolling along the harbor.

Even though it's often crowded with tourists, there's something roman-tic and compelling about the **House of Seven Gables** (54 Turner Street; 508-744-0991; admission), located down the street from Derby Wharf. Built in 1668, the dark, almost black house is framed by ocean and sky. The tall, imposing gables look a bit like witch hats (although this thought probably wouldn't come to mind in another town). Inside, a labyrinth of cozy rooms with low ceilings, narrow passageways and secret stairs add to the ancient feeling of the place. The guided tour includes a good short film about how the house inspired Nathaniel Hawthorne to write his famous novel.

Northeast of Salem, scenic Route 127 hugs the coast and follows Cape Ann, which juts out quietly into the Atlantic to its tip at Pigeon Cove. First you'll come upon the residential towns of Manchester and Magnolia, known for their old money, private schools and magnificent mansions.

Right off Route 127 is **Hammond Castle Museum** (★) (80 Hesperus Avenue, Magnolia; 508-283-2080). Perched on the edge of a steep, windswept cliff, this seaside castle looks like something out of a Gothic novel. Built by John Hays Hammond, Jr., creator of the radio remote control, the house features an eccentric collection of medieval artifacts, armor and tapestries. Guided tours are available.

Three miles from Hammond Castle on Route 127 is **Gloucester**, the oldest seaport in the United States. Home port to approximately 200 fishermen, it has a salty dog ambience that brings you back to the real world after Hammond Castle. Overlooking the harbor stands the town's famed **Gloucester Fisherman** statue, *Man at the Wheel*, commemorating "They that go down to the sea in ships."

There's not much to see and do in Gloucester, but the **Cape Ann Chamber of Commerce** (33 Commercial Street; 508-283-1601) in the center of town deserves a visit. The largest tourist information center on the North Shore, it has a hotel hotline for last-minute accommodations.

A short hop from Gloucester, off Route 127, is **Rocky Neck Art Colony**, one of the country's oldest artist colonies, dating back to the 18th century. Winslow Homer and Rudyard Kipling lived here. Today it is a quainter than quaint seaside village with tiny houses, restaurants and galleries.

Down the road from Rocky Neck is **Beauport Museum** (★) (75 Eastern Point Boulevard, East Gloucester; 508-283-0800), a sprawling oceanfront English manor owned by noted decorator Henry Davis Sleeper. (Ignore the "no trespassing" sign at the entrance to Eastern Point Boulevard. It's to discourage people from driving through this "Dynasty"-like neighborhood, where all the mansions have names.) From 1907 to 1934 Sleeper spent a fortune decorating all 40 rooms with a vast collection of American and European antiques, tapestries, wood paneling from abandoned old homes and much more. An informal pale green dining room has a worn brick floor and two long wooden tables set with a beautiful collection of colored glassware that reflects the light coming in from a bank of ocean-facing windows. Surprisingly, the overall effect is of an intimate English cottage.

Ten minutes from Gloucester on Route 127 is **Rockport**, the quintessential New England seaside village and the North Shore's only resort town.

Until the mid-19th century, Rockport was a quiet fishing village. Then artists discovered its scenic charm, and the proverbial seascape was born. Today tourists flock to Rockport in the summer. The town is rather commercial, but the beautiful harbor and windswept cliffs that originally attracted artists are still here to enjoy.

Bearskin Neck, a narrow peninsula jutting out into the ocean, is Rockport's main tourist attraction. It's lined with Lilliputian-sized wooden fishermen's cottages transformed into restaurants and galleries selling everything from T-shirts and seascapes in every style imaginable to model ships made of cut up beer cans. At the end of the peninsula is Motif #1, a red lobster shack, so named because it has been painted by so many artists.

About two miles south of downtown Rockport is the **Rockport Chamber of Commerce** (3 Main Street; 508-546-6575). The folks here can point out local sights like the eccentric **Paper House** (Pigeon Hill Street; 508-546-2629). At first it looks like a normal cottage, but it's made entirely out of newspaper. Even the furniture and fireplace are papier-mâché. Elis F. Stedman, its creator, started the house in 1920; it took 20 years to complete.

About 30 minutes north of Rockport are the rural villages of **Essex** and **Ipswich**. Essex is famous for its antique stores (see the "Shopping" section in this chapter), Ipswich for its clams. A pleasant day can be spent antiquing and enjoying fresh, affordable seafood at one of the many roadside eateries in this area.

This route takes you right past **Whipple House** (53 South Main Street, Ipswich; 508-356-2811), a steepled, pitched-roofed house built in 1640 and occupied by the Whipple family for over 200 years. As did many colonists, the Whipples built their home in the Elizabethan style popular in England at the time. It has a lovely herb garden and is located in a semirural area close to other historic buildings.

Thirty minutes north of Ipswich, just before the New Hampshire border, lies the handsome 19th-century town of **Newburyport**. When the fog rolls in and the smell of brine and fish fills the air, you can walk along narrow streets bearing names like Neptune and imagine what it was like 100 years ago when this was a major shipbuilding center.

In the late 1970s the downtown area overlooking the harbor was renovated from top to bottom. Today, Newburyport's 19th-century brick buildings are so spit-and-polish clean, the town literally sparkles. As in many European towns, there's a central plaza overlooking the harbor where you can sit and watch the world go by. The shops and restaurants are quite tasteful; T-shirt and souvenir shops are the exception. **Greater Newburyport Chamber of Commerce** (29 State Street; 508-465-0704) is in the heart of the downtown area.

For a healthy dose of the good life circa 1850, walk along **High Street** (Route 1A), which is lined with immaculate 19th-century Federal-style

(Text continued on page 182.)

Exploring Cranberry Country

Hidden away in Carver, a scenic rural area ten minutes east of Plymouth, you'll find one of Massachusetts' most spectacular and least-known autumn attractions—cranberry harvesting (★). If you think fall foliage is a beautiful sight, wait until you see this dazzling display of color.

Cranberries are the state's number one agricultural product, valued at $100 million annually. Around 458 growers work more than 12,000 acres of cranberry bogs. Little Carver alone produces half the nation's crop, while Cape Cod and Nantucket also have cranberry farms.

One of the few fruits native to North America, cranberries were known to Indians as *sassamenesh*. They ate the tart red berries raw and mixed them with venison and fat to make small cakes called pemmicans. The cranberry's slender, cone-shaped flower reminded early European settlers of the beak of a crane—hence the present name.

Harvest time starts shortly after Labor Day and continues through October. During this time, restaurants and bakeries in southern Massachusetts use the berry in a number of creative dishes, ranging from cranberry horseradish and salsa to cranberry soup, bread, muffins, sorbet and tarts.

To explore the cranberry bogs, from Plymouth take Route 44 east to Route 58 south. Bogs line both routes, and the harvest process is very easy to see from the road. Many farmers don't mind if you observe from the elevated dirt paths bordering the bogs, just as long as you stay well out of their way.

The short, scruffy, dark green cranberry vines are grown in shallow bogs surrounded by deep woods. When the cranberries are ripe, they are picked by either dry or wet harvesting. Dry-picked berries are often sold fresh, while wet-picked fruit usually becomes canned or frozen cranberry sauce.

Dry-harvested berries are combed off the vine with a machine. But it's wet harvesting that's the real treat to watch. First the bogs are flooded with about 18 inches of water. Then farmers in bright yellow slickers cut the fruit off the vine with large water reels that look like giant egg beaters stirring up a waterfall of crimson berries. The buoyant berries float to the water's surface, creating a scarlet sea surrounded by a fiery ring of woods ablaze with fall colors.

The wind blows the floating berries to one end of the pond, where they are corralled with wooden booms. Giant vacuum cleaners then suck the berries into dechaffing machines. Helicopters and trucks transport the berries to packing houses, where they are graded according to size, color and quality.

It's easy enough to explore the bogs on your own, but if you want more information and an official tour, there are a number of options. Right in Plymouth is the **Cranberry World Visitors Center** (Water Street; 508-747-1000). Operated by Ocean Spray, it has exhibits of harvesting equipment, historic and current photographs, a small working cranberry bog and free cranberry juice. It's educational, but nothing compared to seeing the real thing.

Plymouth Colony Winery (Pinewood Road, Plymouth; 508-747-3334), off Route 44 about five minutes east of Plymouth, is in a former berry-screening house in the middle of a ten-acre cranberry bog. It offers free tastings, plus a tour of the winery and bogs.

The **Edaville Railroad,** a steam-belching, antique wooden train, takes visitors on a five-and-a-half-mile ride through 1800 acres of cranberry fields. The train attracts a lot of children, so it's not always quiet. But it travels through areas inaccessible by car, and the scenery is breathtaking—acres of crimson cranberries, splendid pine forests and fall foliage. This is Mother Nature at her flamboyant best.

mansions built by sea captains. For a peak inside, visit **Cushing House** (98 High Street; 508-462-2681; admission), home of the Historical Society of Old Newbury. It has 19th-century antiques, plus a genealogical library, French garden and carriage house.

NORTH SHORE HOTELS

Two-thirds of the North Shore's accommodations are in the resort town of Rockport. A sprinkling of motels can be found along Route 127, but they're short on charm and expensive.

Pleasant Manor Inn (Route 114, Marblehead; 617-631-5843), an 1872 Victorian, is located on a historic street surrounded by other impressive homes. A grand staircase leads to 12 good-sized guest rooms. Some furnishings are a bit drab, but the inn's wide hallways, tall ceilings and many fireplaces are impressive. The inn has a homey, laid-back feeling, which is perhaps why it attracts the serious sailors from around the world who come to Marblehead, a yachting center. A tennis court is located behind the house, and each room has a coffeemaker. Moderate.

A modest-looking green clapboard house, **The Nautilus** (★) (68 Front Street, Marblehead; 617-631-1703) doesn't have a sign outside. "People just know about it," says the owner. Four plain and simple guest rooms with contemporary furnishings occupy the second floor (no private baths). The house stands on a narrow street across from the busy harbor and the Driftwood, a colorful, sea-shanty-style restaurant popular with fishermen and locals. Budget to moderate.

The **Daniels House** (1 Daniels Street, Salem; 508-744-5709) is like a trip back in time. Built in 1667 by a sea captain, it is one of the few bed and breakfasts around here furnished entirely with museum-quality antiques. The five guest rooms have enormous walk-in fireplaces, low beamed ceilings and age-worn pine floors. The inn is located on a quiet, historic street within walking distance of everything, although the sign outside is small and easy to miss. Moderate.

If you can't live without a telephone, color television, air-conditioning and room service, stay at **The Hawthorne Hotel** (18 Washington Square West, Salem; 508-744-4080). One of the few real hotels on the North Shore, this impeccably restored Federal-style building is located across from Salem Common. Eighty-nine guest rooms are tastefully decorated with reproduction Colonial antiques. Elegant public rooms have wood paneling, brass chandeliers and wing-back chairs. Deluxe and ultra-deluxe.

Tara (★) (13-19 Shore Road, Magnolia; 508-525-3213), a white Tudor mansion, sits high on a bluff overlooking the crashing Atlantic in a residential neighborhood once favored by wealthy Bostonians. The house needs a little paint, but it has a certain kind of faded charm. Tara's owner, Gladys

Rundlett, a true Boston Brahmin, is a walking history book. Her home and its three guest rooms (no private baths) are decorated with an eclectic mix of old and contemporary furnishings. Guest rooms are large and light with touches of wicker. A full breakfast is included. In the winter, tea is served in a gracious formal dining room. Moderate.

Beach lovers enjoy the **Blue Shutters Inn** (1 Nautilus Road, Gloucester; 508-281-2706), a lovely old house across the street from Good Harbor Beach, one of the North Shore's most beautiful strips of sand. The inn sits on the outskirts of a secluded, affluent residential area overlooking the ocean and a vast expanse of scenic salt marsh. Blue and white throughout, the inn offers ten rooms and three individual apartments, all with ocean views and sporting furnishings that are homey, simple and sparkling clean. Breakfast included; moderate.

Only a ten-minute walk from Gloucester's famed fisherman statue, **Spruce Manor Motel and Guest House** (141 Essex Avenue; 508-283-0614) has economical accommodations to satisfy all tastes. The main guest house, a lovely, 20-room Victorian built in 1900, has bed-and-breakfast-style guest rooms, some with turret-shaped ceilings and oversized beds. Next to the guest house are one-story motel units overlooking Annisquam River, plus a salt marsh and estuaries. The decor is plain and unobtrusive. Moderate to deluxe.

A 1791 Colonial bed and breakfast, **The Inn on Cove Hill** (37 Mount Pleasant Street, Rockport; 508-546-2701) is a five-minute walk from Bearskin Neck, Rockport's main tourist attraction. Eleven guest rooms have wide pine plank floors, beautiful restored moldings, antiques, country quilts and Laura Ashley-style wallpaper. Some rooms have canopy beds. In summer a continental breakfast is served in the garden; in spring and fall it's served in bed. Moderate.

The **Old Farm Inn** (★) (291 Granite Street, Rockport; 508-546-3237) looks like the original Sunny Brook Farm. Built in 1779, the barn-red inn is shaded by glorious weeping willow trees. Only ten minutes from downtown and within walking distance of Halibut Point State Park, it's a good place for getting away from it all without going to extremes. Four guest rooms in the main house (some featuring sitting rooms) have gun stock beams, wide pine plank floors, fireplaces and antique quilts. Four large guest rooms in a newer building (some with kitchenettes) are decorated with country-style prints, but they lack the charm of the other rooms. Moderate.

JFK and Jackie once slept at the **Yankee Clipper Inn** (96 Granite Street, Rockport; 508-546-3407), one of Rockport's finest hostelries. The main inn, a stately white oceanfront mansion, has magnificent wood-paneled public rooms appointed with model ships, Oriental rugs, paintings and elegant yet comfortable furniture. The Quarterdeck, a separate building built in 1960, has panoramic ocean views and a contemporary look. The Bulfinch House, an 1840 Greek Revival building across the street, has fine period details but limited ocean views. Most of the 28 guest rooms are nondescript, but what they lack in decor is made up for by location. The inn has a good restaurant, saltwater swimming pool and nature paths. Deluxe to ultra-deluxe.

The **Peg Leg Inn** (2 King Street, Rockport; 508-546-2352), a white clapboard Colonial, is only steps away from the beach. One of the inn's five buildings is on the ocean and commands the highest rates, but it has spectacular views, a large, sweeping lawn and a granite gazebo. The 32 guest rooms are furnished with chenille bedspreads, braided rugs and reproduction Colonial furnishings and wallpaper. Moderate to deluxe.

The **Seaward Inn** (62 Marmion Way, Rockport; 508-546-3471), a rambling brown-shingle building, sits on a beautiful bluff overlooking the ocean. Surrounded by flower gardens, lawns and stone walls, it has a spring-fed swimming pool and bird sanctuary laced with nature paths. Cottages with kitchenettes, located behind the main inn, are ideal for families. Thirty-one guest rooms, some with ocean views and fireplaces, are simply appointed with homey-looking Colonial-style furnishings. Adirondack-style chairs on a grassy knoll overlooking the windswept shore are perfect for relaxing and reading. Rates include breakfast and dinner. Ultra-deluxe.

A budget bed and breakfast in the heart of Rockport is hard to come by, but **Lantana House** (22 Broadway; 508-546-3535) fills the bill. The two-story clapboard inn isn't decked out in antiques and paisley-print wallpaper, but the rooms are neat and clean and there's a deck where you can sit in the summer. The decor is of the braided rug and chenille bedspread variety. All rooms have private baths, and continental breakfast is included.

Morrill Place (★) (209 High Street, Newburyport; 508-462-2808), a three-story, 1805 Federal-style mansion, stands on historic High Street, where wealthy shipbuilders lived in the 19th century. The inn's 12 spacious guest rooms are beautifully decorated. The Henry W. Kinsman room (named for a former owner) is a rich hunter green with an enormous white canopy bed, while the Daniel Webster room has a four-poster antique bed and sleigh dresser. Rooms on the third floor are less formal but charming in their own way, with Colonial-style antiques. Some rooms share baths. Moderate.

NORTH SHORE RESTAURANTS

Rockport has the majority of restaurants on the North Shore, but few are outstanding. Restaurants with a steady local clientele in nearby towns are generally better.

Rockport is a dry town, thanks to Hannah Jumper, a temperance supporter. In 1856 after a raucous Fourth of July celebration, Hannah convinced town fathers to outlaw liquor. Even today you can't buy it in a store or order it in a restaurant. But you can buy liquor in Gloucester, which is only ten minutes away, and bring it to any Rockport restaurant.

King's Rook (★) (12 State Street, Marblehead; 617-631-9838), a romantic café and wine bar, serves many varieties of hot chocolate, coffee, tea, imported beer and ale, wine, sherry, apéritifs and champagne. Also available are light entrées such as pesto turkey sandwiches, pâté, cheese, sausage, soup and salad. The restaurant's low-beamed ceiling, soft peach walls, lace café curtains, candlelight and classical music create an intimate atmosphere favored by couples. Budget.

The **Driftwood Restaurant** (63 Front Street, Marblehead; 617-631-1145) is something of an institution. Homey, friendly and colorful, it attracts fishermen in the wee hours (it opens at 5:30 a.m.) and young professionals late on weekend mornings. The fare is traditional and plentiful: ham and eggs, pancakes, fried dough, clam chowder, burgers, fried seafood. The interior of this modest little establishment is plain and simple with red-and-white checked tablecloths. Tables are jammed close together, and there's a counter. Breakfast and lunch only. Budget.

If you want to do it up right, try **Rosalie's** (18 Sewall Street, Marblehead; 617-631-5353) for imaginative Northern Italian cuisine. Frequently reviewed by *Boston* magazine, this well-known restaurant is housed in a former brick box factory. Elegant and eclectic looking, the three-story restaurant also offers cooking classes. The menu is short and good: lobster ravioli, chowder with fennel and red pepper, swordfish with pesto sauce, veal chop. Ultra-deluxe.

For sophisticated dining in a beautiful setting, try the **Courtyard Café** (★) (5 Summer Street, Route 114 East; 508-741-4086), on Salem's Heritage Trail. Entrées include grilled quail with pumpkin-cornbread pudding, smoked turkey with cranberries and sage fettucine, sautéed duck breast with a port-cherry sauce and scallop sauté with orange-raspberry cream. In the summer lunch and dinner are served in an outdoor brick patio adorned with climbing roses. Moderate.

A good spot for a casual lunch or dinner, **Tammany Hall** (★) (208 Derby Street, Salem; 508-745-8755) is favored by locals and not as touristy as the restaurants at nearby Pickering Wharf. Complementing the restaurant's political theme, two benches sit in front of the building—one for Republicans and one for Democrats. The cozy wood and brass restaurant serves hamburgers, ribs, sandwiches and entrées with names like Henry Cabot Scrod. Moderate.

The Rudder (★) (73 Rocky Neck Avenue, Gloucester; 508-283-7967), an eclectic waterfront restaurant, is so popular Bostonians drive here just for dinner. The decor features a crazy mix of memorabilia collected by owner Evie Parsons, including hundreds of menus from around the world tacked to the low-beamed ceiling. Eyeglasses left here by Judy Garland are displayed in a glass jewelry box. The atmosphere can't be beat, and the food is good too, offering a little bit of everything—pasta, fried clams, steak, escargot. Two of the best dishes are flounder stuffed with spinach soufflé and covered with hollandaise sauce, and succulent leg of lamb for two. On Saturday nights the place gets jumping to live piano music and after-dinner sing-alongs. Moderate to deluxe.

For a little bit of heaven, come to **The Old Fire House Restaurant** (★) (1072 Washington Street, Route 127, Gloucester; 508-281-6153) for breakfast, sit at the counter and order the local specialty—thick slices of homemade, molasses-rich, anadama bread with a pot of strawberry preserve. Located in an old firehouse on a country road next to summer cottages, antique stores and galleries, this charming little restaurant serves traditional American dishes cooked to perfection: blueberry pancakes, anadama french toast, bacon and eggs, crisp home fries, chowder, salad, hamburgers and sandwiches. Budget.

The North Shore has two first-rate gourmet delis perfect for unforgettable picnics. **Grange Gourmet** (★) (457 Washington Street, Gloucester; 508-283-2639) and **Bruni's** (★) (24 Essex Road, Route 133, Ipswich; 508-356-4877) offer items such as leek and cucumber soup, homemade salsa and chips, tortellini primavera salad, chicken salad with green grapes and almonds, big, healthy sandwiches, gourmet desserts and baked goods. You can also pick up different types of coffee and tea, natural sodas and more.

The Greenery (15 Dock Square, Rockport; 508-546-9593), located near the entrance to Bearskin Neck, has sandwiches, a salad bar, bakery goods and desserts to go. The back dining room facing the harbor serves all these dishes plus entrées such as pesto pizza, lobster, crab quiche and seafood casserole. The restaurant is appointed with blond wood, brass light fixtures and touches of green throughout. Moderate.

Portside Chowder House (Bearskin Neck, Rockport) is a good place for a cup of chowder on a cold, blustery day. Cozy and tiny, the dark wood restaurant has low-beamed ceilings, a fireplace and Windsor chairs. Specialties include New England and corn chowder, grilled sausage, crab and chicken. Budget to moderate.

Like many Rockport restaurants, the **Sea Level Café** (Bearskin Neck; 508-546-2180) serves classic entrées—baked, stuffed jumbo shrimp, linguine with clam sauce, lobster sauté—but it prepares the food with more care than most of the competition. Sit at the counter in front or the back dining room facing the water. The crisp blue-and-white restaurant has a fresh, clean look. Moderate.

Downhome and fun, **Woodman's** (Route 133, Essex; 508-768-6451) hasn't changed anything except the prices since it opened in 1914. This roadside institution claims to have created the fried clam. The menu includes steamers, lobster, clam cakes, scallops and corn on the cob. Sit inside at old wooden booths or outside at picnic tables in back. There's a raw bar upstairs and a full liquor bar downstairs. Locals like to come here after a day at nearby Crane's Beach. Budget to moderate.

Tom Shea's (122 Main Street, Route 133, Essex; 508-768-6931) is a fine quality seafood restaurant with large picture windows overlooking Essex River—a great spot for watching the sunset. The wooden interior gives the restaurant an understated, nautical look. The fare is traditional—baked stuffed lobster, fried clams, stuffed sole, grilled teriyaki shrimp, plus some beef and chicken dishes. Moderate to deluxe.

Chipper's River Café (★) (Choate Bridge, Ipswich; 508-356-7956) is great for casual fare in an idyllic setting overlooking Choate River. Tucked behind the Choate River Bar, the restaurant has a sign that's small and easy to miss. Chipper's imaginative, health-conscious menu, tile floors, natural wood, art prints and juke box make it look and feel like a California restaurant. In the summer you can sit outside overlooking the river and quaint bridge. Dishes include Santa Fe Salad (cheddar cheese, chick peas guacamole, mixed greens), chargrilled mustard lemon chicken, and linguine with scallops and broccoli. Next to the restaurant is Chipper's Bakery, a good source for picnic fare. Moderate.

Chamber music, candlelight, gold gilt mirrors and mismatched antiques give **Scandia** (25 State Street, Newburyport; 508-462-6271) a romantic look. The menu changes with the seasons and the chef's whims. Entrées might include veal and lobster sauté with sweet butter, scallop chowder or seafood sausage—a very popular item. The homemade salad dressings are excellent—fennel herb, maple curry, tomato cheddar and more. Reservations a must. Moderate to deluxe.

Fowle's Restaurant (17 State Street, Newburyport; 508-465-0141) is a nostalgic, 1930s-style soda fountain and tobacco stand. It hasn't changed anything over the years except the menu, which includes everything from granola blueberry pancakes and bagels to homemade stews, chowder, enormous avocado, bacon and sprout sandwiches, malts, sundaes and sodas. Budget.

NORTH SHORE SHOPPING

Marblehead's **Old Town** has quite a few antique stores on Washington Street. The **Gallery of Folk Art** (111 Washington Street; 617-631-1594), the best store of its kind on the North Shore, sells hand-carved, brightly painted wood animals, peacock blue pottery, jewelry and more. Located in a former tavern, **Antique Wear** (★) (82-84 Front Street; 617-631-4659) offers beautiful earrings, stick pins, broaches, pendants and tie pins made out of antique buttons, some dating back to the 17th century.

Across from the House of Seven Gables is **Ye Olde Pepper Companie** (122 Derby Street, Salem; 508-745-2744). Established in 1806, it claims to be the oldest candy store in America. Specialties include gilbralters, black jacks and other old-fashioned candies made on the premises.

Hanna Wingate House (20 Main Street, Rockport; 508-546-1008) sells antique quilts, English pine antiques, reproduction light fixtures and attractive antique linen bed accessories.

New England Goods (32-B Main Street, Rockport; 508-546-9677) specializes in wooden toys, salt-glazed pottery, Maine wind bells and other quality crafts made in New England.

Rockport has almost as many galleries as bed and breakfasts. The majority sell seascapes—some good, many bad. For an excellent selection of Rockport art, visit the **Rockport Art Association** (12 Main Street; 508-546-6604). All the work on view is for sale.

Walker Creek (★) (Route 133, Essex; 508-768-7622), a real find, offers reasonably priced, finely crafted wood drop-leaf tables, hutches, four-poster beds, one-of-a-kind pieces and custom work loosely based on Shaker or Colonial designs.

Essex's 25 antique dealers run the gamut from the **White Elephant** (32 Main Street; 508-768-6901), bargain basement heaven, to **A. P. H. Waller & Son** (140 Main Street; 508-768-6269) for quality antiques. **The Scrapbook** (34 Main Street; 508-768-7404) specializes in antique botanical prints, advertising posters and maps. **North Hill Antiques** (155 Main Street; 508-768-7365) has 19th century furniture. Always ask if a dealer can do better on a price—you're expected to bargain. But don't hope for major savings. Prices are usually reduced by 10 to 15 percent.

Housed in a former movie theater, **Gabriel** (75 Merrimac Street, Newburyport; 508-462-9640), one of the better factory outlets, sells Ralph Lauren, Calvin Klein, Liz Claiborne, Evan Picone and other designer labels at 20 to 30 percent off.

NORTH SHORE NIGHTLIFE

Every Sunday Le Grand David and his Spectacular Magic Company perform a highly skilled magic show at the **Cabot Street Cinema Theatre** (★) (286 Cabot Street, Beverly; 508-927-3677), featuring levitations, vanishing acts, comedy and song-and-dance routines, complete with outrageous costumes and sets. The rest of the week the theater shows first-rate foreign and domestic films.

Symphony By The Sea (P.O. Box 8034, Salem; 508-745-4955) concerts take place in the Peabody Museum's (161 Essex Street) spectacular East Indian Marine Hall and are concluded by a reception with the musicians.

The **Blackburn Tavern** (★) (2 Main Street, Gloucester; 508-283-9108) presents live rock bands. A clean, friendly establishment, it's also good for a beer and game of darts.

The **Gloucester Stage Company** (267 East Main Street, Gloucester; 508-281-4099), under the direction of playwright Israel Horovitz, stages first-rate plays throughout the year in an old brick firehouse.

Rockport Art Association (★) (12 Main Street, Rockport; 508-546-6604) organizes popular social events such as rockabilly night, jazz club and a speakeasy evening with silent films and dancing.

The **Rockport Chamber Music Festival** (508-546-7391) performs in the Hibbard Gallery of the Rockport Art Association (12 Main Street).

Castle Hill Festival (P.O. Box 563, Ipswich; 508-356-4351) presents a wide range of musical concerts (jazz, ragtime, classical) in Castle Hill mansion or on the manicured grounds.

The Grog (13 Middle Street, Newburyport; 508-465-8008) is an attractive restaurant and cabaret with live entertainment ranging from reggae, rock and rhythm-and-blues to oldies and dance bands. Cover.

NORTH SHORE BEACHES AND PARKS

Devereux Beach—On the causeway leading to scenic Marblehead Neck, Devereux is a small, clean beach. There's a lot to see here. The affluent town lies immediately behind the beach on a hill, while across the street lies a windsurfing cove and busy Marblehead harbor. Devereux is popular with families and teens, yet, unlike most North Shore beaches, it isn't always packed on summer weekends.

Facilities: Picnic areas, restrooms, playground, lifeguard, bike rack, snack bar; groceries five minutes away in Marblehead. *Fishing:* Excellent. *Swimming:* Good, but it can get rough.

Getting there: Located on Ocean Avenue, to the south of Marblehead harbor.

Salem Willows (★)—Don't be thrown off by the tawdry-looking Chinese take-out joints and arcade you see when you enter the parking lot. Salem Willows holds some pleasant surprises, including a nostalgic old park overlooking Salem Sound that is shaded with graceful willow trees planted in 1801 to provide a protected area for smallpox victims. Next to the park is a small beach. People come here to stroll in the park, admire the view, fish and rent rowboats. Locals swear by the popcorn and chop suey sandwiches sold in the parking lot.

Facilities: Picnic areas, restrooms, lifeguards, snack bar, rowboat rentals; groceries ten minutes away in downtown Salem. *Fishing:* Excellent from shore and a short pier. *Swimming:* A little rough.

Getting there: Located at the end of Derby Street in Salem.

Singing Beach—This jewel of a beach, only a quarter mile long, has pristine sand that literally squeaks underfoot. Hidden away in a lovely affluent neighborhood, the beach is surrounded by steep cliffs and spectacular

(Text continued on page 192.)

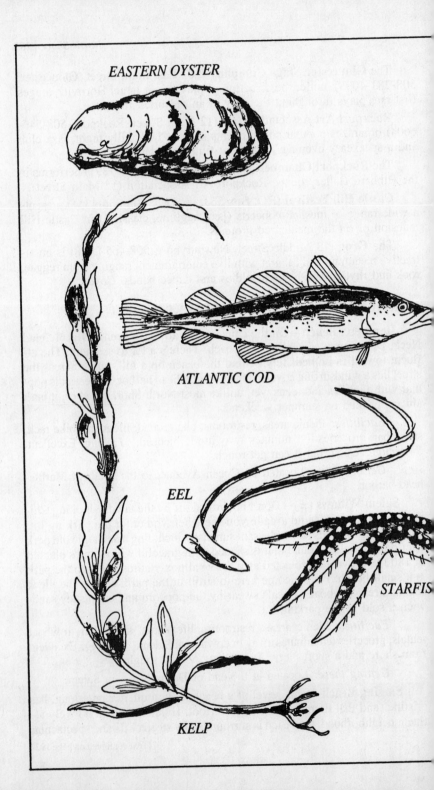

EASTERN OYSTER

ATLANTIC COD

EEL

STARFIS

KELP

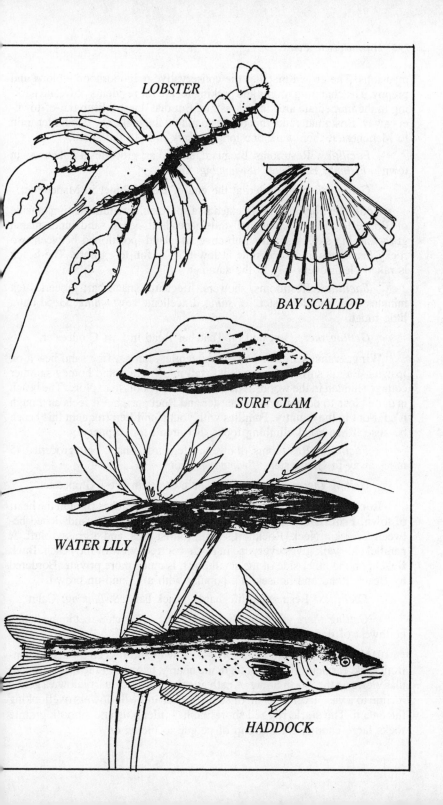

LOBSTER

BAY SCALLOP

SURF CLAM

WATER LILY

HADDOCK

mansions. The crowd matches the conservative neighborhood—blond and preppy. The changing rooms and parking lot are for residents only, and parking in the immediate area is impossible. But that doesn't keep out-of-towners away. Bostonians like this beach so much, they take the commuter train to Manchester, then walk one long, sweaty mile to the shore.

Facilities: Restrooms, lifeguard, snack bar; groceries a mile away in town. *Fishing:* Excellent. *Swimming:* Good.

Getting there: Located at the end of Beach Street in Manchester.

Good Harbor Beach—Located in a spectacular natural setting outside of Gloucester, this sweeping, half-mile beach is all ocean, sand dunes, marsh grass and big sky. A small shrub-covered island, positioned between two rocky headlands and accessible at low tide, is fun to explore. The beach is raked clean every day in the summer.

Facilities: Restrooms, showers, lifeguard, snack bar; groceries ten minutes away in Gloucester. *Fishing:* Excellent. *Swimming:* Good but a little rough.

Getting there: Located on Thatcher Road in East Gloucester.

Wingaersheek Beach (★)—This gentle, sloping, fine sand beach on Ipswich Bay is surrounded by rocks, tall marsh grass and homey summer cottages hidden in the woods. There are also tidepools to explore. The beach is quite close to downtown Gloucester and Rockport, but it feels as though it's far out in the country. Families with young children frequent this beach because it has good climbing rocks that aren't too slippery.

Facilities: Restrooms, showers, lifeguards, snack bar; groceries 15 miles away in Gloucester. *Swimming:* Calm.

Getting there: Located on Atlantic Street in West Gloucester.

Rockport Beaches—Rockport has two small beaches right in the heart of town. **Front Beach**, a favorite with small children, is sandwiched between Bearskin Neck, Rockport's main tourist area, and a grassy bluff. A parallel sidewalk gives everyone in town a perfect view of the beach. **Back Beach**, on the other side of the small bluff, is much more private. Bordered by Beach Road and houses, it's popular with a 15-and-up crowd.

Facilities: Restrooms, lifeguards, snack bar. *Swimming:* Calm.

Getting there: Both beaches are located on Beach Street immediately northwest of downtown Rockport.

Halibut Point State Park (★)—This wild and rugged 54-acre oceanfront park, formerly the site of a granite quarry, has one of the most spectacular views on the North Shore. A path goes past the old quarry down a gentle incline to a vast, treeless plain of scrub thicket and wildflowers overlooking the ocean. The stark, rugged shoreline has tidepools and smooth granite rocks large enough for a group of people to picnic on.

Facilities: Restrooms, walking trails, guided tours; groceries nearby in Rockport; information, 508-546-2997. *Fishing:* Excellent. *Swimming:* Permitted, but not recommended because the shore is covered with big, slippery rocks.

Getting there: Located north of Rockport on Route 127.

The Cox Reservation (★)—Formerly the home of famed muralist Allyn Cox, this 31-acre salt marsh farmland is now headquarters for the Essex County Greenbelt Association. Peaceful and pastoral, it has paths leading through gardens of perennials and roses, salt marsh, woods, orchards and open farmland down to winding Essex River. Artists come here in the late afternoon when the river and graceful marsh grass are bathed in a soft golden light, creating a dreamlike environment. It's easy to see why a muralist lived in this romantic and private place.

Facilities: None; groceries nearby in Essex; for information, call 508-768-7241.

Getting there: Located off Route 133 in Essex.

Crane's Beach Memorial Reservation—This massive, two-mile, dune-backed beach is surrounded by over 1000 acres of salt marsh farmland, shrub thicket and woods. In the off-season, the wide beach seems to go on forever. In the summer it's wall-to-wall people. Nature and beachgoers co-exist peacefully, however. At certain times of the year, sections of the beach are fenced off to protect nesting birds. A boardwalk leading to the beach protects sand dunes and marsh grass.

Facilities: Restrooms, showers, lifeguards, snack bar; groceries nearby in Ipswich; information, 508-356-4354. *Fishing:* Excellent. *Swimming:* Good.

Getting there: Located on Argilla Road in Ipswich.

Parker River National Wildlife Refuge—This magnificent ocean-front wildlife refuge on Plum Island is only about ten minutes from downtown Newburyport, but it feels very far away from civilization. One-third of Plum Island is covered with ramshackle summer beach houses; the rest is the refuge—4662 acres of bogs, tidal marshes, sand dunes and beach. A boardwalk leads to the beach, and a trail meanders throughout the refuge. The abundant wildlife includes seals, geese, ducks, deer, rabbits and over 300 species of birds. Parker River is dearly loved by Newburyport residents. On a sunny day in the dead of winter, they can be seen strolling with their dogs along the shore looking for snowy owls.

Facilities: Restrooms; information, 508-465-5753. *Fishing:* Excellent winter smelt fishing. *Swimming:* Strong undertow.

Getting there: Located on Plum Island in Newburyport.

Plymouth Area

This area is a mix of cranberries and Pilgrims, small scenic villages, pastoral farmland, clean beaches and one main town, Plymouth, about 50 minutes south of Boston. Plymouth, of course, is where the Pilgrims landed, and it draws over one million tourists annually. It has enough historic sights to occupy an entire weekend, although most people can't take more than a day of Pilgrim lore.

To reach Plymouth from Boston, go south on Route 3 or take scenic Route 3A. It hugs the coast, a beautiful area with affluent old villages, lovely harbors, vintage lighthouses, stately mansions and numerous historic sites.

A few miles southeast of Boston along Route 3A lies one of the area's most attractive coastal communities, **Hingham**, settled in 1635. Sailing yachts bob in its picturesque harbor, and Hingham's downtown retains the characteristics of a small village, with mom-and-pop shops, restaurants and a vintage movie theater surrounding Hingham Square. A drive along Hingham's long and wide **Main Street** rewards you with views of stately 18th- and 19th-century homes painted pastel colors and sporting neat black shutters. A number of them are on the National Register of Historic Places. These houses are private, but many are open to the public during the **Hingham Historical Society's** (617-749-0013) annual house tour in June, reputed to be the oldest historical house tour in the country, held since 1924.

Two private houses worth a drive by are the **Hersey House** (104 Summer Street), a handsome gray mansion in Italianate style, with a flat-roofed, pillared porch, which dates to about 1857, and the **Joshua Wilder House** (605 Main Street), a beautifully restored house that probably dates to 1760. Both are opened during the house tour.

The Old Ordinary (21 Lincoln Street; 617-749-0013; admission), a house dating to 1680, numbered among its many owners tavern keepers who provided an "ordinary" meal of the day at fixed prices. Halfway on the day-long stagecoach ride from Plymouth to Boston, the Old Ordinary did a brisk business, and counted Daniel Webster among its patrons. Additions were made to the house in the mid-18th century. Now a museum of Hingham history, the house has an 18th-century taproom, complete with wooden grill, pewter plates and rum kegs. There's also an 18th-century kitchen outfitted with large hearth and butter churn, and a den, dining room and front parlor. Upstairs are four bedrooms furnished in period style. There are a number of rare objects among the collection, including "mourning" samplers, made to honor the dead; a 17th-century Bible box; an 18th-century Queen Anne mirror; chinoiserie; and paintings of Hingham ships that sailed to China.

The Puritan congregation of the **Old Ship Church** (90 Main Street; 617-749-1679) gathered in 1635. Built in 1681, it is the oldest building in continuous ecclesiastical service in the United States, and the nation's only surviving Puritan meeting house. Unlike later New England churches with white spires and sides, Old Ship is built of somber gray, wooden clapboards in Elizabethan Gothic style, as its Puritan worshippers saw fit. Crafted by ships' carpenters, the ship has curved oak roof frames like the knees of a ship, and the unusual roof structure resembles an inverted ship's hull.

Not far from Hingham, on a peninsula jutting out into Boston Harbor, is **Hull**, site of **Boston Light**, the oldest lighthouse in America. Immediately south, on Jerusalem Road, is **Cohasset**, known for magnificent homes with sweeping ocean views.

Scituate, a village directly south of Cohasset, is famous for an event that took place during the War of 1812 involving Abigail and Rebecca Bates, the young daughters of the lighthouse keeper. When the girls noticed two barges from the British frigate La Hogue approaching the shore, they hid behind some trees and made so much noise with a fife and drum, the soldiers mistook them for an entire regiment and hightailed it back to safety. Scituate has quite a few historic homes plus many elegant shops along Front Street.

Continuing south, you'll arrive in **Marshfield**, where Daniel Webster lived for 20 years. His law office is located in the **Winslow House** (Careswell and Webster streets, 508-837-9527), a historic home built in 1688, where you can also see a blacksmith shop and old schoolhouse.

A few miles south of Marshfield lies wealthy **Duxbury**, an aristocratic residential area of elegant homes just north of Plymouth. Stop by **The King Caesar House** (★) (King Caesar Road), one of the state's most beautiful historic homes, located off Route 3A on a winding coastal road. A fresh yellow-and-white, Federal-era mansion with green shutters, a sweeping lawn and climbing roses, the house stands across from a massive stone wharf where ships were once rigged. The house has finely crafted wood cornices, moldings, fanlights and balustrades, plus original hand-painted French wallpaper and fine antiques.

From Duxbury head south for **Plymouth**. "America's Home Town" can't seem to make up its mind whether to be a tourist trap or a scenic, historic village. The town is a jarring mix of historic homes, cobblestone streets, '50s-style motels, souvenir shops, a tacky waterfront and tour buses everywhere you look. It's not particularly scenic in parts, yet the town is rich with historic sights.

Plymouth is small, and without trying you bump into everything there is to see. The **Plymouth Information Booth** (North Park Avenue; 508-746-4779 summers or 508-746-3377 year-round) has walking-tour maps.

The first thing everyone heads for is **Plymouth Rock** on Water Street on the harbor. Believed to be the landing place of the Pilgrims, it is housed inside a Greek canopy with stately columns. Don't expect to see a big impressive rock; it's only large enough to hold two very small Pilgrims.

Right next to the rock is the **Mayflower II** (State Pier; 508-746-1622; admission), a brightly painted reproduction of the real *Mayflower* that looks like the pirate ship at Disneyland. The tour conducted by guides in period costume is worthwhile, even though there's usually a line to get in. The *Mayflower* is shockingly small. It's hard to imagine how 102 people ever survived 66 days at sea in such cramped quarters.

For more Pilgrim lore, head for **Pilgrim Hall Museum** (75 Court Street; 508-746-1620; admission), on the main drag. The museum houses the nation's largest collection of Pilgrim possessions, including richly styled Jacobean furniture and the relic of a ship that brought colonists to America. Its hull is made out of naturally curved tree trunks and branches, a crude but effective design.

Three miles south of Plymouth is **Plimoth Plantation** (Route 3A, Warren Avenue, Plymouth; 508-746-1622; admission), a "living museum" where men and women in period costumes portray the residents of a 1627 Pilgrim village. This sounds contrived, but it's authentic and well-done. The re-created village, on a dusty, straw-strewn road overlooking the ocean, is comprised of many ramshackle wooden dwellings with deeply thatched roofs. There's not a modern detail in sight—just the village, the ocean and settlers going about the daily tasks of the time, tending the vegetable garden or building a house with 17th-century tools. The villagers speak in Old English, and you can ask them questions about anything—including the politics of the 17th century. There's also a Wampanoag Indian settlement that re-creates a typical native encampment with woven dome-shaped dwellings.

From Plymouth go west on Route 44, then south on Route 58 to rural **Carver** (★), cranberry capital of the world. In the fall the harvesting process, a breathtaking sight, can be witnessed from the road. There's also an antique train visitors can ride and a cranberry winery. (See "Exploring Cranberry Country" in this chapter.)

PLYMOUTH AREA HOTELS

Plymouth has an abundance of very ordinary motels that attract families and tour groups, but there is also a sprinkling of hidden bed and breakfasts that are quite special.

For a romantic getaway, 15 minutes north of Plymouth, try the **Windsor House Inn** (★) (390 Washington Street, Duxbury; 617-934-0991). This graceful old inn stands on a street lined with houses listed on the National Register of Historic Places, and it's next to a classic white-steepled church. Down the street are a few elegant little shops, a French bakery and small wharf. Windsor House has two tastefully decorated guest rooms and a beautiful suite with pale blue wood-paneled walls and blue-and-white stenciling. All

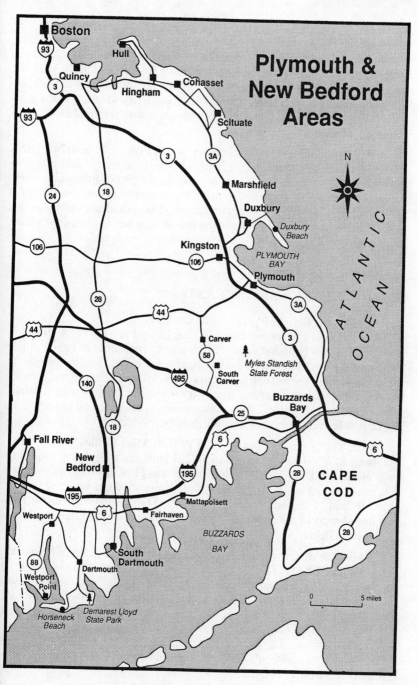

Plymouth & New Bedford Areas

rooms are furnished with Shaker and Colonial-style antiques. A dark, cozy restaurant on the ground floor looks like an old seafaring tavern. Deluxe.

Cold Spring Motel (188 Court Street, Plymouth; 508-746-2222) is one of the most attractive of the many motels lining Route 3A. The 40-year-old, reasonably priced motel is in pristine condition and beautifully landscaped. In the summer thick yellow marigolds border brick paths leading to the guest rooms. These are spacious and simply appointed with standard-issue motel furniture. Moderate.

The **John Carver Inn** (25 Summer Street, Plymouth; 508-746-7100), a large, imposing, Colonial-style hotel, attracts tour groups and gets very crowded in the summer. But it's in the most scenic part of Plymouth, across the street from a row of 17th-century historic homes and a beautiful grist mill. Seventy-nine guest rooms are decorated in soft shades of beige and Colonial-style reproduction antiques. A full-service hotel, it has a restaurant, lounge and pool. Deluxe.

PLYMOUTH AREA RESTAURANTS

The **British Relief** (★) (152 North Street, Hingham Square, Hingham; 617-749-7713) is a welcoming spot indeed, housed in a red brick storefront and modeled on a British soup kitchen. Vintage signboards and photographs following the soup kitchen theme hang on the walls. The homey furnishings include a massive carved oak table that seats at least ten, and ancient wooden booths. Cafeteria-style service dishes up hearty homemade soups, salads, sandwiches and desserts. The restaurant also operates a deli counter with gourmet take-out. Breakfast and lunch only; budget.

There's no cozier spot in town than **Ye Olde Mille Grille** (8 North Street, Hingham; 617-749-9846), housed in a 1723 building, with dining rooms upstairs and down. Dark wood tabletops and booths glow lustrously in the warm light of shaded table lamps, and the vintage bar is a favorite watering hole for locals. Robust Yankee seafood and meats fill the menu, from fried clams, scallops and shrimp to a hamburger plate, roast lamb and hot turkey sandwich. Moderate to deluxe.

A ramshackle brown-shingle restaurant a few miles north of Plymouth, **Persy's Place** (★) (117 Main Street, Route 3A, Kingston; 617-585-5464) claims to have "New England's largest breakfast menu," and that's no joke. The menu takes about an hour to read, but some of its offerings include fish cakes, buttermilk pancakes, chipped beef on toast, catfish and eggs, hickory-smoked bacon, raisin, corn, wheat and pumpernickel bread, finnan haddie, no-cholesterol eggs, waffles and much, much more. The restaurant looks like a cross between a coffee shop and a country general store. Breakfast and lunch only; budget.

Station One (51 Main Street, Plymouth; 508-746-6001) embodies 19th-century elegance. Located in a former fire station, the restaurant has a lovely brick sidewalk café and a cavernous, honey-colored, wood-paneled dining room with crystal, brass and handsome arched windows. The menu has something for everyone—veal thermidor, Cajun shrimp, baked stuffed sole, chicken with raspberry vinaigrette, crab meat and avocado salad, and hamburgers. Deluxe.

Hidden and lovely **Crane Brook Tea Room** (★) (Tremont Street, South Carver; 508-866-3235) is a must if you're touring cranberry country. Located in a former iron foundry, the cozy, antiques-filled restaurant overlooks a pretty pond and is surrounded by woods, pastures and cranberry bogs. The restaurant started out serving only tea and pastries, but now it also offers lunch and dinner. A perfect place for a long, leisurely lunch, the Crane Brook has a changing menu of dishes such as grilled duck breast sandwich and imaginative salads for lunch; rack of lamb and spicy pork loin roast for dinner. Deluxe.

PLYMOUTH AREA SHOPPING

Cordage Park (Route 3A, North Plymouth; 508-746-7707), housed in a former brick cordage rope factory, is the most attractive factory outlet on the South Shore. The lovely old building is surrounded by ponds, fountains, gazebos, rolling lawns and flower gardens. Some retailers include Hanes, Van Heusen, Crazy Horse, Harve Bernard and Maidenform.

PLYMOUTH AREA NIGHTLIFE

Free concerts at the **Village Landing Gazebo** (Water Street, Plymouth) range from swing bands to Irish balladeers and children's performances.

Live jazz can be heard free on weekends at the **Sheraton Plymouth Pub** (Village Landing, Water Street, Plymouth; 508-747-4900).

PLYMOUTH AREA BEACHES AND PARKS

Duxbury Beach—This five-mile stretch of clean white sand is one of the finest barrier beaches on the Massachusetts coast. The beach juts out into the ocean and is bordered by a little harbor on one side and the Atlantic on the other. Stretches are dotted with salt marsh, and parts are accessible only by four-wheel-drive vehicles. Located in an affluent residential neighborhood, it attracts a well-heeled crowd.

Facilities: Restrooms, showers, changing room, lifeguards, snack bar, restaurant; groceries in Duxbury. *Swimming:* Good.

Getting there: Located off Route 3 on Route 139 in Duxbury, north of Plymouth.

Myles Standish State Forest—Locals joke that once you're in this 14,635-acre park, you'll never find your way out again. The park is enormous, and the roads winding through the forest and meadows seem to go on forever. Because of its size, it feels remote and peaceful even in the summer. Beautiful and clean, the park has 15 ponds with beaches. Bicycle, bridle and hiking paths wind through the forest.

Facilities: Picnic areas, restrooms, interpretive programs; groceries and restaurants in Plymouth and Carver; information, 508-866-2526. *Camping:* Permitted in 570 sites with restrooms, hot showers, fireplaces and picnic tables, available on a first come, first served basis. *Fishing:* Good in most ponds. *Swimming:* In College and Fearings ponds.

Getting there: Located off Route 3 on State Road in Plymouth.

Plymouth Beach—Located in a half rural, half residential area, this straight, three-mile beach dotted with beach grass and clear stretches of sand serves as a nesting ground for migratory shore birds such as terns and sandpipers. The nesting area is fenced off for protection, but the birds can be easily observed. In the summer this busy beach attracts families and local kids.

Facilities: Restrooms, showers, lifeguards, snack bar; restaurant within walking distance. *Fishing:* Excellent. *Swimming:* Good.

Getting there: Located off Route 3A, three miles south of Plymouth.

New Bedford Area

About an hour's drive southeast of Plymouth lies the former whaling town of **New Bedford**, which gained immortality in Herman Melville's *Moby Dick*. It still looks and feels a lot like a 19th-century whaling city, with a bustling waterfront and large Portuguese population.

Until the early 1980s the waterfront area was in disarray. Then, to attract tourists, the town restored more than 100 buildings. Fortunately New Bedford didn't go overboard with cute, contrived tourist attractions. Today it has a number of fine museums, restaurants, antique shops and galleries alongside the harbor. There's something genuine and tasteful about this miniature city.

The New Bedford Visitors Center (47 North 2nd Street; 508-991-6200) occupies a restored brick building, sharing space with a French bakery and chowder shop.

Three sights that shouldn't be missed include **The New Bedford Whaling Museum** (18 Johnny Cake Hill; 508-997-0046; admission), **Seaman's Bethel,** a church across from the whaling museum, and **County Street** (★), where wealthy sea captains built homes in the 19th century.

Start with the Whaling Museum, then enter Seamen's Bethel, and New Bedford won't look the same again. The museum depicts whaling's profound impact on this town, telling the story beautifully with large, dramatic paintings of life aboard whaling ships and an enormous mural created in 1848. You can climb aboard a half-scale model of a fully rigged whaling ship housed in a large room with harpoons and figureheads. The museum is spacious, airy and absorbing.

Across the street is Seamen's Bethel, where whalers prayed before setting out to sea. The pulpit of this plain, sturdy church is shaped like a ship's bluff bows. Its walls are covered with memorial tablets to men who died at sea. A visit to this church is a sobering experience.

"Nowhere in America will you find more patrician-like houses," wrote Herman Melville of County Street, located a few blocks up a slight hill from the whaling museum. The impeccably restored Federal-style mansions and elaborate Victorians along this street illustrate how grand life was in 19th-century New Bedford.

For a unique change of pace, consider visiting **Cuttyhunk** (★), an island 14 miles offshore from New Bedford accessible by ferry (see the "Transportation" section in this chapter). It's part of the Elizabeth Islands, a chain of 16 tiny islands, 14 of them owned by the Boston Brahmin Forbes family. The island is practically all sand and scrub bushes with a rocky beach. It does have a general store, one hotel, two restaurants and about 100 homes. Cuttyhunk is the opposite of busy, crowded Cape Cod—there's nothing to do but walk and fish—and therein lies its charm.

Immediately southwest of New Bedford off Route 6 are the affluent rural communities of Dartmouth and Westport, where you'll find some of the most exquisite coastal farmland in all of Massachusetts. Like Kentucky bluegrass country, this area has miles of ancient stone walls, lovely old houses, shingled dairy barns, rolling pastures and elegant horse farms.

Off Slocums Road in South Dartmouth sits **Padanaram,** a fashionable yachting resort on Apponagansett Bay. It's home to the famous boatyard Concordia, where beautiful old wooden yachts are restored. The village is only two blocks long, but it has a number of fine restaurants and shops.

Not far from Padanaram is **The Lloyd Center for Environmental Studies** (★) (430 Potomska Road, South Dartmouth; 508-990-0505), a non-profit organization that studies coastal and estuarine environments. Open to the public are an aquarium, resource library and changing exhibits featuring such work as naturalist photography. The best thing here is the dazzling view from the observation deck, which overlooks winding Slocums River and miles of wetlands. The center offers weekly walks, canoe trips and a variety of educational programs.

Heading back to New Bedford, you can take Route 195 west to **Fall River** 15 minutes away. Factory outlets and Battleship Cove are this town's claims to fame.

At the turn of the century Fall River had more than 100 textile mills, but in 1927 the industry sagged and the town went through serious hard times. Today its large granite mills are occupied by electronic and metals firms and factory outlets, but the effects of the Depression still linger.

Fall River's downtown has been spruced up, but there are so many "for lease" signs tacked to its grand 19th-century buildings that the town looks a little lost.

Columbia Street (★), the Portuguese section of downtown, is a colorful place to stroll, sample treats from the many good bakeries and discover the beautiful mosaic sidewalks. The **Fall River Office of Tourism** (72 Bank Street; 508-679-0922) is housed in the former Armory, an impressive granite building.

There's also an information center at **Battleship Cove**, a harbor and park area right in town off Route 195 at exit 5. Docked in the water at Battleship Cove are a World War II battleship, destroyer, attack submarine and PT boat that you can tour (508-678-1100; admission). Not surprisingly, these vessels, which are in excellent condition, are filled with children playing war. Hundreds of scout troops make pilgrimages to this John Wayne playground.

Next to the boats is the **Fall River Heritage State Park Visitors Center** (200 Davol Street; 508-675-5759). It has an attractive waterfront park and a building with a number of exhibits about the town's former textile industry. A moving slide show documents the appalling working conditions, accidents and deaths suffered by children and adult immigrants who worked in the mills.

NEW BEDFORD AREA HOTELS

The Melville House (★) (100 Madison Street, New Bedford; 508-990-1566) stands on a historic street lined with stately Federal and Victorian mansions built by 19th-century sea captains. The 1855 French Empire house was once owned by Herman Melville's sister, and he often stayed here. A spacious inn, it has lofty ceilings, wide halls and sweeping stairways. Tastefully decorated with soft, subtle colors and antiques, the three guest rooms

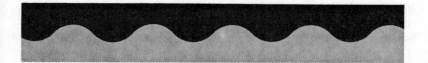

Hiking the Coast

The Massachusetts coast offers excellent opportunities to hike through deep forests, salt marshes and swamps and past ponds and beachfront. Many of the hikes are short and easy, while a few offer a more rugged challenge. For more information on hikes, contact the **Massachusetts Department of Environmental Management Trails Program** (225 Friend Street, Boston; 617-727-3160).

Art's Trail (1 mile), in Dogtown Common, a 3000-acre park near Gloucester, winds through red oak forest past a highland of scrub oak, grey birch, blueberries and huckleberries. Several low areas flood in late winter and spring, forming frog-breeding ponds. Of moderate difficulty, the trail is rocky in parts and requires careful walking.

Whale's Jaw Trail (4.5 miles), a rugged, rocky, hilly hike, starts at Blackburn Industrial Park off Route 128. The trail meanders through former grazing land and past Babson Reservoir, birch groves and cattail marsh. It ends at the top of a hill, where you'll see an enormous split granite boulder that looks like a whale's jaw.

You need a rowboat to get to get to **Hog Island Trail** (1.5 miles), but it's worth it. Located near Crane's Beach, the easy trail leads through vast expanses of salt marsh, beside pastures and along the shore, past a 1725 house and barn, to a hill where you can see Maine on a clear day. The Crane Refuge Visitor Center at the beginning of the hike has bathrooms, picnic areas, a museum and trail maps.

East Head Reservoir Trail (3.5 miles) starts behind the Myles Standish State Forest headquarters building in Plymouth. The best thing about this hike is that it covers the full spectrum of habitats in the 14,635-acre park. The relatively flat trail winds past deep forest, marsh, hard and soft wood groves and a pristine pond. A pamphlet available at the start of the hike explains the flora and fauna of each environment. A couple of benches are located along the way.

The **Flora B. Pierce Nature Trail** (2 miles) at Acushnet Cedar Swamp State Reservation in New Bedford follows along a river spanned by several large wooden bridges and travels through deeply wooded inland wetlands.

The **Massasoit State Park Trail** (2.5 miles) in East Taunton meanders through white pine forest and hardwoods and past swamps and brooks. It edges Lake Rico and arrives at a large, secluded sandy beach. Along the way, you'll spot wildlife such as deer, fox and owls.

are quite large and have working marble fireplaces. Two rooms share a bath, but guests often have the bath to themselves in this little-known place. A full-course breakfast is served in an elegant solarium. Moderate.

Off-the-beaten-path **Mattapoisett Inn** (★) (13 Water Street, Mattapoisett; 508-758-4922) is in a scenic little seaside village of doll-sized clapboard houses with white picket fences and window boxes. The inn stands right across the street from the harbor. The village which is only one block long consists of a small dock, a liquor store, a coffee shop and the inn. The white-clapboard inn with black shutters has a restaurant and pub on the ground floor. Three spacious guest rooms are upstairs, and one has a balcony overlooking the ocean. The rooms aren't "decorated," but they're neat, clean, bright and comfortable. Budget.

If you want solitude and natural beauty, try **The Allen House** (★) (Cuttyhunk; 508-996-9292), the only inn on Cuttyhunk Island. Cuttyhunk— remote, unpretentious, noncommercial—has no shopping, nightlife, tennis or golf, and practically no cars or bicycles. Allen House, a plain Jane sort of place with limited services, reflects the island's no-frills atmosphere. It's perfect if you like long, quiet walks along uncrowded shoreline. The inn serves meals in a glassed-in porch with ocean views. Twelve rooms in the main house share baths, and two cottages are available. Moderate.

A 1760 brown-shingle bed and breakfast, **The Edgewater** (★) (2 Oxford Street, Fairhaven; 508-997-5512) is so close to the water you'd swear you were on a boat when you look out the window. The inn seems miles away from civilization, yet it's only a five-minute drive from New Bedford's historic wharf district. A perfect spot for romance, the handsome house has soft taupe walls and crisp white arched moldings. The blue-and-white Captain's Suite, the best room in the house, has a sitting room and spectacular views. The other four guest rooms are attractive and comfortable, but not all have views. All are appointed with contemporary and antique furnishings. Budget to moderate.

Salt Marsh Farm (★) (322 Smith Neck Road; 508-992-0980), a 200-year-old farmhouse, is in the heart of pastoral South Dartmouth. A perfect retreat for nature buffs, the house is on a 90-acre preserve with trails leading through hay fields, woods and wetlands. Only 15 minutes from New Bedford, Salt Marsh Farm feels like another world and time. The floors are uneven, the doorways low and the rooms small, but it has comfortable, homespun charm. Sunny guest rooms are furnished with antiques, and a full breakfast is served in an attractive dining room with a beautiful old fireplace. Moderate.

One of the best things about **The Little Red House** (★) (631 Elm Street, South Dartmouth; 508-996-4554) is the beautiful backyard overlooking a stone-walled horse farm. Guests can relax in the gazebo and throw apples to the horses. The barn-shaped red bed and breakfast is new but has an antique appearance. It's located in a pleasant residential neighborhood of mostly 20th-century homes. Padanaram village is close by. The house is spotless, the decor country cute with pineapple stencil wallpaper, wooden hearts, ruffles, canopy beds and more. Budget.

NEW BEDFORD AREA RESTAURANTS

Candleworks (72 North Water Street; 508-992-1635) is housed in an 1810 granite candle factory half a block from New Bedford's major sights. During the week it attracts the town's white-collar lunch crowd. A pink, atriumlike room in front is appointed with wooden tables and Windsor chairs. The main dining room has a low-beamed ceiling and rich wood. The menu is continental with an emphasis on seafood and includes such specialties as fish filet stuffed with oysters in béarnaise sauce. Moderate to deluxe.

Jeggrey's (47 North Second Street; 508-990-0557) is right next to the New Bedford Tourist Information Office in one of the town's restored historic brick buildings. Open for breakfast and lunch, the informal café and bakery offer spinach and sausage calzone, deep-dish pizza, pita sandwiches, antipasto, clam chowder, a wide range of gourmet coffees and a cappuccino bar. Croissants, muffins, bread, bagels and cookies are baked on the premises. Takeout is available. Budget.

There are many Portuguese restaurants in New Bedford, but one of the best is **Café Portugal** (★) (1280 Acushnet Avenue; 508-992-8216). A large, festive restaurant popular with Portuguese families, it features house specialties such as an enormous platter of succulent shrimp and marinated steak served with eggs on top. With its acoustical tile ceiling and plastic flower arrangements, Café Portugal looks a little bit like a banquet hall. Moderate.

A white clapboard building with bright blue awnings, **La Rivage** (★) (7 Water Street; 508-999-4505) overlooks the water in Padanaram, a chic yachting village within South Dartmouth. An outdoor deck with red umbrellas is a good spot for lunch in the summer. The elegant yet understated interior has large picture windows and white tablecloths. Lunch features dishes such as brochette of shrimp, scallops with fresh herbs, salmon with orange sauce and caesar salad. Dinner ranges from veal in madeira sauce to lamb chops with fresh thyme and endive and watercress salad. Deluxe.

Bridge Street Café (10-A Bridge Street, South Dartmouth; 508-994-7200) in the heart of Padanaram, attracts a young, well-dressed crowd. Clean and crisp, with slate floors and skylights, the café has an outdoor deck overlooking the town and harbor. Daily specials range from Creole-grilled swordfish, scallops and pesto pasta, to tuna and shrimp brochette and grilled sirloin. Specialties of the house are smoked brook trout and smoked eastern salmon served with capers and mustard sauce. Deluxe.

It may look like a coffee shop, but **Bayside** (★) (1253 Horseneck Road, Westport; 508-636-5882) serves classic clam-bar fare and other dishes such as chicken burrito and eggplant parmigiana. More "in" than it seems, the restaurant has a clientele ranging from construction workers, senior citizens and families to yuppies and arty types dressed entirely in black. Bayside overlooks rolling pastures, salt marsh, stone walls and the ocean. Budget to moderate.

Lizzie's (★) (122 Third Street; 508-672-7688) is in an 1894 brick office building in the heart of Fall River. Architectural buffs appreciate the authentic, impeccably restored interior, with dark green tin ceiling, paddle fans, brass light fixtures and wood paneling. Warm and inviting, Lizzie's serves hamburgers, pizza, quiche, sandwiches, salads and entrées such as grilled salmon. The attractive bar is a good spot for a beer. Budget.

NEW BEDFORD AREA SHOPPING

This is outlet country. Fall River has over 100 outlets, and New Bedford has quite a few, too. Until the 1980s these were novel, but today there are so many discount shopping places across the country that they don't seem unique. Choices are somewhat limited because the same brands are sold everywhere: Bass, Farberware, Crazy Horse, Jonathan Logan, Van Heusen, Vanity Fair, etc.

Howland Place (651 Orchard Street, New Bedford; 508-999-4100) is the Rodeo Drive of factory outlets. Located in a restored brick building that could pass for a fancy mall, it has retailers including Perry Ellis, Vakko Leather, Adrienne Vittadini, Alexander Julian, Carlos Falchi and Royal Dalton, to name a few. Discounts range from 30 to 75 percent.

Calvin Klein Outlet (100 North Front Street, New Bedford; 508-999-1300) has great bargains on sportswear (tailored shirts, T-shirts, jeans, cotton sweaters) and fine quality leather handbags and totes. Discounts on the better quality merchandise (wool skirts, silk blouses and cashmere sweaters) are not that impressive. Housed in an enormous brick building, the outlet displays everything quite neatly so you can see the merchandise. Discounts range from 20 to 70 percent.

Salt Marsh Pottery (1167 Russells Mills Road, South Dartmouth; 508-636-4813) specializes in hand-painted pottery and tiles designed with windflower motifs.

Fall River Outlets: Driving the expressway in Fall River, you can't help but notice the mammoth, six-story granite textile mills transformed into factory outlets. To visit them from Route 195, which runs through town, take Route 24 south to the Brayton exit and follow the signs. All the outlets are close together, and each building has between 50 and 100 retailers selling clothes, dishes, sheets, towels, jewelry, handbags and more. Prices are rock bottom, and the merchandise is pretty low-end. Natural fiber clothing is difficult to find.

NEW BEDFORD AREA NIGHTLIFE

Zeiterion Theatre (684 Purchase Street, New Bedford; 508-994-2900) presents a wide range of musical and dramatic performances—everything from Chuck Mangione, *Dreamgirls* and the Mantovani Orchestra to *Carmen* and the stars of the "Lawrence Welk Show." Located in historic downtown New Bedford, the Zeiterion is a masterfully restored 1923 vaudeville theater with gilded Grecian friezes, elaborate crystal light fixtures and a glamorous atmosphere.

NEW BEDFORD AREA BEACHES AND PARKS

Horseneck Beach State Reservation—This vast, breezy beach is one of the state's most spectacular and least known. Bordered by fragile dunes that create a barrier between the enormous parking lot and the beach, it has crunchy white sand and fine waves. Follow the road past the beach to **Gooseberry Neck** (★), a narrow, mile-long stretch of sandy, grassy land jutting out into the ocean and laced with paths. There's an abandoned World War II lookout tower at the end that you can climb. Right before Gooseberry Neck is a clam bar, a small parking lot and a tiny beach popular with windsurfers.

Facilities: Restrooms, showers, lifeguards, snack bar; groceries nearby in Westport; information, 508-636-8816. *Swimming:* Good, but can be rough.

Getting there: Located at the end of Route 88 in Westport Point.

Demarest Lloyd State Park (★)—This little-known state park has everything: natural grassy areas for picnics, rambling hills of beach grass, winding rivers, abundant wildlife—deer, hawks, egrets—and a fairly isolated beach. At low tide a long sand bar juts out into the calm, warm waters. Located in the bucolic Dartmouth area, Demarest is a real find.

Facilities: Picnic areas, restrooms, showers, lifeguards; information, 508-636-8816; groceries nearby in South Dartmouth. *Camping:* Permitted in 100 sites on a first come, first served basis. *Swimming:* Calm.

Getting there: Located at the end of Route 88, east of Horseneck Beach in South Dartmouth.

The Sporting Life

The North Shore and the Plymouth and New Bedford areas don't attract such vast numbers of sports-oriented tourists as other parts of the state; hence activities are limited and most golf and tennis clubs are private.

SPORTFISHING

Blue fish, stripped bass, tuna, cod and flounder are abundant on the Massachusetts coast. No license is required to fish, and tackle shops are everywhere. For detailed information on what to catch when, where and how, call the Massachusetts Division of Marine Fisheries (100 Cambridge Street, Room 1901, Boston, MA 02202; 617-727-3193).

The North Shore has Captain Bill's Deep Sea Fishing (9 Traverse Street, Gloucester; 508-283-6995) and **Hilton's Fishing Dock** (54-R Merrimac Street, Newburyport; 508-465-9885).

In the Plymouth area, try **Captain John Boats** (Town Wharf, Plymouth; 508-746-2643) for fishing and whale watching, and in New Bedford, **Captain Leroy Inc.** (Route 6, on the Fairhaven Bridge; 508-992-8907) for charter and party boat excursions.

SAILING, SURFING AND WINDSURFING

Marblehead on the North Shore is sailboat country. **Coastal Sail School** (617-639-0553), the only rental outfit, has 24- to 30-foot boats and gives lessons. Windsurfing equipment can be rented from **Eastern Seaboards** (Pleasant Street; 617-639-1929).

GOLF

Public golf courses are rare on the North Shore, but there is one beautiful municipal course surrounded by deep woods, the **Beverly Golf and Tennis Club** (134 McKay Street, Beverly; 508-927-5200).

There aren't any public golf courses close to Plymouth, but about 30 minutes out of town are **Pembroke Country Club** (West Elm Street, Pembroke; 617-826-4994) and **Bay Point Country Club** (Onset Avenue, Onset; 508-759-8802).

Hilly **New Bedford Municipal Golf Course** (581 Hathaway Road, New Bedford; 508-996-9393) offers golfers a challenging course.

TENNIS

The best spot for tennis in the North Shore is the **Beverly Golf and Tennis Club** (134 McKay Street, Beverly; 508-927-5200). It has ten clay courts open to the public. A limited number of municipal courts are available throughout the North Shore towns.

Municipal courts can be found in New Bedford's woodsy **Buttonwood Park** (Rockdale and Hawthorne avenues) and at **Hazelwood Park** (Brock Avenue), a city park with playgrounds. For park information, call the **City of New Bedford Parks Department** (508-991-6175).

WHALE WATCHING

The Massachusetts coast offers an enormous number of whale-watch excursions, some conducted by naturalists. On the North Shore, Gloucester is the gateway to whale watching. **Yankee Fleet** (75 Essex Avenue; 508-283-0313) is the oldest and largest whale-watch outfit, plus it offers charter and fishing party excursions. Also try **Cape Ann Whale Watch** (415 Main Street; 508-283-5110).

In Newburyport, there's **New England Whale Watch** (Hilton's Dock, 54 Rear, Merrimac Street; 508-465-7165) and **Hilton's Fishing Dock** (54 Merrimac Street; 508-465-9885).

Several excursions depart from Plymouth harbor. Try **Captain John Boats** (Town Wharf; 508-746-2643) or **Cape Cod Cruises** (State Pier; 508-747-2400), which also goes to Provincetown.

CANOEING AND SEA KAYAKING

One of the most beautiful canoe trips in New England is along the North Shore's Ipswich River through the 2000-acre **Ipswich River Wildlife Sanctuary** (★) (Perkins Row, Topsfield; 508-887-9264). For rentals contact **Foote Brothers Canoes** (356 Topsfield Road, Ipswich; 508-356-9771).

South of New Bedford in Dartmouth are many rivers ideal for canoeing. The **Lloyd Center for Environmental Studies** (430 Potomska Road, South Dartmouth; 508-990-0505) organizes day-long canoe trips along beautiful nearby rivers, and **Bibeau's Boat Mart** (Route 6, North Dartmouth; 508-993-6120) rents canoes.

SKINDIVING

In Gloucester, the brave and the bold bare the chilly waters with **Underwater Explorer** (19 Harbor Loop; 508-283-0028), an outfit that teaches scuba diving and rents equipment.

HORSEBACK RIDING

Pleasantview (★) (225 Bedford Street, Lakeville; 508-946-1781), a 500-acre horse farm off Route 18, 25 minutes from New Bedford, offers guided rides past cranberry bogs, sand pits and forest.

ICE SAILING

Ice sailing is a tradition on Watuppa Pond in Fall River. This graceful sport takes tremendous skill and specially designed sailboats. Rentals aren't available, but it's fun to watch these lighter-than-air boats glide along the icy pond.

BICYCLING

The Massachusetts coast has limited bike riding areas, but a few choice spots are described here.

Cyclists in the North Shore area recommend riding along scenic **Route 127** from Beverly to Magnolia. The tree-lined road dips and turns past seaside mansions and historic homes. It's cool and peaceful in the summer.

The **Westport** and **Dartmouth** area south of New Bedford doesn't have many cars, and the flat country roads wind past elegant horse farms, pastures and ocean. From Route 195, take exit 12 and head south to Chase or Tucker Road. At this point it doesn't matter which road you take; they're all lovely, and as long as you head south you'll wind up at the beach.

BIKE RENTALS   On the North Shore you can rent bikes at **Seaside Cycle** (23 Elm Street, Manchester; 508-526-1200).

In the New Bedford area, try **Sumner R. Crosby** (484 Russells Road, South Dartmouth; 508-992-2176) and **Yesteryear Cyclery** (330 Hathaway Road, New Bedford; 508-993-2525).

Transportation

BY CAR

On the North Shore, **Route 128** is the main artery connecting Salem, Manchester, Magnolia, Gloucester and Rockport. Route 95 is the major north–south artery to Essex, Ipswich and Newburyport.

Route 3 links Boston to Plymouth and ends at the Sagamore Bridge to Cape Cod. **Route 195** is the main east–west artery connecting Fall River and New Bedford.

BY AIR

Many people visiting this area come into **Logan International Airport** in Boston (see Chapter Two). Also serving the southern coastal area is the New Bedford Airport.

Airlines servicing **New Bedford Airport** currently are Edgartown Air and Express Air.

BY FERRY AND BOAT

Ferries and boats between Boston, Plymouth, New Bedford, Cape Cod, Martha's Vineyard and Nantucket require reservations in the summer.

The following ferries and boats operate seasonally and do not transport cars: **A. C. Cruise Lines** (28 Northern Avenue, Boston; 617-426-8419) goes between Boston and Gloucester. **Cape Island Express** (1494 East Rodney French Boulevard, Billy Woods Wharf, New Bedford; 508-997-1688) operates between New Bedford and Vineyard Haven on Martha's Vineyard. The **Cuttyhunk Boat Lines** (Pier 3, New Bedford; 508-992-1432) connects New Bedford and Cuttyhunk Island.

BY BUS

Greyhound (617-292-4700) offers frequent service to Newburyport, Boston, Plymouth, New Bedford and Fall River.

Bonanza (17 Elm Street, Falmouth; 508-548-7588) runs buses to and from Logan Airport, Hyannis, Woods Hole, Falmouth, Bourne, New Bedford, Fall River, Connecticut, Rhode Island and New York.

CAR RENTALS

Avis Rent A Car (508-999-6900) serves New Bedford Airport.

PUBLIC TRANSPORTATION

Many Boston commuters live on the North Shore; hence **Massachusetts Bay Transportation Authority** (617-722-5000) runs numerous buses from Boston's Haymarket Square and trains from North Station to Salem, Beverly, Gloucester and Rockport. **Cape Ann Transportation Authority** (508-283-7916) provides bus service from Magnolia and Essex to Rockport.

Plymouth does not have public transportation. **Southern Eastern Regional Transit Authority** (508-997-6767) provides bus service throughout Fall River and New Bedford.

TAXIS

New Bedford Airport is served by **Standard Taxi** (508-997-9404) and **Yellow Cab** (508-999-5213).

Index

Abbreviations used for chapter areas are: (B) Boston; (CC) Cape Cod and the Islands; (MC) Massachusetts Coast; and (OB) Outside Boston.

Abbreviations are used for parks, beaches, sightseeing attractions, and some natural features, but not for towns or cities. Hotel and restaurant names are not included here, unless cited as a historical or sightseeing attraction.

Also Available From Ulysses Press

HIDDEN HAWAII

A classic in its field, this top-selling guide captures the spirit of the islands. 384 pages. $13.95

HIDDEN MEXICO

Covers the entire 6000-mile Mexican coastline in the most comprehensive fashion ever. 432 pages. $13.95

HIDDEN NEW ENGLAND

A perfect companion for anyone exploring America's birthplace. 564 pages. $13.95

HIDDEN COAST OF CALIFORNIA

Explores the fabled California coast from Mexico to Oregon. 468 pages. $13.95

HIDDEN FLORIDA

From the Keys to Cape Canaveral, this award-winning guide combs the Sunshine State. 492 pages. $13.95

HIDDEN FLORIDA KEYS AND EVERGLADES

Covers an area unlike any other in the world—the tropical Florida Keys and mysterious Everglades. 156 pages. $6.95

HIDDEN SAN FRANCISCO AND NORTHERN CALIFORNIA

A major resource for travelers exploring the Bay Area and beyond. 444 pages. $13.95

DISNEY WORLD AND BEYOND: The Ultimate Family Guidebook

Unique and comprehensive, this handbook to Disney World and its surrounding area is a must for family travelers. 200 pages. $8.95

CALIFORNIA: The Ultimate Guidebook

Captures the best of the Golden State. A Book-Of-The-Month Club selection. 504 pages. $13.95

TO ORDER DIRECT   For each book send an additional $2 postage and handling (California residents include 6½% sales tax) to Ulysses Press, P.O. Box 4000–H, Berkeley, CA 94704

About the Authors

Ryan Vollmer is the author of *Affordable Spas and Fitness Resorts* (Ventana Press) and co-author of *Hidden New England.* She has written for the *New York Times, Rolling Stone, New York Daily News, San Francisco Chronicle, Self, Psychology Today, Ladies Home Journal* and *Woman's Day.*

Patricia Mandell is co-author of *Hidden New England* and author of *Massachusetts: Off the Beaten Path* (Globe Pequot Press). A member of the American Society of Journalists and Authors and the Travel Journalist Guild, she has been published in the *Christian Science Monitor, New England Monthly, Caribbean Travel and Life, Dallas Morning News, Miami Herald, Washington Post* and *Denver Post.*

About the Illustrator

Norman Nicholson, a graduate of the Art Center College of Design in Los Angeles, has successfully combined a career in illustration and painting. His artwork has appeared in national ads, book and magazine illustrations and posters. His paintings are included in a couple of important government collections as well as private and corporate collections throughout the United States. He currently teaches painting at the Academy of Art in San Francisco.